broken caterpillars

a book of irrelevant literature and magical nihilism

BROKEN CATERPILLARS

A BOOK OF IRRELEVANT LITERATURE

"...the dead caterpillars emerge living animals; so it is equally true and miraculous, that our dead and rotten corpses will rise from the grave."

A PROPHECY OF WEEDS AND LIKENESS

Weeds had grown on top of his head, a single flower, a Stargazer-Lotus grew out of one of his eyes, it had a bloom with a cherry color that spread out, coughing into the air, dropping sprinkles of chocolate seeds that twirled back down into the grass.

His feet had rooted into the dirt, his body was prehistoric, his toes would sing to the ancient trees that accompanied him. When the rains came, he would stick out his tongue, roll it around his face, catching the ants and moisture, bringing them into his mouth, into his body. A nest of insects made a home inside the mud in his head. They whispered to him of dreams he had long forgotten, dreams that pressed into him and made him laugh, but the laughter was short, it never escaped his lips, it drooled in strange colors as it dripped down his beard, a beard that was green with moss and white Chick-Toad flowers that weaved around full of aphids, aphids that sometimes exploded into memories, memories that were robotic, broken into time-lines that would corrode into romantic flavors that he once had of lovers and those that had once loved him, those that had escaped into the dirt without him, those that went back to the primeval slime of bone and dirt.

He was unmoving, like a rock, like a tree stump, how long had he been here? A hundred, a thousand years? Did it matter? Time was the abandoned passage of insanity, a sleepless reasoning, or so the insects whispered to him. The insects in his head rolled out of his mouth, they brought in a clump of dirt that was tangled with dandelions, they spoke of something walking, near-by, as they packed eggs between his teeth. He tried moving his eye but it fell out, rolled onto the ground, immediately it cracked open, a lizard crawled out, yawning, eyes specious and yellow, rushing off into the greenery of the distance.

A creature walked out from the trees, a mutant that walked with legs and arms moving to the rhythm of its body. The creature had a robot head that looked like a makeshift television screen, something old that kept up with the static of the great and beloved script-leaders, but the rest was flesh – it was alive but not like him, it was alive like a dream is alive, distant and remote, like a tree far off in the distance, like an old memory. This creature danced, spun like a ballerina up to him, it pulled the Stargazer-Lotus bloom from his head, its hands were melancholic and full of tenderness, it took a moment to smell the fragrance from this flower that was as ancient as the stars, it had moved through the dark waters when tadpoles still dreamed of being creatures that marched upright, that marched full of terrible voices. Those voices that were eerie and absurd and strange with brutal undertones.

The creature put the flower in its mouth, chewing the memory, digesting the dreams of leaf and tree. It had visions of planets far off, vines curling around men and robots and cities in flames, fish walking from great oceans, waking to the fresh scent of sunlight and air. It watched the wars of monkey-like creatures, the madness of animals, the wilting of sunflowers, the horde of insects that consumed the robots, infesting their electric brains. The robots that then, in their insect insanity, murdered the monkey men, that murdered anything plant like, anything that had a pulse, a heart, a scent – all were dead now. Nothing but the trees remembered. Nothing but the lizards would speak of the horrors of disciplined rockets that cannibalized young men and sent widows to sip champagne that carried not victory, but the misery that death brings to all creatures. Even the insects would eventually forget men and all the terrible virtues of his disparity.

The creature bent down, looking at this strange tree stump, one that resembled something alive, something that it might have known in some other life. It pulled at the weeds and grass around the stump. It washed its head with water that smelled like honey and bumble bees, it uprooted its legs from the ancient soil. It stood this man up, insects fell from his mouth, he vomited earth and clay from his eyes. This creature picked up his eye from the ground, put it back in his head, it picked up his arms that had fallen off long ago and attached them back on his body. The creature smiled at this man that had been born again. A man born out of the dreams of romance and insects.

He awoke to see her in front of him, she was ancient, like him, smiling with warmth and love. He moved towards her, looking at her arms and legs, moving his hands across her face, amazed at the life in her face, the way her lips pressed and felt against his fingers. She took his hand inside her hand.

'I found you,' she whispered.

The words were like butterflies the way they danced around him. He attempted to smile but his lips slid off. She laughed, covering her face. She moved his lips back to its proper place. They both laughed now, they danced in the clearing, under the new suns, grasshoppers watched with envy and then they too joined in, the trees shook their leaves with the same merry laughter.

'What took you so long?' He asked her when they had sat down in exhaustion, sweat and laughter twirling down their faces. She took a moment to pull her hair back, her eyes were exploding, the scent of lavender touched him.

'They're all gone, you know,' she said as if remembering

something that was distant and terrible. Her eyes fell from him as they gazed off to the clearing, towards the storm that was approaching. She looked back at him, this magnificent creature, this creature of television and flesh, how she loved him. She took his hand, she spoke to him and it flowed out of her like a song, a song he might have known when he was a child, singing to the aromas of family and community. But that childhood was lost, forgotten, it would slither into unknown rivers he would never swim in again.

'The people, the metal ships, everything. Everything is gone,' she sang, 'I hid like you. I became earth and insects. I had this lovely dream, my brother in a field surrounded by so much beauty, by so much life. It took years but I uprooted myself. I swam in lakes full of lily pads, giant frogs leaping out of my hair. It was all so beautiful. It was all so full of madness and majesty. Oh! I cried, I did, I'm not ashamed of being alive. I'm not ashamed of any of it. I hadn't cried in years. I took off my mask and I saw I was a woman, and I knew that was beautiful, somehow I knew. I was alive. I remembered you. I went to find you.'

He cried. The tears that came out of his eyes were worms.

'Remember,' he said while flies escaped his mouth, 'remember what the script-father used to say? That god gave man fire and love, but man, man in all his infinite wisdom, found love unprofitable.'

She took his hand.

'Don't think such terrible things,' she said, 'life is a drunken wraith and its poetry is in the motion of these landscapes. Why should you be afraid to die if you were never afraid to be born?'

She laughed at her melodrama, she picked him up and danced.

'Love,' she cried, 'love all and nothing and you will always be free.'

They put their arms around one another, melting together, their mutant faces shedding thunder, rain washed down their red cheeks. In the landscapes they walked together, hand inside hand, to the mountains of motionless metal beings that had long gone to a deep and undisturbed robotic sleep. They crawled on their giant heads, they pulled the weeds from the dead and sleeping creatures, they cartwheeled together, they built their arms and legs with forest and flowers, they filled their heads with mud and rolled their eyes into insect bubbles, they remembered the script-phantoms that sang of perfect motions, they laughed and portals opened up inside their mouths.

They had visions of giraffes grazing in the wild lands, snow falling like feathers against red tipped oaks, ants crawling on the belly of a beetle. They melted into a clearing, they became tree bark, silent and still, unmoving and dead. The rains came, with it brought the insects, they crawled the tall towers of their legs, they nested in their hair, bringing ancient seeds, growing great flowers, flowers that would always dream. The dreams were broken, fragmented with forgotten weeds, serpent-like faces. Behind them an army of dead robots ... one robot stood frozen in place, moss and fungus grew in the palms of its hands. Thousands of caterpillars crawled out of its vacant eye sockets, twitching in fervor, falling to the ground. The sunrise was suspended, clouds slithered into broken pieces, trees and lakes turned into opal and marble, ferns blackened, stars melted into dust and glass, armies of beetles with haunted faces marched out in formation... the world became strangely quiet, terribly lonely. God's love made sure to destroy everything completely.

They cleared a way through the forest, to an open ocean, where they found the head of an ancient robot. They picked up the head, cleared out the insects, blew balloons into its electric brain. The robot's eyes twitched on with a strange glow, it asked many questions. The children that were once trees answered as much as they could in their rhythmic and poetic tongues. They came to a clearing, and sat in an outside, old playhouse. The chairs were the stumps of heads that had once been great statues. The stage was made of insects. A small gathering of people came to witness the show. A spectacular show. A beautiful and irrelevant show. A man with termite mounds in his teeth sat beside them and told them colorful jokes that seemed to make them feel comfortable and jolly. Sometimes the termites would spit out of his mouth as he spoke. The hive of dirt eating through the porcelain in his mouth gave him a cryptic appearance. If he was a dream, they were delighted. A strange couple opened the show dancing slowly. They danced and spoke softly. They melted into the stage as the insects consumed their bodies. A man with a top hat and a golden cane walked out. He spun his cane. He twirled his top hat. He pranced around and clicked his heels.

'Welcome, welcome,' he said, 'welcome to the magical theater of starlight and groomed corpses. Where none are beautiful and all are ridiculously dead. Come closer and let me tell you a tale. A most magnificent sermon. For life is the watery substance of dreams and we float merrily through it. Where all conscience is decayed, drunk on the caterpillar's tonic, radiation and television in its metamorphosis. Listen now, my friends, for this is the beginning ...'

From the sky a giant caterpillar floated down. It flew through the great light socket that was suspended in the curved arch of the heavens. In its eyes was the endless curiosity of a thousand different lives. The musical started, the sun dimmed, all through the land it was quiet, an echo that seemed lost like a murmur inside a fantastical execution. None were beautiful and all were dead. And so the show began ...

COME FORWARD, YOU BEAUTIFUL MONSTER

Where the lovers are outlawed the savagery of men will be seen in all its flames. The trees will no longer bend, thoughts will twist sideways. Leaves shall wilt as they fall upside down and quiver in the abstracts of insects. The rivers will ripple no longer to wind nor will the dreams of children ever be known under mothers with a weary kindness. They will bend their breast as they take the small fingers in dismay, undressing their despair in gestures of shame ...

Where the lovers are outlawed ... Poets shall lose their blood, their teeth, their skin. Streets will fall beneath the tyrant's following, they will break under the footing of ridiculous myths. Notes of fear will be musical inside the eyes of animals who snarl at the fading stars falling softly like snow on red deserts.

Where the lovers are outlawed ... Wicked women will poison meandering men. Meandering men will rip apart the weeping women. The gasping of the environment, a limited death inside consciousness, the taste of ash upon culture. Wrinkles on the tongue, warped lips, the pending pause before a lover's disaster ... Sinking thoughts in the pale grip of a god's last exasperation as it digs its claws in the earthworms and buries the sorrows of widows in the lack of conscience.

The sure-footed drops of suffering will be seen in the water logged paintings, howls of desperation when remorse is melted under indoctrination, passion crumbling in dissolving nature ... All ahead now - Staring into the vastness with blisters in their eyes and the dead among their feet. The fraudulent minded performing for the machines shaped like bleeding faces and paradoxes. Uniformed idiots singing praises, imbeciles like ballerinas marching to apprehension to please the cynics and thieves. Music of a lazy destination, nonsense will be the texture of senses.

Let it be known where the lovers are outlawed ... All are bound to defeat ... All are lost to the murmurings of soldiers who lie naked in fields of swollen rocks who dare not dream of what the trees dig for underneath. All are lost to the silence of rebellion as they tear their clothes from the wombs they built in their children's future. None speak of adventure when all are doomed to superstition ...

Let it be known that where lovers are outlawed the republic becomes a sinister stranger, flesh inhaled on the slopes of witches and hysterical jesters, critics of ignorance will be beheaded.
The complaining of oceans will sleep beneath the bringing of flesh eaters, fish heads in garbled costumes, rising the great sigh before the gasping of death...

Where lovers are outlawed ... All will be forever lost to headless suicides, serviceable deviants looking out windowless palaces. Always lust in their brains and never will lovers be found in singing and hands abound by fits of merry ... Imposters inside a resurrection, swarming in decay and monsters. Where education will have two tongues, one that perfumes the inept and one of transparent conspiracies dressed as divinity and fantasy.

Where lovers are outlawed ... Let them know that I too once was a man. Never did I lose my tongue to vulgar nests, madman trinkets, hardened cavities from lies spoken, broken lips against madness. That I wished to be the ocean. The sun burdened by beauty that weeps underneath it. The petals of flowers were in my veins and the sting of bees hid underneath my eyelids.

I was inside the reforms of existence.
And ... my dreams, my beautiful dreams, they were frozen lightning trapped inside lakes, slowly drowning, in a sea of lost liveliness ...

OH, SING FOR ME YOU BEAUTIFUL HERETICS

(1)What epileptic inventions share their jest with fellows of fire among my maiden's fury, winery that amuses the wits with delicate irony, slippery songs of mad women realms, the gunpowder dresses ... the fools with a head full of decay and snowflakes.

she, who was a representative of nature
she, who rolled water under her eyelids
she, who spoke of shadows that fell flush in knives between the metal faces ...

she, who was bored with miscalculations inside the compliments - how the earth bound up inside her hands in swirls of insects, how she felt so alone when told to laugh at her own expense ... and when age grinds into her flesh, she complains about being grossly invisible (the compliments fade, no one ask her to smile anymore, she is amused by the men's lack of chivalry ... a playful blight on the lips). When the heart is meek, pain penetrates capital, and who laughs more happily than those in silent errors? (a spirit lost without flesh to tempt is a tongue lost to spoil a thought) What are words when lovely turns elusive from the snare of pain when comes a lack of spirit from unending burns to the heart's cavity? A phantom propaganda cools the tongue and the stomach fills itself with cruelty, a spirit of fetishisms among indignations ... identity becomes a mockery of reality!

(2) It seems my teeth were made for cavities and rot, garbled bits of gravel and rocks, blood for bark, gunfire with melody, monsters inside hearts, cities on the wings of mythical species who tongue-speak of unruly democracies ... laughter made for women while despair for men in armory, who cry remorse for reward and recruits in cultist expansions ... the time slimes inside the walls of conversation so commercialized the merriment is understood to be a disaster, among fools setting the corporate carnival, (how delightful is the brittle bits of frantic screams upon frantic battles of hellish belittlement ...)

(3) Despair! Despair, my friends! Despair for the blood in my blood, the skin inside my skin, what is love but a river of muscle inside your chest, what is a whisper but a dream between the flocks of disease caught inside your regrets... abandon the skin, abandon the blood, abandon the heart, because the unknown washes me in pockets of ferocity hidden in my brows and nothing is gentle when all are shattered by suffering, what a terror that man has for a face! What a virtue that woman commands in the bellyaches of roaches inside the cathedrals of men-genitals ... that's not a man of men but a busy-body womb with metaphors hanging with incoherent animations ...

(4)I remember the glass lake beside the fantastical ducks whose bodies were populated with feathers and scripts... the ballerina trees that grumbled over sullen giants .. the thieves of stars, pieces of good stomped on by capital police ... I watched a woman grow into a beast, slaughter three hens with her teeth, a man felt foolish under her charity ... and she was stone, she was madman, she was passion, she was colors and she fell to her knees ... her caved in stomach spent such a lovely brood for blood ... we plunged into sea and horizons and the distance was dismantled by slogans and the gods were abolished to shame cursed with poison ... within a dream mankind was banished from the garden for killing animals, drinking their blood, not for eating the fruits of trees ... they mocked god by wearing the skins of its creations ...

(5)I remember when god was a subtle defect, a strange memory dipped in blood, nails against a frenzy of contradictions ... where eternity is an inconspicuous drama and i decided to wait out my superstitions ...

(6)It was not the lovely love of love's love we lack but the heart of reflections turned terrific and what does despair do for such beauty but tempt it to vibrate in a world of soundless righteousness, deathly dialogue that creates leisure in disappointment ... send off those cannibal rockets! ... despair in your identity! ...

(7) Come quickly, I cried to the body
Here, I have a knife to my tongue, a pleasure stirring between the songs I sing when lonely ...
Do you not know me? I have never loved or repeated a slogan ... I have never loved a caricature nor worshiped an ideal ... I am a tadpole licking the underneath of a poisonous lily called oh beautiful funeral from misery ...

Oh, you beautiful monsters!
Oh, you beautiful bodies inside dream-like machines!
Let our blood bond in this earthly commentary ...

Be beautiful! and be dead! be the miserable cretins you have been since history sprung you from a skeptical malefactor - your lives are an intolerable impasse, a mixture of loathsome and insecure scoundrels, robbed of modesty, sense and reason - who would suffer cannibalism if it proved an adventure past stupor - your faith is an evacuated treaty of conviction, a vile spectator possessing a soul that contradicts the spirit ... you will be forgotten, your superstitions of country and gods is your dishonor ... your ambitions are a false vitality, overwhelming civilization in your hypothetical insanity, your stubbornness is a tyrant and your dreams are liars ... you sell your soul not to god but to death and pestilence.

Run lightly, tread heavy with those insect bodies, enchant yourself with desire and mischief, love eternally and dance among the springs of stars …

Oh! Oh! Oh! fly those cannibal flags, you beautiful monsters … you are heretics of your own anti-utopia …
(be free, free, free to frolic in the breeze licking this dreamer's lips …)

A MURDER OF MUSES

This house seems to burn loudly during the nights. There are old rituals performed daily by the walls, death is haunted by more of what we call life - that spirit lives in these bricks. The people from the temples don't really trust anything. They burn the books but keep the fetus. We have to show cards that we pray to the correct gods, we have to hide our breath from those around us, lest the whispers be fouled with exposure. There's a vaccination for everything except our ideologies. We suffer the poor, but exempt them from participating. Seen a tiki-maiden in a white dress splatter a dog for being the property of heathen. The young hate the old but only because they are mirrors of one another.

I suppose they didn't love the love anymore. They took it outside. Put it on its knees. They put the gun to its head, shot twice, the music blasted out like doves fornicating in oil. Love fell face forward, dead and illegal ... Everything is so illegal here. I tell the strangers I walk by how I will never love them. They close their eyes, they flex their eyebrows, they seem to understand. They are not concerned with me. They are not concerned with anything.

We lie around this house. Reading books from thrifty stores haunted with bed bugs and ghosts. We bleed sonnets from the blood, critters ashamed with age and spirit's sniff beside us. We die in flames caused by what we hold between our legs. I look at the trees between her legs as she digs in the dirt between mine. We are old and bitter like the ancient temples under oceans. Our arms and legs fall off, the creases in our foreheads unwind, our eyes roll like waves behind our heads.

Is it odd that I don't find any of this beautiful? The lands, the prayers, the dreams, the sunsets, nothing rolls out as special to me. There's nothing beautiful about getting old, age seems to be a terrible solitude. I tell the young to die quickly and don't give any of this much thought. But they don't listen, they want to be beautiful, fresh like warm bread. They pray for sexual favors still and the night always runs out too quickly for them. I get up in the mornings, I watch the water splashing, giggling, it comes out naturally but I know it's all a falsehood. Nothing is real in this world of mine. I am the dreams of trees and the imagination of ants. Everything falls like a fog rolling from the mountains, into my mouth, reminding me that one day these thoughts will be forever lost for someone else to decipher. I will leave them clues under the rocks and the dirt. Will they find the little notes I hide in the grass? Will they find pieces of my skin in the cracks of insect eyelashes? Will they whisper those wonderful words while I decay under the roads?

The highways here are nothing more than an assembly line of broken dreamers, economic gutter-feeders, workers with gold and snowflakes in their brains, they have tree bark for blood. They are dressed for disease, cursed with a disorder, going super speeds into a future of imaginary inventions. I want to pretend that these people are all something profound, something beautiful, but I know they are just afraid like everything else. They have this reasoning problem, almost like a lover being unhooked for the first time when it comes to questions about our mortality, they simply work harder, hook their veins into the system. Like the whale whose tail bends in captivity - the human also bends - since civilization is a break and apart from nature, then it becomes a psychosis that is made up of madmen, mad ideas - the brain breaks - the man can never go back to nature, he would die since he was born in captivity.

Psychopaths becoming puritanical conformists fill the churches. It wasn't just the fascists and rednecks applauding lawlessness. It was toxic individualism, psychotic isolationist, the ultimate freedom for them meant no responsibility to anything but melodramatic hypocrisy, the more disappointing their horror at endless empathy the more inconvenient their anti-human revolution became. They fantasize of nihilism to create a temperament for soft totalitarianism. They scream about being silenced on machines that transmit their words to millions. They have few emotions, mostly indignation, hate, appeasement or fear. They have all become deviant romantics easily entertained by madness, stupidity. They wait in long lines for the last mirror in the cities. One by one they look upon themselves. They don't do it for self-reflection, they do it because they want to remember how they look, and what they look like in the newest trends that set their glands ablaze with tragedy. It was stupidity combined with near fatal levels of narcisism. They preserve the last mirrors in an attempt to gratify youth that will eventually become as despicable as the big top boomers they hated and so could act out in their violent temperaments. Nothing separates the blood of barbarism except technology and age. The common market for them all fits the same purpose of ransacking nations and ecosystems, fostering class divisions, scapegoating into fear to propel capitalistic fascism masked as neo or new wave or something beautiful for them to pet or call property. The mirrors disprove responsibility comes from civility, but from conformity to beauty and that resentment towards being ugly is only too abstract for them to understand. Being cruel and vindictive is the humor, their generation is a generation of self-mutilation. But, their eyes are abstracts of consciousness blended into an existentialist lethargy that creates a leprosy of the spirit. They enjoy punishing themselves for no other reason but to resent the coming panic. No one cares here. They don't even pretend to care. The mirrors are fun, they say, but are off limits to those too poor to participate.

This country, this city is a machine that runs on human misery. Misery is its currency, it's how it survives, it's how we survive. But these are just thoughts, electricity running between my neurons creating a human costume. Does it really mean anything? Do these words bleed and feel pain? The language I speak is dead, I see the adages on the billboards - they speak and I listen. We snub our noses at the utopian empire because we prefer chaos, we prefer subversive behavior over complacency. Everything, including people, has to be beautiful for us to experience it. To get to love and hope - we have to murder a lot of people first and then we will love one another. We can only experience hope once we feel the extinction of hate inside our bones. In a world run and operated by psychopaths, apathy is the only way to survive. Apathy is how you stay alive.

When the weirdo creatures from a different culture unearth our remains three thousand seasons from now, what will they say about us? What will they see in these bones? What will they explore inside this city? Will they know Henry likes to shit behind wooden fences while drunk on fireballs? Will they know the sounds of horses feet who carried tourist gods to point out the decay in our sidewalks, the violins in our voices? Oh, they will say, this is where the witches danced so long ago. There was a temple for shopping, their cities were theme parks masquerading as churches. And they speak in echoes and say: Well, I think the furniture is on fire and the cats have been threaded with a broken back. The stars are satellites of rich men and rain is a dream is a fire is a season is what we call the eloquent generation.

Will they find us, dressed and curled and ugly, coffee mugs and old books, against each other? What would they say then, love?

They bring us back using special technologies. But, only for a day. They ask us questions about our planet and our communities. When they are done, they take us outside, three gunshots. One to the head, one to the chest, one for our fathers. They set everything on fire with their strange tongues and language.

They won't remember us, my love. They won't remember much of anything. This land belongs to dreamers with insect bodies. And something caught in my throat, it said: We will murder the muses so the poets will have no future.

VULGAR.
VACCINATION.
VULTURES.

Reality is an evil hallucination disguised as a sexual degenerate ....

This adage was spray painted across the body of a giant cartoon mouse that stood mimicking human ailments. The amusement park was unusually crowded on this day. Global tragedies were rampant. The Earth was beginning to resemble a neurotic child with a desire for self-destruction and mass murders. Time-lines and parallel universes were corroding into deserts and hideous parades with poetic-like graves. The politicians were all cynics and thieves and the working class was deciding whether or not being poor was a projection of a dead god with a lunatic agenda.

People were shuffling about, spreading more diseases, pesticides were the names of the next generation of children floating about like poisonous clouds. Fleas and dust-mites were jumping from their eyelashes and earlobes. Bed bugs had nested inside their brains, creating an abomination of spirit that whispered mocking dick jokes. They had silent thunder for orgasms between their cavities. Most of them were armed with drug-infected minds. Curly-blonde psychos with no imaginations foaming at the mouth to dry-hump the carnival sisters spreading mange and syphilis down near the river attractions. Doppelgangers with no reflection stood in bathroom stalls as a robot attendant recited the new American slogan: *Please practice social decay. Wash your melancholy every time after using our suicide nurseries. Stabbing our handsome specimens with sharp objects is discouraged but quickly forgiven if you praise our park with an immediate blood lust.*

Most of them had their teeth replaced with digital devices that created a virtual psychosis reality which made them feel like they were made of rubber chewing gum. People wore masks. Name marketing brands slithered on their clothing and advertisers were printed into the neurons that electrified their dreams with tasteless infections and bad bedside etiquette. They were here to manipulate their reality through strange adventures of entertainment. Which was enlightenment if enlightenment was a homicidal maniac with a learning disorder. Two hour lines for a sixty second thrill. They feared boredom because boredom reminded them of reality or a shadow reality. An electric reality. Everyone hated being alive, surviving, so they mimicked the idea of dying on thrilling coasters, haunted houses, boats flying through slimy waters. They secretly hated their children while they stood in these lines.

Some of them wondered if murder was possible through a type of osmosis. They waited patiently to be entertained. They were angry with being human. Someone lied to them. Reality was a whore that charged too much for admission and there was no fantastic orgasm at the end of this. They coughed insects from their mouths, they shit their souls into crowded bathrooms that warned that not washing your hands could lead to politically fallacies, bad crazy, dreams brought to you by superhuman preachers with bullhorns screaming in a burnt-out arena.

Nothing was subjective here. It was meant to harm self-preservation through fits of mania. God was a psychopathic suicide. It made sense that most of Its creation would follow in the steps of Its son and try to generate an excuse to eventually die for some reason like dying for a dull romance in a bland kingdom of endless imbeciles.

Reality was meant to create servitude through the lie that being alive was the paradise and being dead was the fear. Since boredom felt like death, it made sense that they thought being bored was like being dead and just surviving meant being both dead and bored. No one wanted to die, because death was boring. They had even figured out a way that even in death you would live in a continuous cycle of repetition and nineties advertisements. This scared the shit out of people who had put their futures in being born again virgins. A virtuous mutant with a placid slime ball between their legs.

They had been waiting in line at this amuse-men-rent park for at least fourteen days. They heard the screams but never saw anyone return to life once they boarded the rides. He had been picking his nose while waiting. There was a strange taboo about picking your nose in public. How far could you really put your finger in your nose before it made others uncomfortable? How did slime from the nose or the hardened nuggets that collected in the nose hairs make people feel so uncomfortable? He wondered about this insecurity while the person he was having a conversation with stood speaking symbols from his face with one of these nasty creatures just sitting slightly below his nose, caught in his mustache. He thought if he picked his nose in front of this goddamn freak of nature, maybe it would subconsciously let him know that he had a nostril mutation hanging from his nose. When this didn't work, he shoved his finger so deep into his nose, it started to bleed.

'I've heard some people that get their second shot of the vaccination become slightly altered.'

'Altered?'

'Mutations, my friend. Their DNA melts. They become depressed with reality. They start dry-humping inanimate thoughts. Some turn into roaches, peel away warning stickers from cigarette lighters. Mass abortions of realty. Robot funk. Necrosis of the skin. Nasty shit, like real nasty.' He said this while a part of his face became like static and flaked off into someone else's history. A godless approach for the problem with demonic dementia that was starting to manifest from too much sugar. The line they were waiting in was moving, but it was moving slowly. He still couldn't look his friend in the face because of the nose creature. But, he continued picking his infected, bleeding nose in hopes of his friend finally doing something about it. He thought of the universe of bacteria that was building up in that snot universe. How many lives had they lived? How many wars were fought? Did they have space travel capabilities yet? Time travel? The universe for bacteria was a thousand years to a microsecond of their universe. Time flows differently for bacteria that live inside snot. One conversation and already the bacteria had lived a million lives.

'I heard the fourth shot creates abnormalities in your streaming networks. Some people turn into televisions with a never ending advertisement that has a 'skip ad' button but every time you push it the ad just becomes longer and longer before your reality suddenly snaps and you end up breathing through a dirty dish-rag.' His nose continued to bleed. Bacteria was harboring on his lips. His throat felt sore. He wondered when the last time he had an erection and if thinking this while his friend talked made him homosexually generous.

'Seventh shot is even worse. Your lungs turn into liquid shit. You breathe polluted music through your eyelids. I heard of some people turning into carpet zombies.'

'What the fuck is a carpet zombie?' He could feel a blister forming inside his ass from the constant sweat.

'DNA infusion. Electric nematodes of the brain circuits. The DNA just goes fucking berserk, man. Creates millions of time-lines, parallel worlds, like sucking cat hair in a vacuum cleaner. Every piece of hair is it's own multiverse. The vacuum eventually succumbs to a reality overdose. Worse than heroin. Reality junkies. They hallucinate being alive. Imagine that! Being alive.'

'I'll probably skip the vaccinations. My liver is already altered by bad decisions.' He said this while he wiped the blood coming from his nose on the handrail.

'I mean, I don't blame you. How many of these goddamn shots do I need? They are up to sixty-seven shots now.'

'And adding at least eleven more everyday.'

'Fucking communists. All of them. Their reality is a typo.'

'They want to murder all these virus types. Living creatures. They just want to live like us. What makes us so goddamn special? In fact, since this pandemic, traffic has been nice.'

'Really? Because it's still a nightmare for me. This pandemic fucking sucked. It didn't even get rid of the lines at Mcdonalds. The highways are creamed with these bloated bastards.'

'My neighbor got the fifth shot. We were talking about the football game and he just melted in front of me. Like he fucking melted into a puddle of slime. It smelled terrible. Nothing but clothes and jewelry left. He wore women's underwear. I never knew that about him. Fifteen years of living next to him. Odd how we never really know anything about people.'

'I think about that too.'

'What?'

'You know. How we don't really know anything about who or what we are. We are designed to function and create personality by having opinions but we never really know if our opinions are created because we want to belong or if it's something we heard or if we actually created them and they are real opinions. Like, when someone asks me what my favorite color is. I tell them but it's more of an exaggeration. I don't really believe in a favorite. I have a color because it placates them and gives my personality or reality a more defined definition. It makes me think that our reality isn't even really ours but just a series of exaggerations and definitions we give ourselves to present a reality of what we are towards other realities. Do we really even know who we are? Are we defined by our dreams? And, if definitions and words and symbols were created by other people then are the personalities we accept about ourselves even ours? I mean, if someone else created these words, aren't we just living under someone else's reality?'

The line wrapped on forever. They heard the screams of the people on the giant snake like coasters. Men and women dressed like nightmare cartoon characters pranced around, giving children complex anxieties, freedom necrosis, Hollywood erections, pornographic images filled with diseases created from melting ice-caps.

'Freewill is probably the greatest lie we were ever told. Even in religion. How we respond to good or evil is only perspective. Do you really think God gives a shit what our definition of evil or good really means? Evil is usually associated with death but death is how you communicate with God and everyone knows God is a fucking tyrant, a nemesis of creation and man bound laws. That poltergeist is constantly changing Its views about what being alive should be like or what it means. Why would It give a shit about how or why we die? What if God doesn't even understand language or what evil means? What if talking to God is like trying to communicate with a fucking ant?'

'Do you think God dreams?'

'I think God is a neurotic alcoholic with a personality disorder. All Its fanatics have inferiority complexes. I would invite some of them over for cheetos and fishsticks if they weren't all either rapists or practicing mass murderers. God's reality is abusive and cruel. I'm pretty sure Its invention was to cure our infected consciousness. Where's the fucking vaccine for that?'

'I really hope I have enough skin left to get all eighty-eight of these vaccination shots. The last one made me feel slightly annoyed that the movie I was streaming didn't have enough ads in it. I feel like my life is just a series of bamboozlements, my personality is just one long advertisement meant to trick people into letting me inject them with my DNA and whatever parasite runs those neurons in my brain-mud. Man, this line never ends.'

'Wait until you get the thirty-third shot. Your fingernails and eyebrows grow at an exaggerated rate. I had to get my eyebrows cut by a professional at least twice a day. It also has nano-robots inside it that turn your dreams into liquid garbage where you dream in 256 resolutions. I felt like my eyes were going to explode. I really need to get a drug addiction. Maybe I'll swallow vitamins until I turn purple.'

'I really need to upgrade my anime pillow.' Blood poured from his nose. Crickets were jumping from his hairline. He secretly wondered if werewolves were natural basketball players.

It was true. The vaccinations were getting out of control. People started to fear them more than they feared the actual diseases they were supposed to cure. Some people woke up and started to become afraid of the strange shortages caused by the pandemic. They needed a constant desire for mundane objects or they lost their will to spend frivolously. The worst was the shortage of critical thinking. No one had been able to upgrade their sex-bots with the new 3090 TXG card. This caused a sort of panic and would eventually result in the extinction of a few thousand more species throughout the reality of hallucination.

Modesty was darkening. Heretic gardens were growing into metaphysical soups. Spicy criminals with terrible haircuts. Everything was a cage of gloom. No one was worried but they were experiencing mild forms of epilepsy. Most people even stopped updating their Facebook pages in fear of becoming too great and causing the American landscape to explode into an even bigger theme park of chaos and stupidity. The line curved through the many hallways. Dreams were becoming overpriced. No one was alive but no one could die either. At the end of the line they were given enough vaccinations that they became addicted to them. Junkie vaccinologists. Lines wrapped around grocery stores with people twitching and screaming for their shots. Many started to wonder if murder was their best possible route to avoid responsibility.

People were melting, sliding across the gutters and sewers. A fire caught in the horizon. Diseases were a currency and most of them had a nationality. The new strain of flu could speak in certain languages. No one wanted to admit it but the new breed of human was becoming contagious. It was outgrowing its own mutations and evolution. Everything was affected. Plants, animals, insects, viruses, bacteria, universe, Gods, language. The story was slowly starting to climax. The end was coming soon. No one cared. No one thought about it. They coughed their godless imaginations into the sky. They traced their fingers across the lost constellations their ancestors had created. They were now orphans in a world that would never love them.

As they sat down on the ride and fastened their plastic belts they noticed that this wasn't a roller coaster. It was a giant needle. They were trapped in a vial attached to it. The needle exploded into space and time and dimensions and mutant portals. It injected the human audience into the arms of Jesus, Zeus, God, the Whatever - they were going to vaccinate the heavens and infect the entirety of reality with the human disease. Everything was becoming a type of sexual scum. The screams throughout the universe was the pale passage of hopelessness. The televisions continued to show the reruns of last year's humiliation. But God was in mourning and the human condition carried on.

LITTLE MIRACLES OF IGNORANCE

There's a fish. Lying in a parking lot. It's temporarily alive. Gasping. Slightly floating with oil in its gums. A woman is pondering this mystery. How did a fish still alive get to her? In this parking lot. Why is it here? It must be a miracle of pacifism and tyrants (those shifty characters of transparent plot contrivances and superficial window dressings leaving vague inspirational quotes in italics and sassy literature). There's a man beside her. He has a cruelty in his hairline. His heart flutters at the sounds his phone makes when it reminds him of trending social fires. These fires make him feel confused and angry and give rise to opinions he feels like he has to pursue even though those opinions will mean absolutely nothing to anyone except the ghosts that linger from his phone. He scratches his head (it's infested with made-up ideas and dandruff). He looks around the parking lot. He secretly believes in invisible humans. He believes monsters are alive in spaceships, on certain tongues, festering inside dirty fingernails. When he votes, he puts the voting sticker right over the left side of his chest, where he used to place his hand when he had to pledge his allegiance to the greatest flag of the greatest country when younger - stronger - when his dreams were made from frog eggs and decaying muscles.

The woman beside him is using her phone to record this

miracle, this fish gasping in the parking lot. To prove to the world the fallacies of the universe, of our reality, for her this is proof that something is wrong with the world - it just doesn't make sense and when the world doesn't make sense for her type of people they believe it must be poltergeist, gods, aliens, secret conspiracies, she is too smart to be fooled by her own ignorance, so everything she doesn't understand is a massive trick. When she was younger she wanted to be a ballerina, she wanted to twirl on a stage to the presence of thousands watching her. But that was hundreds of years ago. She's overweight, her knees don't bend in the correct direction, she complains of precision and materialistic demons and needs constant validation for her misery. She still dreams of being that ballerina. She falls to her knees, she screams and begs, she wants god to command her to perform dirty deeds. She secretly licks pastries and puts them back in a perfect motion on the shelves. She twirls in the mirror and pretends thousands are watching her. With a swarm of brain matter and decayed teeth she eats her children's goldfish. She doesn't dream anymore, she sleeps and the fantasy of being a swan melts through her broken eyebrows. She digs the quasi-millennial jokes that create a real wrinkle-bender in all that tap-talk on the online party think machines. She's addicted to that outrage, a junkie for the real low down sickness of being constantly manipulated by a phony politeness on the lips. Chaos in her face, destructive hands, bloodless fingers, a soul full of bastard vomit ... bastard chaos .... consciousness in the bloodlines, energy, strings like jellyfish for eyelashes. Her eyes were like chewed jelly-beans, a corroded liver, a brain full of parasites and electric junk metals, she had her rotted uterus pulled out and eaten, her tongue was full of slime. But a coward, she reminded herself, is one without a strong sense of self. And in this sick and diasbled society wouldn't it be more productive to survive by being just as disabled and sick?

This man. This woman. They are recording this fish. This

fish is lying in the parking lot. They have proof now. They will submit this to the electric world that lives inside their phones. They will show their families, their distant friends, their decayed lovers, their ghostly fantasies of this little miracle they found in the parking lot. Millions of up-votes and likes will pour in from the world. Videos of scientists and world leaders will converge from their metal skyscrapers. They will discuss this little miracle, this fantastical illusion, they will award and congratulate these two beings for their pursuit of truth through a universe full of demons and liars. Old friends and lovers will send them secret messages about how they always believed in them and knew they would someday find the true and awful mystery of this world. They will bleed from their eyes and bite their lips while tiny fish brains will swell from their gums. For them, a few minutes of fame from ignorance is better than a lifetime of being gross, invisible, annihilated by silence (for in a world that fears boredom more than they fear death, solitude is a miserable god that promotes a slacker psychosis). They understand the world is pushing a need for profound attempts at shopping. That agitators and homosexuals and communists have taken over the news centers. The handicapped are coming for their parking spots. Murderers and rapists and gender-swapping ghouls are foaming at the mouth under dark lagoons to steal their precious freedoms where the price is so ambiguous that no one really understands what type of freedom it is or what it really does. This fish. This little mermaid miracle. This will finally show the world that they are not insignificant decaying flesh with hyper-manic brain circuits.

A few feet away some teenagers are riding skateboards, laughing, they are recording these two people recording a fish. Their skateboards race across the pavement like static against broken glass. A man in his car is recording the teenagers riding in a shopping mall that specifically states that skateboards are not allowed to ride in shopping malls. Behind this man someone is recording him for double parking and above that person someone is recording them all for being ridiculous and above them someone is recording and showing their recording of those recording while simultaneously recording everything that they record. At the end of the day all of these videos of people recording will flood the electric world and though nothing will change everyone will wait in secret anticipation of the next recording as they record themselves reacting to another recording while someone behind them records that reaction and then reacts with a video recording as they respond to the recording they recorded of themselves recording someone else while recording their stupid fucking cats. Nobody will understand it but at least thirteen different groups of people will claim that whatever they are doing while recording is offending their desire to exist. Existing as loud as possible is their only hope of fighting off the existential soup that whirls around in their oh-so-beautifully-made-up genitalia.

This fish. This little miracle that laid eggs before it was snatched up by a bird and dropped in this parking lot will gasp out and suffocate from this ignorance. In a few days its eggs will hatch, those fish will slowly evolve, they will grow snails in their brains, fingers from their heads, slime will mold into seashells, and in a few million years those fish will mutate and crawl from the oceans seeking revenge and they will come with shark teeth spears as they burn the shopping malls and bite the heads of babies off. They will swarm the cities with their mutant armies. Sacrifices and fires will sweep through the world. The songs of whales will lure people to jump into the oceans so the dolphins can rape them while sharks tear through their faces and limbs. A great bolt of energy will explode through the sky and a commercialized Zeus made of every gender and every color and every handicap and every stereotype to be utterly unoffensive to existence that it will technically not even exist itself - in fact, it will be so unoffensive it will not be human or alive or even a figment of anyone's imagination - it will exist as some mutant Frankenstein created by the fear of those that record themselves being in a state of constant anger and phony melodramatics - and this creature named Zeus will come riding a tractor with a leather jacket and a pack of cigarettes in his ears and mouth and this motherfucker will proclaim that he is the fish master and these fucking fish will believe him and start praying to him and with every prayer this dude gets stronger and when they are busy looking for subversive acolytes he will be eating their fish eggs.

A revolution. A comet. A sacrifice. The fish will evolve into grass. The grass will evolve into an ocean made of cheese. The cheese will create a new sentient race of salted crackers with speckles of black with ironic heads. Trees will mutate into giant tentacles that portray themselves as radioactive recordings pursuing outdated identities while fondling their mutilated genitalia. A new species of human will evolve from the septic tanks of shopping centers, they will blink their eyes in the slowly dying star that hovers in the distance. A million different billboards and advertisements floating in the sky will remind them how fucking special they are and it will make them feel so phony and gross that they will eat their overpriced pets while raping television robots and electric vehicles. Everyone will scream. The planet will melt. The last garbled words will be from some commercial selling oxygen purified in the volcanoes of Mars and someone will probably be fucking recording it while hoping to justify their existence by validating the hopes and dreams of a million losers that need to record and occupy opinions to justify having the personality of a sitcom messiah. The stars will explode into cat food. Artists will sell their piss stained carpets. Suicide will be easier than living. Alcohol will be cheaper than water. Smoking will be easier than breathing. Porn will be more gratifying than dating. The rich and crudely wealthy will receive applause for arrogance, mockery, and an audience that will hail them as convictions of mania. Addictions to a pursuit of pseudo-spirituality that will only rob the populace of its inhibitions … greed is evolution is conversation is paradise is intelligence is muddy swamp water plague for rotting teeth covered by plastic caps. Conversations will be lacking in color so we will shoot those who we believe to be already dead. We will fear death by dying in daydreams brought to you by traffic. Love will be a narrative anecdote for commercial people with corporate brain-toys who wish to purchase borrowed happiness from certain hormone glands and they whisper to the fish and ants and trees how they love them but those things won't exist except as stereotypes and corporations so won't be human enough to understand. The beautiful will cannibalize the poor and the poor will rape the trash between their bones and the gods will laugh in a complete mockery as everything slowly decays into a musical number as seen on certain programs for those special socialites with proper love to give to the parasite infested tombs inside a whimpering happiness pretending to be a song pretending to be a dance pretending to be a human gland pretending to be alive while twirling on the dreams of fables and madmen.

Everyone will scream: Life is so beautiful, oh my fucking god, isn't life so fucking special and beautiful? … and if you refuse to agree with them they will murder you and then they will also die and no one will understand the irony.

These proper little miracles will circle us forever in pieces of ignorance and one day we will all die so happy we will explode into rag-dolls of friction and pragmatic imaginations.

And so … and so … and so … and so …

THE DESPERATION

Love, he said, as his face melted into a sense of confusion.

Possessive love, she wondered, is progressive treachery.

They were in love with all manner of things - the way the music lays, it rides through them ... yeah, they fade in the loveliest of ways.

Lizards sing, the stray cats pounce, the insects are mounted in mathematics, and the dreams of ant queens are the imagination of trees.

The smell of poison and rain, heat and wind, came upon them.

They were perpetual readers so they were always bored or drunk or dancing or in love.

Mass-man was mass-insanity and the poisonous outnumbered the sufferers. Oh, how they suffer, they are alive but there is an emptiness to them, to their world, to their dreams, to the singing of substance, to the spiders in the corners spinning - oh, how they spin to be in love, to be dead and to be in love. There is nothing more beautiful for them. There is nothing more dramatic than them.

What does a poet know about anything, she said, you are surrounded by murderers, thieves, cynics, rapists, everyone will always denounce you. You will be alone.

It's true, he said, I am no different than them. But I know something they refuse to accept.

What, she said, could a poet possibly know in all this absurdity?

I know, he said, that it doesn't mean anything. All the dramatics, the politics, the hate and love. They are all following a script that was written long before they were born. They need to be dramatic because they think it's the only way to remain human. They think that humanity is going to save them from their vanity. It's not.

Oh, she said, a nihilist! That's original.

I'm not a nihilist, he said, that assumes I want to participate in the world they created.

Then what are you, she asked, a pretentious bastard?

I don't know, he said, maybe a bad decision on my parent's end? I mean, don't you feel like you have been tricked in this world? Not only tricked into it, but forced to laws and ideas you never agreed with? All this depression and addictions and no one seems to think that maybe it's because we are living in a world that promotes insanity. We are the tricked children of a revolution that will never happen. But watch them! They love it. They fucking love it!

Sometimes, she said, you scare me.

Sometimes, he said, I love you.

Why, she said.

I have nothing else to do in this world, he said.

You only love me because you are bored, she said.

No, he said, I love you because I want everything from this world. I want the insects, the trees, the books, the heavens, the gods, the wet dogs. I demand everything.

Well, she said, you can't have me.

But, he said, I already do have you. Here. Now. Everywhere.

No, she said, this is a dream. I'm not real. Everything about this is a fantasy.

I don't care, he said.

So the television became gospel - beautiful, ugly, static gospel.

They were made from trees and plastic, they were filled with everything - a bird, streets, mold, toasters, cold coffee, the cats would turn into statues, sometimes weeds, people climbed into their eyes, they bled from their tongues. The television was on its daily crusade. It was filled with infidels, agitators, atheists. They all wondered the same things ... is this the landscape where I die?

Her personally was artificially stimulated with chemicals and romance novels. He went to purify the human condition with an inconsistent dream. Her dream.

Love, she said, as her face melted into a sense of desperation.

THERE ARE GHOST INSIDE HER BONES

We hooked phones into our brains before we slept - everyone would share the same experience inside dreams - we would slide into a constant state of deja vu together ... they advertised commercial-souls that promoted designer slime-pits made of cavities and orgasms -

(when the show ended she took off her clothes and became a stereotype in front of me ... we floated into the bedroom, where we dug a grave, we hid secrets in corners of our hearts that contentment would never find)

the ocean spread the cunt-minded between her legs, her vagina opened up with an eyeball staring at us from the inside, we feared the extinction inside her genitalia ... her skin was smooth yet slimy while our skin was rough and full of scars - we injected the magic into our veins, our blood was full of gods and stars and our eyes were an ethereal fluid - there was an elegance to her lips, a transformed iconoclast - disillusioned, over-civilized madmen (adventurers of conformity) who were not normal and since they were not normal they were not alive or allowed to surrender to stupidity and destiny, they poured out from her like a liquid, intoxicated by their resistance to sensation, rebellion, happiness, superstition was their illusion, suicide was the prophet of a schizophrenic god - in our television-dreams the universe was applauded for its absurdity, it became a magical land of celestial beings living out ridiculous myths of insecurity and inferno, free will became a complimentary gift of culture and cult religions ... boredom reminded us that we were alive, being entertained made sure we were dead -

(she reaches in, she stabs at the television screen, she embraces its radiation, she slices open the screen, she drinks the slime and static that spills out ...) mutations designed itself across our necro-skin, our eyes frizzled into mathematical molecules, our tongues became passive, we traveled through time with melancholy's grace, spreading unknown diseases to the bacteria (living in the suburbs of sitcoms and villains) that was still evolving, wiping out human history, creating madmen monkeys in love with incoherence ...

eventually the universe would expand faster than light and all the stars would forever burn out and disappear - our brains became entropy, electric toasters, it pulsed with energy none of us could understand - we were magnetic - we were invincible - we were genius.

THE GIRL WITH THE SHOPPING CART OF TOILET PAPER

Grocery store. Somewhere near the end of the world. The weather is its own perfect devil. Life here has mutated into hysteria, insecurity, immoral vigilance, anxiety, destruction, disease, people's faces are monasteries burning with perfect wounds. God is on the bullhorn bellowing from thunderclouds screaming for people to waste more time in mortification and torment. Of course, the people in this goddamn town comply. They are, after all, outraged suspects of degenerate commentaries, indolence, gluttonous, thirsty, fanatics, extremists, greedy, desolate, ambiguous monsters holding their children to the terrors of immortality. God is the aggressive womb in their inexpressible literature (whatever the fuck that means). Hopefully, paradise is full of leeches and muted funerals followed by eternal groveling. I bet it smells like sex and rape in heaven.

And, by all the fucks, I am surrounded by these goddamn mutants as I shop in this grocery store. Someone is being stabbed in the front of the store for not wearing their protective gear, there are three people rioting in the parking lot, fighting with shopping carts with squeaky wheels because they believe these protective helmets they are forced to wear might be affecting their ability to get an erection. Those of us that wear the plastic bags around our faces are slowly dreading the future. We know we can kill ourselves at any time because we realize that being a corpse makes us stronger than any disease. Piles of bodies are littered all over the store. The manager is pouring cheap wine on them and setting them on fire. Someone is screaming about toilet paper. Someone removes their hazmat suit and lights themselves in extravagant complaining. There is a cemetery in the eyes of the old, and the bellowing misfortune of birth in the hands of the young. We all understand what is happening here. God fucking hates us and our mothers and fathers did this to us by having too much of the fucking fuck because growing up with too much electricity bores the shit out of all of us.

You were shuffling along in aisle three with a shopping cart of toilet paper. I was following people around that were coughing or sneezing, rubbing my face on everything they touched. You said: "Hey! Why are you doing that, psycho-face?"

I shrugged and said: "My poor upbringing has brought me into a mood for self-destructive behavior. I don't really have a choice, I just follow the script my parents laid out for me. I'm only a product of my parent's lust for each other. I understand my need to gratify my existence by embarking on petty shenanigans but since I'm a product of poverty and an institution that would rather indoctrinate instead of educate, I have no choice but to follow the commandments of the stereotypes and cliches my type of people have become. I don't want people to hate me. I want them to love me for my ignorance. I rather like it when they pity me."

I asked you about the toilet paper. You told me you were afraid you didn't have enough Instagram followers so you would fill up shopping carts with toilet paper and then have your grandmother take pictures behind you. "Your followers jump by fifteen percent if it's about panic shoppers." You smiled. Some of your teeth were missing. I secretly knew you were selling them on the internet at a two-hundred percent mark up rate.

In aisle seven two people were dancing to the disco tunes of dead superstars. No one understood a goddamn thing. But, for whatever reasons, we watched them and thought they were beautiful. We might have joined if they didn't have a sale on hand sanitizers ... buy fifty and watch three people die.

In line, the grocery manager stood on a 'Happy Birthday' balloon that had traces of pink and the picture of some Disney princess we might have all known in some other life, some other world, somewhere none of us belonged anymore. He sprayed us all with disinfectant - we danced like it was 1993 - bubbles of soap surrounded us. Our limbic system cracking under the violence of infectious revolutions ... everyone was guilty of grandeur, vanity, beauty, love, murder or the suspicion of murder. None of us really minded ... capitalism made sure that we were safe as long as we kept spending money on items that would never have a soul.

You lit your toilet paper on fire. I started to get sick from the years of alcohol abuse that was probably causing a slow psychosis. My liver was growing its own universe. It was election year. As Americans, we knew we would have to vote eventually. None of us wanted to - we all dreaded it - We would either vote for the man that the media told us to pick or the man that our communities told us to pick - which was paradoxical because our communities always picked the man the media told them to pick and then hated anyone that actually listened to them. Elections were like buying something. We were buying our freedom. We were buying personality cults. None of us really believed the world would ever change, we didn't need it to change, we just wanted some validation for believing we actually ever had a choice. In America, the land of freedom, we didn't vote because we wanted to - we voted because we were forced to have an agenda and that agenda made us angry and mean and hate each other. We were voting for ideologies, stickers to boast proudly of the mad citizens we had made gods, nothing would ever change - it was never supposed to.

In the court of kings, the jesters will always be ironic to please the masses.

Down in the gutters of this America, between the alcohol-washed faces and Burrrr-gun-dee, a homeless man is walking forward with his hands up, listening to the fireworks, he's screaming: 'It's not me, man! I didn't do it! Don't shoot me, motherfuckers! I ain't even black, I am shades of shadows and shit.'

The tourists are doing hula-hoop dances with snakes around their necks. The slums are built under the faces of deformed children, sexual cultists worshiping dead fetuses they shove inside vagina goons they navigate by turning their cocks into steels and chains and chimneys made from the bone-dust of slaves and rape. Priests and wizards and warlocks smoking insects in front of cloudy alleys. Electric enthusiasts with homosexual eyes blinking in the weird sickness. Tarot card fingers flipping through the past and present. Teeth, trash, old junky lovers lying wasted on the cracked and dented concrete. The buildings smashing downwards into the earth. Waves of broken sidewalks like jagged mouths swallowing the venom and piss of the city.

America isn't meant to be beautiful. It's a country where the shit and grime and dirt and dust are the aesthetics, the attraction. All the horrors of what poverty does to men, the insanity of boredom when there's nothing left but booze and bad hookers and fresh dirt to lie inside. People come here to witness the dirt come alive and wrap everything like giant tentacles from the cemetery ghouls. There is filth and old evil under the fingernails here. People's eyes are stained, flaking skin from the tongues that rot dried lips and songs from a past no one quite remembers.

The artists love it here because everyone is sort of walking under the life. The shadows have names. The buildings lurk with a menace, the con-artists look to shine your eyebrows for a flick of rust from your tin tobacco. Even during the day the shadows don't dissipate - they twirl inside with the ghosts and poltergeist that haunt every word, every time someone vomits, every tune from an instrument, every drink and the constipation of booze that squeezes from the tit of the serpent that lives underneath it. The gloom of the city wraps itself against the sludge of our souls, it twist and burns until everyone in the city becomes silent like a soft sore under your tongue festering during that hour around midnight when no one is really sleeping, they are staring into the dirt, the shadows stirring inside their flesh, the voodoo whores inviting the degenerates of a paradise run by poverty and shit and the graffiti of a soulless god. You can see the stains of their shadows on the streets and buildings in the morning when smoking your cigarette. You breathe it in ... you melt inside the filth ... the city consumes you and you smile in anticipation of the coming witches. Nothing was subjective here. It was meant to harm self-preservation through fits of mania.

Somewhere between the parking lot and mass hysteria I lost you ... my disco queen ... between love-victory, a city full of cynicism, and the end of the world - where none of us understood anything.

FLORIDA

On the side of a thrift store across the street from me someone has spray painted: *If you stop doing drugs you will die.* This has somehow destabilized people's mental anguish. They believe America will be ruined because of this slogan. That freedom will somehow disappear into the ground and become some lost and ancient monster people will daydream about when high on alcohol. There's a bee, or maybe it's a wasp, that lives underground here in Florida. Nancy, the old woman across the street is waving her arms at me. She says these bees are attacking her cats. I immediately ran over to save her from embarrassing herself. I assure her that these are in fact, not bees, but wasps. This doesn't seem to calm her down. Nancy is now running around her lawn in her pajamas screaming for someone to save her cats. She is going in a perfect motion of circles. I think maybe these things are carrying some type of disease, a new type of schizophrenia that will call an end to us all with more madness. America doesn't need more madness. It needs less of it.

I've become a stranger here.

I pretend not to understand this ending of the world. I care little for vowels or petty driveling of newscasters who always seem to have sensationalist eyebrows and sneering lips. The internet has become full of poltergeists that want to haunt people's reserve. Estrangement is spreading everywhere. Nothingness clouds the windshields of cars here. Florida doesn't require a vehicle inspection. Rage and hatred is hustled out to street poets and park benches - even the Republicans here have renounced their duty to the metaphysical and given up to television. Romance has become the ignorance of criminals. Darkness is a cannibal and it is eating our livers. Environmentalists are running around in black robes, hockey masks, beating anyone that knows the definition of plaster, or is it plastic? People have become scared here. They spray paint words on their cars and homes that say: *Electric only. Don't raid.*

There's a treasure in the hearts of the cashier and women and a pornographic imagination of the men whenever they see them wearing short skirts and shorts. Even though these men have seen a thousand women naked, they must, for whatever reasons, see one more. It is the curse of being a man. We are all citizens of Florida and a failing god of the world. Stray cats are running around like thugs, stealing people's food and water and perhaps even their inhibitions. The language they sing seems to be only known by old or lonely ladies.

The place I live in is small. The carpet is stained. It has the constant smell of cat piss. I'm sure the antichrist is living in my refrigerator. There is always a dog barking in the neighborhood. Someone is always landscaping their lawns or power washing their kids faces. None of it makes sense. It's like a dream but the dream is only half-created like an old VHS tape where most of the movie has been erased. There's a sense of pending doom here in America, in Florida, the weather is constantly moody, nothing ever dies, everything is on drugs, grocery stores are littered with hoodwinking programs for the communist minded, even the cockroaches have started to complain.

Someone should tell God that his creation has become bored and that boredom is spreading brutality. Absurdity is spreading like a sickness. The churches here are starting to worry. They have begun building their worship with thoughts of self-validation inside a song about how consumerism will set your soul free and wild. People are now shopping with thoughts of making Jesus happy and Satan angry. Satan is and was never a capitalist. Everyone who has ever been to Sunday school knows this. It's the law they feed our minds when young and full of vulnerabilities. Evolutionists are asking questions like: Did tadpoles dream of being grocery clerks? Do we really need another billboard advertising Jesus holding an M-16 rifle but with a look of subjective identification in his eyebrows? They are pulling skepticism from the thoughts of the lower classes. Young girls are now inert materials as seen in certain social media clubs. Everyone is married but no one is happy. Speech is free but language is dangerous. Everything is familiar but extremely vague. There is no God but there is a mathematical code to the universe. Okay, there is a God but it is such a ridiculous dilemma we have decided to pray to state lotteries instead. Politicians here are denouncing everything, well, except absurdity. That they love. One politician from Orlando pulled out his motorcycle pamphlet and started reading passages. People were so bored some wondered if God had already committed suicide and this was the cause of the universe being born. Someone fainted from humility. One person laughed. That person was immediately destroyed. Everyone is entertained and everyone is bored. Everything is paradise, everyone an exaggeration, a pedestal of suggestive thinking. Everyone is beautiful, nothing is allowed to be ugly. In fact, it's sort of the law.

Everyone here has psoriasis. Patches of red appear all over their bodies. Faces look dull, a sort of blush with traces of blood. They have red wine foreheads. Since everyone has it. No one seems to mind or do anything about it. It is their genetic leprosy, a mutation caused by random acts of chocolate shortages. Which causes chaos during the shopping seasons. They have babies. The babies come out all red, patches of scabs festering all over their bodies. They look like swollen balloons that have lost their purpose to spread static electricity across carpets and children's perky heads. No one cares. No one minds. Everyone has it. The sun rips it apart in the summer anyway.

In Florida, no one is really dead and no one is really alive. We are at the end of the world. Somehow we know that America is ending. The men are no longer pleasant to be around and the women have started to find mediocrity pleasing. Women have never found mediocrity a pleasant substance. Everything is oversensitive, even the streetlights here are flicking in Morse code. In America, in Florida, where we are in the kingdom of plastic, unforgivable soldiers, the citizens are not afraid as much as they are annoyed. Termites are practicing osmosis by eating books. Beetles are eating the imagination of trees. The stray cats are pondering human cruelty. Nothing is real. I slip into my Styrofoam uniform. Conformity continues on the minds of insects. The year is 2020. There's an army of love sick enthusiasts marching down the street. Nobody understands them. Nobody wants to. They are an absurd fiction of America. They are the drunk assassins of Florida.

SONGS FOR THE LOVE POETS WHO SMOKE CIGARETTES

The exploitative critic (culture-cropping men that depend on narcissism as self-identity, they create the neo-poet who cares little for the human condition as much as they care for the individualist - they will unwind you with more filth until you are a dark sewer foaming with dead stars arriving in poisonous ironies) ... the dysphoria circus - when nothing seems real or you don't feel like you exist at all ... the last poet gasping for more lines in the sickness of sonnets, the violence in his world is so passive it becomes absurd ...

- the sudden glass weeping in black purgatory - the miracle of neon eyelashes swooning to men-masked with shades of alarm and somber greys - oh how my mortality stumbles towards impurity - oh how the haunt of no-life is persistent in my musical tongue - where did my gods go? Where do fathers escape to inspire young women with stacks of sexual limbs? - curse this goddamn summer and the forgotten stars -

oh dear, the walls are coming apart in conversation, the ceiling is about to fall, my mind is mud and wires and my body is scaling inward - the living are the counterfeit and the dead are impatient for more chaos -

- they and all are made into dirt and tree parts - it is not i that is suffering, it is you, you, and you that are reading this - how the monsters in my fingernails grovel to life and all its amused amusements (error and silence bit into his lips at this precise moment, the audience gathered and began to stab him with knives) ...

- the loveliest people live in my songs, my stories, they are the loneliest people i've ever known - everyone else is a superficial paradox looking to eat me with slime and advertisements (apathy becomes the only sane choice here, free speech is only identity which offends other identities which creates moderation for abstract thinking, the language is no longer interesting unless it abides by rules and regulations from mutants that ooze horror poems from their mouths, their desire to control through symbolism creates the worst of all skeptics - a poem is a movement of the mind, a movement of forbidden language, hiding between tiny fragments of magical gangsters who wish to destroy the horror of identification)

- the poet's pores open up into small portals, earthworms and trees crawl out in certain formations - the poet is no longer a part of identity (shadow object), he is no longer superstitious of language and abstracts, he becomes a heroic nihilist that uses poetry to expose the language of horror that pretends to be of free virtue when it only wishes to suppress offensive fictions (in this exact moment the audience becomes bored and starts to cannibalize themselves and their children ... a new world forms from the slime in their heads ... the new world promotes apathy as the only servitude ... the signs all glow in the same colors and they read: *Don't be dangerous and will we entertain you cretins ...*) ...

- grocery clerk poets smiled at the hoodwinking products they were shoving down the throats of the goblins, no one understood this vanity, they simply continued to be polite and meander around in epileptic brains gone weird within nationalist dreams of comfortable sounds ... oh identity (they scream to invisible creatures living in television screens), oh superfluous identity, enlighten me with your a-musings ... they become angered - they scream all at once towards the loser poet:

... Hey! You! Stop disrupting the social order of things! Turn your eyebrows off! You are obviously raising them too high. We measure the length of someone's forehead and apply a rule that your eyebrows can only go .2 centimeters forward - anything above that we believe you are being subversive and subject to nasty bouts of passive-aggressive lip snarling - you have been warned, sir!

Police! God! Police! God! Fire and Twitter! Arrest this cretin! It's trying to modify my existence!

(...(part poet and cigarette)...)

poor petty penny, curving into her cigarettes

drawing gentle shrills from the audience, twisting her cigarettes with her fingers, gnarling the filters with lipstick

her inverted intimacy, the hundred thousand eyelashes, who each impassion conspiracy

(...(part poet and solitude)...)

blurr'd cosmic boys with curly blonde hair,
treating gardens, clapping with phantom hands
(yah! yah! yah!) this is how they sing for love's love and love love love

superhuman thirst and fevers and weather-beaten limbs, they fold into the destiny of peasants in thrift store boardrooms

(homeless men sleeping on bed bug infested furniture while smoking cardboard cigarettes)

rose water liquor in his swollen lips, a cripple with an obsession for vulgar celebrations ... the utopian empire was a barbarism (his face is illiterate fusion and his teeth are melted stars) this mutant was easily god-smacked when drunk, a fantasy of the cerebral pleasure centers ... oh! this beautiful mutant cried: To the hysterics of love! You brain-arousing mystics! (he fell to his knees and proclaimed to the enchanted savagery between her legs) We have seen the face of the universe and it is strangely human ... The threat of drama always brings us disorder and vanity! Let my art be degenerate - lick me with mannerisms and modesty! Pinch the belly and let us spread this deadly and contagious boredom where they sell our dreams for profit! Let our lives be rational, concise, let nothing disturb our rest!

(...(part poet and beggar)...)

love is a lantern cast by flesh, in the car accident where Shakespear died, black cast coals etched my silhouette.

i can see flickers of light from the room close-by, small tiny flecks of retreat, like tiny toad-crickets exploding.

i can still remember, the pain in, trembling over one's birth, the pause before silence gathers silently.

she, the queen of woe, drifting on the bed, lighting her cigarette, against the lampshade

a proper wife for pluto

(...(part poet and a mask of suffering)...)

(note): the words are an abstract. they are illusions, mirrors of something shallow most of the time. love isn't meant to be a constellation of profound emotions or an intimate desire in any of these poems. love is more of a person, a bodied resemblance to something unknown or alien. i, myself, think the word is often used to gratify self-indulgence, self-esteem, or simplify one's affection. also, the 'she' or 'her' in any of these poems do not represent anyone at all. they are used as subjective plot devices to give the abstract some personality, or embody it with romantic characteristics so as to prevail over any corruption of identity. because, those of us that look for the human condition, eventually drown within it. we know people don't want truth. they want lies and illusions. and, if ever, you were to tell them the truth, they would rip you apart and eat you. thank you for understanding (lights a cigarette and drops it which creates a blister on my right finger).

(...(part poet and the last poet of cosmic worlds)...)

her figure(a composition of tainted family gatherings mixed with a suicidal flavor, her father was a ghost and her mother brought in all the real boys - her last marriage was to an unmanageable maggot with bad bedside appetites - this man grew up in afternoon slums anchored with flower shops and palm trees infested with gravel and beetles and homeless men) -

she hangs slightly over the bed frame, her breathing is attentive, delicate, her breast kept close in her arms as if some trophy. i sketch her eyes and breathe slowly with nicotine against my lips, its air flowing out of my mouth and lungs like a breeze through the window (there's only two windows in this house - they all point eastward so the sunlight always wakes us up).

i notice the shitty light staring heavy through the blinds, i can see particles of dust wide-eyed; caught nesting on the clouds of cigarette smoke i exhale throughout the bedroom. she stirs, stretches, and yawns. her eyes are scorned with sleep and shit and those pretty dreams she speaks about, but only on the weekends will she tell me about them, or maybe a rainy afternoon when everything's spent, the ground soaking heavens spit, and the flowers we planted imagining some silent fear or the kids next door kicking away their blooming-heads.

she moves in slow motion, her hands go over my side to the desk as she grabs a cigarette and the small green lighter. she lights the cigarette and for a moment her face is eclipsed by light, but just for a moment(nose hairs pruning to the fire in her literature). she drags, inhales, releases. her neck, her lips, her hair, her fingers, her shadow and all the emptiness is grained into the earth, into the bed, into the pillows.

we don't know it yet but we are in a dead relationship ... i tell her i want to have knife fights with borges. She tells me about a vampire novel she's writing. she says it's a parable of metaphors hiding within an obscure allegory ... i tell her i want to inject a conjecture inside her semicolon. i tell her it's a shame she was born too late to be a genius and too early to be a decent poet. she doesn't agree (at this moment she extinguishes her cigarette between her legs).

(...(part poet and cosmogonies in casualty)...)

His face is a thunderbolt. His eyes are tragic cradles. His breath is prone. His tongue is marble, ruined teeth, mustard expressions, murder in his sneeze. He yelps like a conquering mosquito wrestling in the hairs of someone's scalp. His name is written backwards. Someone points to the tower in the center of the city.

That's his lair, they say in hushed tones.

His friends walk up the spiraling stone to his den. They don't notice the burnt marks from gunfire and explosions drawn on the walls. They don't see the dead, they are invisible unless they are wearing the same colors or carrying the same flags.

They get to the top. They find him face down. Someone turns him over. His eyes are death-phobic. His face is gray. His stomach is turned out.

"It's Hansen," one of them says while lighting a cigarette.

(...(part poet in disembodied faces)...)

He was a janitor that worked the night shift at a grocery store. She was a lesbian with a penance for collecting stray cats. People made fun. People laughed. But, the crime rate dropped and their costumes matched.

ATOMIC SPECTACULAR

"Hypocrisy is a rotting cat named Irony"

I say this even though I know everything that comes from my mouth is a blister of lies piled on fictions I have created to partake in pretensions so others around me feel comfortable. I have never been honest, even when I pray to god I lie about everything. Most of the time I write my prayers down instead of saying them because I know god is illiterate. I mean, that's why other people had to write its books, right? We wish for all these cruel sounds to crumble from our tongues. Yes. We understand beauty is a trick and a disturbing one. Everything beautiful is boring. Every time I hear someone say, 'That is beautiful.' I secretly think they are devils. Yet, I don't tell lies, I theorize the truth - I theorize situations to commit them into rumors which therefore make them into works of fiction and fiction is never a lie, they are simply stories. When I tell stories, I am not a liar, I am a writer.

I have thought all day about this moment. I practiced all morning in the mirror for this. To wait in line, to gather resources from this store, to connect in the most superficial way possible with other human beings. This is being alive for me. My fingernails are cut, trimmed nicely. My hair is combed. My clothes I washed and ironed for this moment. To wait here, in line. I am vaccinated against the gods and their heavenly poisons. I wear a witch's bridle across my face. I am focused under my eyelids. I dance in a fevered lust amongst the others with me. We are waiting in line together. Hands rubbing our wallets and purses and coins and pendants and we are all well mannered while we stare at the advertisements, the celebrities who seem to live in terrible melodramas, the political fires across our hairlines. We all got up this morning and decided that we should wait here, in line, together. We quietly judge those who take too long with their credit cards, who fumble with change, who speak the weather-speak in hopes of connecting some facetious conversation with strangers. We are waiting our turn to exchange brain-moss with this mythical creature they presume to be a clerk.

These clerks are minstrels and priests and guardians of the items we need to purchase. We must pass their tests to acquire these and so to level up in this capital quest to own more than everyone else. We applaud space travel but understand we will never taste it. The clerks of sorcery and uselessness howl out their questions and we must answer them or be destroyed. Their teeth are like chipped fingernails, their lips bloodied from their last meal, their eyes decayed with a boredom that goes deeper than any hell.

'Hello. Did you find everything okay? How is your day? Would you like to feel guilty for crippled children and the poor by fulfilling us with more of your monies? Would you like to register your secrets and all the numbers that make you human for a discount?'

They scream this out as pieces of dead souls cartwheel from their tongues.

We answer these questions while biting back our humanities. We are afraid if we answer wrongly someone might intervene and continue this baseless interaction with more banality. We want to say yes to everything because we fear the confrontation of being negative might upset the order of these creatures. We don't want to be an asshole because it takes too much energy, too much responsibility, and someone might be recording us. But, we don't really care about the crippled children, the poor, the dead mermaids devastated by our civilizations. We only say we care because we are well-mannered, good citizens, and easily amused by clever adverts.

We are only concerned with acceptance. We push buttons on small keypads, secret numbers, numbers that have all the codes to what universes we belong to and what gods we worship. The clerks of divinity look upon our glowing faces and teeth. They secretly wish they could be like us, they could fulfill their human needs with what we carry, silently, in vaults that this oh so secret number on this plastic card carries, hides, those dark universes we worship with every job we work. We look at them as well, we smile together, even though we secretly hate each other's existence.

The women around me smell like demons and strawberries, they hold onto crypto philanthropies which they believe is therapy for the brain coupons creating living landscapes behind their mirrors that are slowly killing them. Mass deception is open and voluntary. Drugs to promote suicide, and drugs to promote birth rates to recreate new human generations from failed ones. Manifolds of deprivation and poverty and ugliness are sought over logic and love, adaptation into insanity is a natural evolution of humans in a disturbing culture. An announcement is overheard: the suicides of self interest will continue until morale improves.

Some men are weeping behind me like insects burning in plastic. Some women are biting at their fingers and barking at their animals. Someone drops to their knees. They scream in a prayer that sounds mad and terrible and though I pretend they don't exist, I am secretly in love with them. Everyone of us is a biomech maestro piloted by stomach bacteria, reflexes, proteins, and a chain of neurons like a haunted conformity. An atomic spectacular. And I, a poet con artist that identifies as decadence as my mouth explodes and goes … blah blah boom!

My head cracks open like an egg and out from it comes a slimy bird vomiting word miracles. I don't want to commission my compassion to faith, a fashion from illusionary myths sedating this disaster, I would find my absence of god in my lack of a beloved master (my soul is a grifter in this nostalgic and imperialist grandeur) ... this world belongs to disco and danger ... this world belongs to beauty among the anger, my very own and to no one else's tune. I fight back the imposters and abstractions of behavior that mimic my own vanity in the most antisocial way possible.

I understand that the demon they call Consciousness is constantly trying to mutilate us with language, thought, identity, till we become a harbor of dystopia and confusion. We forget what being alive and human means as the cultural grooming bipeds, harboring millions of miserable little fountains full of secrets, take what little aspirations we have left. Gender hysterias have come to sink their teeth into this functional disaster, our disaster, my disaster. An authoritative representation of identity that promotes through degenerate acts of violence to soothe their own self-hatred. We must accommodate every shade of identity so the revolutionary filth may devour us into their self-mutilated foyers disguised as contrived excuses of the infinite. We are crypto-conformists at heart and our extinction self promotes through this prophecy.

This manipulation of reality or mutilation of the human element defines our human experience as anti-nature, deprivation of substance, there is no spirit - it has been mutated into plastic and deviance, violators of peace, prosecuted by stupidity ... who identifies with mental illness except those who are already weaken? The people in line shout in unison: We are not anti-human or lack humanity, we are simply pro suffering.

And I remember the dream I had of the poets who were priests upon the fabric of humanity whose time bellowed and wept when it came to an empty gasp. For I am one who weeps constantly. The citizens, the ones not tied to corporations, will always be the livestock, the minions and deserted gullible - to be used as servants and turned into beautiful corpses, and oh how beautiful they are! There is a wicked sorcery in this store, one that turned the residents into (calculated) mediocrity. It is by will and conscience that I become conflicted ... I am conflicted by the conscience of others and willed by my bemusement of their behavior, perpetuated hierarchies of institutional oppression corrode into my genitals and I cry for more pain to be fed into my being.

Oh oh oh ... how I ride the soul and chase my woes!

We, orphans of schizophrenics, where the cost of morals are indifferent to the suffering it causes, a one way street for hypocrites and tyrants, and the adrenaline junkies hooked to its fear as it produces compulsive behavior that in return promotes consumerism. The line of people becomes restless, we all start to panic. They scream out: there is no morality without our theology, and god is an evil king.

Mutually suspicious gossip is how we survive, in this world. We whisper garbage in each other's heads, a distraction for our domesticated extinctions. We share that death together, with every piece of plastic, poison, extinction, and song we consume. We are the great singularity inside a non-relative monolith experiencing life within the mathematical debris of behavior - and If you are born, or find yourself in thought and recognize how beautiful it is that you are capable of thought ... then, my friend, you are a failure.

The line continues to move. None of us understand anything. We execute our individuality for complacency. We shrug our shoulders, laughing nervously. Rubbing our wallets, gripping our children tighter. The line never breaks, its formation is the last human thing left about us. We see the end and we confuse it with more bizarre entertainments and insane politics (lest the worms grovel from the sum of their thoughts and start to scream). The sun is brighter these days, heavier even. The mountains are all on fire in the distance. Sweet lullabies sing politely in our ears. Madmen on the television are foaming at the mouth, dead cats are lying neatly in piles of rot next to the roads. We fold peacefully into the glowing screens while screaming … but the scream is quiet, the scream is quiet because we are well-mannered, civilized, tamed and beautiful. Lovely, even.

STORIES OF MEN

I'm beginning to think everyone has three stories that define their personality. Some of these stories are never told, some are dull, some vomit it all over your face. Like this English guy here. I've never been to England but if they're all like him ... I'm never going. I have heard all his stories because he tells them all the time.

He's married.

Now all I can think of is how one of those stories got him laid. Some poor woman heard one of those stories and said - -Yes. I think I would like to put more of this man in the world. One is just not enough.

This is now spreading across the city. Everyone wants to share their story. People are lining up everywhere, combing their hair, tucking in their shirts, they all have a story. They are screaming stories from the streets. Some are whispering stories in bathroom stalls. Some think to get laid, some think to be interesting, some just want to be heard. The entire goddamn world is shouting stories. And I want to tell them all to shut the fuck up.

I need some insanity to balance out the sanity of this work environment. I'm afraid one day I might conform to them, that

I might morph into the same shade and colors as them, that I will forget my dreams, that I will forget the movements of stars and galaxies, that I will huddle around in circles sharing stories.

And then a woman will say - - Yes. I like him. I think there needs to be more of him in the world.

And that, for whatever reasons, scares the shit out of me.

INTO THE SEAS OF
LOST LIVELINESS

(1) Today (and only today) I am lovers lived, mathematical equations that twirl on the tips of fingers, the saliva dripping between teeth, the crack in the concrete where the building has become too heavy,

too much, the superficial explosions of weeds and poisons in the wasp nested head of shameless losers (who vote for crude losers to become even more shameful).

(2) I am the yellow-tinted coloring of wilted leaves, pebbles and rocks and the fractured curve in the church bell. When they sing to clouds and space and to the vast emptiness of the universe - they are singing songs that were formless, populated by a perpetual dissolution when only muddy waters and stones and barren vague shapes scattered to secrets (like insects when the light-bulb energy creates an explosion of life) - shameless, ethereal, unhinged.

(3) The dance: Awakens.

(like two different colored shoelaces bending and tying into one another - tongue melting cartwheels, a hug - the dissolving into chemical elements that splash waves of kisses and little lips parted)

and:

the way the keys of a piano play that reminds me of the heart of a woman in love. Or the violin that reminds me of the sound a man makes when he groans in anguish over lost love. If only I had one of those social media type brains. I might be able to see through it all and press against the fluff of optimism and let it enter inside me while I spend the rest of my life lying to myself that a true human experience is found in faceless ideologies, psychotic institutions, men with brooding eyes and women who appear lost forever like some ghostly apparition ...

- drowning into seas of lost liveliness -

(4) I invent all these dreams. I invite the horde of illusions, dancing insects into my stomach. I pick lint and dandruff from my hair, I bite my lip in anticipation.

If I am a poet then I want all the damned and forsaken to be heard singing. They can sing to me. I can sing to you, right outside your window.

I would sing:

You are the world, which is life. When I think of you I think of you thinking and then when I think of thinking I think of all the wrong things thinking. We are free to seek love in those fatally flawed beings with simulations engineered in their brains. May my mind carry you with it, away from those that seek explained worlds, away from difficulty, metaphors, towards where the flesh crawls - because, it crawls in the meadows of the world - where everyone is sleeping.

(5) This is only a demonstration of embrace.

This is only mind-patterns of love. Of spoken-word-dreams.

Come away, and come away, stray with me.

Come away, and come away, stray with me.

There is a taste in our brains - it says: Hello God. I want to be in love.

Hello God. I want to believe in superstition.

My mind! My heart! It is boiling in jolts and tranquility.

My mind! My Heart! It wants to be content in the extraterrestrial. It wants to wither like a growing caterpillar in her stomach. It wants to be naked and unruly like some cave-monster. It wants to be painted. Awkward. Inviting. Friendliness with a body and nothing but a thin strip of sheet between us. It needs darkness and mortality.

Hello God. Kiss me. I am frightened.

Outside. The world is still insane.

Inside, we still have the sky to unwrap and wrap again with our music.

(6) Unholy ghouls with orgasms for lips. They know lovers can read souls through the eyes. A glimpse, idea, swimming in glances. Their voices are the wind. The sounds of piano plays between their legs. It was a fruitful speech that they followed. They understood the individual's reason for love. The man shows his soul. The woman shows him to the liquor store. The man removes his clothes. The woman reassures the man that god is not done with us yet.

They say:

Kiss me. I am alone. I came for the love and the ability to be loved. Do not turn me away. Everything already has turned me away. I am willing to give up responsibility. Heaven. Magic. The mysteries of life and universe ... but first you must kiss me.

When you kiss me I will love you.

Kiss me. I adore you. I want to love you.

Kiss me.

Forget God. He has forgotten you.

Come away, come away.

Come away, come away..

Come with me, Love - think little and gratify the forbidden!

Stimulate and intoxicate the consciousness, abandon the fever of social conventions,

Let us be love larva ...

Come, come and love with me .. come, come away (I want to be young and loved and bitter with songs of confetti singing to this superficial litter)

THE DEVASTATED
ONES

We were in bed. Lying close to one another. Being unhooked like lovers usually are. It must have been winter because everything was dying around us. Even we, even we were slowly dying. Our skin becoming like blisters, our fingernails melting through our pores. She had street lights for eyes and all that make-up made me think she was probably one of those skeptical ones.

Love. Who believed in love these days? There was nothing to believe in. Not anymore. The world was ending in stupidity and plagues and no one even remembered to bring reason. It seemed our lives were perfect elements of half-broken circles. There was a calculating loneliness in the eyes of the poor and degenerates. Scoundrels, madmen, insecure modesty knifed us in our hearts. Social media was filled with heretics, ghosts, devils, pathos of disease. Nostalgia was the intolerable frenzy feeding off our abused thoughts. None of us wanted to be cynical, none of us wanted to be ugly, but banality cursed us with laziness, debauchery, rebellion, religion, hopelessness, shame, work and suicide seemed to be the same monster with eighteen different faces.

So, for many of us, optimism and love were tricks. Phantoms of false mechanics. And you seen it in everything. The weariness made us all skeptics and if you weren't a skeptic, then we thought you were a secret horror looking to assassinate whatever freedoms we had left to endure and the remedy of that injustice was to suffer ... calmly.

The horrors of this world didn't live in the corners or shadowy buildings. It lived in our apocalyptic imaginations - starved, begging, hunched over, staring, ready to drag us into humiliation. Our heroes were rapists and murderers, our gods were dust and tricks, our leaders were thieves and cultists, our families turned into conspiracy fanatics looking for a religious experience in a madman's appetite. Social media portrayed the human condition as a cartoon fantasy world where humans were caricatures meant to be in shades of bright colors that turned us all into mediocre drones. It came off as phony. A falsehood. We didn't really believe these people cared for beauty or the sick or the weak or the poor. They only cared for abstract notabilities, their beauty gave them an artless gloom that only reminded us of our inevitable spiritual collapse. When we brought this up we were called nihilists, shoved into the gutters of damnation, the yolk of hell, doubted within incoherent poetry written by wretched iconoclasts under the pretense of prophetic regeneration.

Culture was an evil word swimming in a cesspool of contradictions. Hypocrisy was it's emperor, anxiety was its misfortune, ignorance infected inside its conscience. The masses had all gone to fornicate with dead prophets. Critics of humanity were called pessimistic when critics of movies were called film lovers. The loudest of all opinions were usually from those with the dullest of minds. Culture was becoming an institution of meaningless drivel, mundane programming where wit and satire were dead arts looked upon as a dark mystique because everyone cared more about being beautiful, civil, polite, than they did with being honest.

So the story began. A man. A woman. A womb and inside this mass-womb an idea dreaming of existence. They moved to songs and yawns and stretched against dirty pillows with bed bug civilizations warped against their dream-fictions. Drugs and booze and cigarette butts and old pornographic magazines rotting from the humidity of broken shower heads lay like insect corpses across the floor, collecting brick dust. Which some assumed gathered some type of power, deep and laid in the fountains in the swamps it was created inside, nested in the nightmares of the old slaves bringing in the shovels and wagons carried by thin horses that crumbled under the humidity of man's desire to work everything into the ground.

She has a habit of staring into the walls. She can smell Jesus and proclaims he smells like peppermints and hardwood floors. We don't really exist here. Not really. We are flakes of a fantasy. We have to constantly be stimulated or we become bored with being human.

She looks at me, stares. She looks back at the ceiling. She says while biting her nails: 'I haven't had any physical contact with another human body since July. The only exception being a very brief interlude in November when my doctor listened to my heart beat to confirm I am still alive. At that moment, she expressed concern because my beats per minute increased significantly as she held her stethoscope to my back. Was there something wrong? (she sighs as she reaches over and lights a half-smoked cigarette she dug from the ashtray) Once we realized the excitement was simply a response to the contact, she put her arm around my shoulder and gave me a little squeeze, a gesture that was incredibly generous and one that revealed a potential problem neither of us wanted to address. If it were possible for her to write me a medical prescription for hugs, I believe she would have. Extended release, to be taken daily, side effects include deep exhalations, crying spells during the acclimation period, sentience.

I've been alone a lot in this lifetime, but I've always found ways to sneak in contact when I've really needed a fix or a reminder. Putting my hand on someone's shoulder to communicate during a moment of concern or understanding, strategically giving a compliment to the colleague categorically defined as a hugger, brushing against a stranger at the grocery store who stood close enough to me while we were both admiring tomatoes to suggest they wouldn't mind. But those tricks don't work anymore, and I suspect they're not going to work once this imposed isolation is over. I'm forgetting what it feels like to feel. That's terrifying. I imagine myself slowly transforming into one of those whimpering dogs at the shelter who were malnourished and abused and cower in the corner of their kennels too afraid and uncomfortable to be touched or approached or even be around people.

In a lifetime before this one, I didn't rely on words to communicate like I do now. Everything I had to say I said through movement and through contact. It started during my ballet years, but after I had taken what I could from the constraints of my ballet training, I dedicated my efforts to studying somatics and the fundamentals of moving. During that time, I learned how to fall and to fly in ways I'm not talented enough with words to describe. I've learned how to use words at least somewhat effectively since then, and I haven't had an opportunity to dance like that in a very long time, but my point is my limbs are lonely and my skin has become so sensitive and hyper-aware in the absence of touch that I feel like I'm glowing all of the time. Wasting away with a brilliance of light like some radioactive bioluminescent spectacle. Let's call that the beauty in my destruction. I feel like I'm dying. Not in a melodramatic way. In a spiritual way. I want to cry often. I don't know. Maybe I'm just depressed. I want to love. I want to grow. But I hate people. I hate men.'

I said: 'It's a shitty gift, isn't it? To be human and alive. To work towards being profound or beautiful. They always talk about humanity as if it's something to be proud of. What have humans done but destroyed everything? They have destroyed sex, love, beauty. Nothing is authentic unless it is plastic and reluctantly agrees with everything. Love is certainly a type of acceptance that exposes us to vulnerabilities - the type we hide from the mutants around us ... a demonic animal that lives in the gut willing to tear through everything to take hold of that they wish to touch and protect and would dive into the deepest of the darkest oceans to drown in a complete irrational and primeval way to eat and devour the soul of all that it inhales into its chest ... an animal that is willing to die and live recklessly to be captivated by a force that flees beyond its instinct of survivability, an unimaginable disturbance that haunts our skin and dreams and the existence between our legs. A disturbance older than all the stories! Through stupidity and crudeness it crawls, a child of every devil and every god, inescapable, immortal, elastic, never victorious but never quite defeated. A trophy of transcendence and wretchedness. And they have drowned it in their despair. Despair for the optimistic children looking to rebel with diseased imaginations. I think about how culture has created the perfect monster in its hate of criticism.'

She moves like a liquid fire. She says while she drags her flaming comet: 'I saw this movie once. It was one of those old movies. I like the black and white movies. I don't know. There's peace in those films. The way people looked then was tragic. Sad even. Or, that's how I imagined them. Maybe it reflected something inside of me. I don't know. I don't know anything. Anyway, those movies always made me feel more alive but in a distant sort of way. Like, it made me feel peaceful, serene, vulnerable, soft even. This movie was about a kid after the second world war in France. He was lost. He didn't have a place anymore. At the end of the movie he's on a beach and he laughs at the ocean. Yes! He laughs at it. Is that not tragic? Who laughs at the ocean and why?'

I melted. I formed into a jellyfish, a seashell, a pebble, a fog along the harbor. My memories were painful. I said or I dreamed I said: 'Maybe it was a metaphor. The ocean might as well be a god to us. The way it vomits jellyfish and seaweed. It has no love for us. It wants to murder us.'

She says or speaks or sings. I don't remember: 'No. It was something else. His laugh wasn't condescending. It was tragic and sad. It's like you. How can someone claim to be a poet and hate mankind and humanity? It doesn't make any sense to me. Where did it go wrong for you?'

I grabbed her cigarette, and inhaled its poison. I sighed, deeply. I could feel the lines on my face deepen. I wanted to say: 'Probably my poor upbringing. Being poor does terrible shit to people. I want the world to be a beautiful idea. I do. But who will listen to some poor poet that lives in some ghetto on the edge of a swampland? Who will listen to someone with no agenda? Who has no desire to vote? Who cares little about conquest? Who cares nothing about identity and being something? Who cares nothing about the color of his skin, his eyes, the manhood between his legs - who dreams he is the imagination of trees, the immortality in the sway of leaves, who lies down at night and prays for his extinction. Who will listen to me when the world is run by madmen? Who will care in a world where men only care about killing gods, setting fire to romance, to the violence and melodrama of their movies and music? Who will listen to me - the uneducated and poor? Who found love in the books he couldn't afford. Who believes social media to be a cult. Who would listen to me? No one listens to people like me. They just keep murdering each other and then making jokes about it. I feel this presence of melodrama from my own abstract ideas. I want to smash everything about identity because I believe it's a trick of the conscience. Everything they believe to be wholesome, I think is fucking evil. I want to make fun of everything they love and hate and show them the hypocrisy of being alive, being free, being beautiful, being anything. I understand what I am doing will make me forever alone. But, I don't care. I don't care about anything.'

She has a dream. She's in a shopping mall. Everyone looks like Frankenstein monsters. Tentacles and spider legs hanging from their heads. It's raining. When she wakes up, she pretends to cry but has forgotten how to produce tears. She says: 'They'll never love you if you just make fun of them. If you act like a defeatist and tell them they're awful people. They want hope and love like anything else. They don't want to be this way. What choice were any of us given? But when you hate them then you are no better than those you claim to be at war with. Not all of us were born to be beautiful.'

I said: 'What's so beautiful about being beautiful? Being beautiful is a treason of humanity. Fucking vampires litter the movies and billboards.'

She says: 'Nothing. Everything. You're right. We all can't be beautiful but there's something beautiful about that. There's something tragic about our lives and what we are. Sure. Yes. We are children of devils and evil thoughts. It's like that movie. That kid on the beach. Looking at the ocean. He was at the end of the world and he saw his own humanity. He saw it and he laughed because it was beautiful. Not beauty in the superficial way you are talking about. But beauty in the way only a child can see it. Without remorse, cynicism, it wasn't a metaphor. He saw true beauty because he was still innocent and hadn't been corrupted by the world yet.'

I said: 'Why do you take up for those people? They'd kill and rape you if they could get away with it. They'd drink your blood and then celebrate it. Look around you. Look at the beautiful condition of humanity and all the beautiful things it has done for itself. It's a goddamn horror show. They hate and spite one another. There's no love in this world. Love is just another item on the consumerism menu. You should be weary of them. You should be afraid of them. They are cannibal mannequins that would eat their own stomachs in an attempt to celebrate their vanity.'

She says: 'But I'm not afraid of them because I'm not a coward. I think it's unbecoming of a poet to have such a nihilistic view of the world.'

I said: 'In that movie. That kid. When he was at the ocean. Did he throw pebbles in the ocean?'

She says: 'He did. Why?'

I said: 'Then he didn't love it. He was afraid of it. The mystery. He was seeing if it would react to his acts of violence. He ran from the horrors of his life to drown in the horrors of the ocean.'

She says: 'Sometimes I wonder why I am even with you. Everyone is afraid. It would be nice to escape somewhere where those things exist only in the abstract parts of our own heads. The only noise would be laughter and the flicker of flames from the camp. I'm a bit of controlled chaos flowing into that delicious disaster. There's this theory that lingers in my brain, chaos and disaster is somewhat essential in most situations- keeps us aware. I'm thinking that means something beautiful - but maybe not. I don't believe you. I don't believe any of your cynicism. I always thought a poet would try and see the beauty in the world. But, you only care about the pain of our existence. You should love more. You would be happier. Our lives aren't dismal catastrophes of life like some would like to believe. We aren't a cruel trick or abortion of the gods. We are animals who have and can create something beautiful and that beauty lies in the rational minded, The wholesomeness in our ability to love and care for nature and the nature of all things. I don't think I would ever love a man like you.'

I said: 'I wouldn't blame you. What type of man would you love?'

She says: 'Hm. Maybe someone with a beard. Who loves all and everything! He would be as tall as skyscrapers.' (She laughs and covers her mouth. She stands on the bed and starts singing a song about all the critters and rocks she loves and she has named them all. They have names in all languages and most of those languages she has made up. A gibberish song about mankind and the universe before him and his creations. She does a cartwheel and floats through the air).

I said: 'If he was that tall how would you make love to this mythical creature of yours?'

She says: 'With my eyes, my fingers, my voice, my soul. You will never know what it feels like for me to love you and you should be devastated.'

I look at her. She is staring at me. Her thin and long fingers against her neck. I smile and hug her. We are at the end of the world. The streetlights are flickering on and off. The moon has collapsed. The stray and lost animals are howling something violent. And, at the end of this make-believe world we stare at one another, holding each other, hoping for a miracle.

TEMPTATION IN REJECTION(A MOST BRILLIANT SACRIFICE)

Inside the offices of degeneration and mediocre anxiety - dingy faces, masturbation and pandering - an outcast, he - his appeal to create begins in mockery, the fabrication is absolute - he cries for more suffering, more fate, more civilization with a history of hostility ... his poetry lacks life, purpose and production, he exiles himself inside aggressive ignorance - the poet outcast, he - he sits, waits with a finger covering his mouth, he is severely judged by his self-mutilation (he once told a woman that every time he loves he feels a piece of him die), identity is somber is faith is salvation is messiah is rhetoric is aggravated and it is sufficient to his servant like sense - a bastard junkie, he -

I'm here to renew my subscription to inescapable suffering ... I would like to try the original metaphysical, reinvigorated with sarcasm - He says this with a poetic mask ...

The worm like goblin, known for cretin acts of exaggerated bravado (this stems from his habit of thinking with his thorn and wanting to stab it into someone's flesh) ponders this creature - the birthmarks on the teeth from years of poverty abuse, the eyebrows sudden and reaching out like cat whiskers, the thin lips, the unshaven face, caterpillar eyes on his hands, his features are cynical, an agony perfumes his hair, this goddamn mutant is measured by his failures ... he has an impure void eating him from the inside ...

I'm sorry sir but you have not cultivated enough suicide credits, you are too anonymous, calamity isn't to be compromised, you have a deficient identity, a superficial intellect, you are not proper properly, you need more disorder ... for the love of all that is rotten, get yourself a haircut and maybe a woman that will domesticate you with daylight and mildly inconvenient orgasms ...

A poet, he - uproots his desire to be conformed ... a primordial monster of adventure, he has no country, no honor, no muses, his ideas are contradictory, he is a fanatic of excess ...he is surprised by his lack of ambition, he longs for exile ... he is only an ordinary man, a most insignificant man, a cosmic prisoner of his own design, he dreams in monologues, he is only subversive during the miracle of commercial breaks between live updates of cult like parades (balloons and confetti while blood sacrifices are made in freedom's name) ... a poet with the heart of a coward ...

A stranger, he ... goes home, watches the television, it pets his face with generous optimism - he becomes vagabond, myth, lint trapped in belly buttons, stupidity transforms him into rabble, his death is a paradox understood only by shame ... ridicule becomes his escape, to live here was to sacrifice his irony - drama is vomit is madness is heritage is the apocalypse in his speech ... he winks at the passing silence, it forms into a woman, she transforms his soul into a comfortable moral, he thanks her by combing her hair as she waits in grocery store lines ... his humiliation is inevitable, he becomes a respectable recluse ... eyes of iconoclast and invention, a formal hobgoblin with no legitimate future ... a poet, he ...

CARDBOARD ZEN

I am living alone. My chairs are perfectly aligned with the stars and table. A dead palmetto bug twitches on my kitchen floor. I kick it under the oven. There must be a graveyard of dead palmetto bugs under there. One day they will rise and demand a proper funeral. This thought scares the shit out of me.

The floors are swept; my shoes hang near the door, music plays and I am drinking cheap beer and writing this. I have no idea why. I have little money, my car is about to explode into ugly syrup, most things people find wholesome I find evil, the dissolution of common sense is expanding faster than the universe.

Yet, for reasons unknown, I am strangely beautiful.

Sometimes I wait until dark to stand inside these internet darlings, covered in confetti and cat food, I throw humor and bad poetry and flowers down the throats of anything that resembles the female form. You would think this rousing demonstration of desperation would entice people to love me for my peculiarity but no one ever sticks around long enough to dance (insert a grumble face here).

I'm going to share pieces of myself. You will probably not care. But I'm going to reach out anyway. I want to say hello. So, hello, I'm byron (lower case because my dad was upper case).

Without names civilization would crumble into ash. Men would climb back into the trees slinging their slime at each other. Yes, the slime of men. You know what that is. The creation that sits inside us all. That primeval ooze that all men want to put inside women. They walk up to a woman and say -- 'I think you are beautiful. I want to put my slime in you.' And the woman says -- 'Yes. Yes. I like you. I want you to put your slime inside me.' So they do.

Slime is being thrown everywhere. In the local watering holes, men with brooding eyes and a whiskey drink are looking for a woman to put their slime in. Women are looking for a man to carry his slime.

This is how the world started.
This is what the world is.
A river of slime ... and we are just floating in it.

I want to do something fantastic. I want fantastical things. All around me people are praying to gadgets and Redbox machines. Everyone is walking around completely unaware that they are mathematical equations that will never be solved. I hang 'out of order' signs on the Redbox machines and then wait on the benches to see the reaction. Families come by, they scratch their dirty heads, their children start to cry, a wife points her finger at her husband and nags: 'Goddammit, Wendell, I told you. This machine is always broken. You never listen to me. I am not letting you put your peasant slime in me tonight.' I imagine in the far future they will find a septic tank under a Wally-mart and extract the shit and use the DNA to mass market stupidity. I know this because my brain knows this. It's almost never wrong. Well, except for math.

I get bored. I jump in piles of leaves. I whip out my cock and twirl it around in the mirror. I run outside with my Lord Of The Rings underwear on and scream at the stray cats to get off my lawn. They hiss at me and promise revenge.

I walk around with a constant erection. I don't know what to do with it. I feel like I'm walking around with a broomstick stuck in my pocket. Well, not really. But I like to exaggerate.

So I go on dates.

We sit and have a staring contest. We talk about every fucking mundane thing about human beings you could possibly talk about. Sometimes when they are talking I stare at their eyebrows. I wonder if you are supposed to shampoo your eyebrows. Oh god, I think, do I have greasy eyebrows?

I want to be interested. I want to convince them why they should come to a dark room with me and get naked and twerk our flesh muscles for ten seconds. Sometimes we hold hands. Sometimes we do cartwheels. Sometimes I sit in front of them and play my usual game: How many beers do I have to drink to make myself interesting?

I want to shove pretty flowers and shitty poetry down their mouths. Sometimes I wonder why I'm doing any of this. Sometimes I pretend to pour gasoline on myself and lit myself on fire when they start talking about their ex-boyfriends. Sometimes when they go to the bathroom, I smell their fork to get an idea of what their breath smells like - in case you're wondering - it usually smells like lipstick and bad decisions.

I tell her: 'I want to rub my weird on your weird.'

Her eyes become passive-aggressive. She calls me a creep. She starts to leave. I yell after her: 'I was being metaphorical! Come back! Please ... I don't have any money to pay for this dinner and you were my ride home.'

At work, I ask Gary the gay guy for dating advice. Since Gary is gay he knows everything about having a vagina. I ask Gary about the transvestite vampires from Mars and if they really are coming to steal our children. Gary looks at me like I'm crazy. I tell him I read it on Facebook. 'Facebook has never lied to me, Gary! Everyone is beautiful.'

Gary finally came out of the closet at a business meeting during work. The room was very quiet, people were looking at their phones, some were shuffling their legs around. Gary stood up and screamed: 'I'm gay! I'm gay! Why doesn't anyone understand me?'

Everyone looked at Gary. No one said anything. The room was completely noiseless, except for Brad's phone ringer going off which, coincidentally, was a song we had never heard.
Gary then did a ballerina twirl and sat back down. No one really cared that Gary was gay. I mean, we all had our suspicions because he kept telling us he was gay but we thought he was one of those trendy homosexuals that was only looking for Twitter followers. Some thought it was nice of him to share. Some thought it was weird that he picked this moment. Some started to pray to obscure gods (Crom was many of these types of gods - you had to find the riddle of steel and give it to him - if not, he casts you out and laughs. That's Crom. Strong in his mountain). Some wondered when the food was going to get here. Some hoped to god whatever Gary had wasn't contagious.

With Gary's sage advice on dating I feel like a new window has opened up for me. I think I now better understand nothing about women but feel like I have a new friend to annoy the shit out of by giving meaningless high fives and asking if these jeans make my ass look fucking awesome.

Gary looks at me. He licks his lips. I'm pretty sure Gary wants to put his slime inside of me.

I'm feeling really good about myself.
I go outside. I breathe in the polluted air. A stray cat comes from the corner. It meows at me. Another one comes from the other side of me. And then another and another before I'm

surrounded by hundreds of stray cats. I try to back into my door, but one of them closes it before I can. One cat jumps on my neck and sinks its teeth into me. I scream and throw it across the yard. The rest all hiss and jump on me. They chew and tear into my skin, my eyes, my tongue. Their breath smells like seafood poultry with just a hint of beef.

They completely devour me until I am nothing but bones and some clothes.

They lay around my lawn, yawning, sleeping, licking themselves, fucking, spreading mange and dirty thoughts.

Some of them look up into the trees. They see the sunlight fragment into a million different equations of life and light. One stands on two legs. It looks around at the other lazy assholes. It sniffs the air and finds it's full of bad pussy and foul rules. It puts its paws on its hips. It wonders of this mystery that is life. It starts to wonder if all life is filled with both the god and devil. That the blood that streams through its system may be made of dust and dreams, universe and time, if all things swim back towards the source of its birth. Are we born to dream? Do we learn to dream? Is it possible that we are a thousand lives and a thousand different people all mixed into one fraction of this multiple verse? It looks around and sees that nothing else seems to ponder or stand like it does. It no longer cares for those that exist in the moment but wishes to find those that exist for life. It scratches one of the other cats in the head. The cat hisses and runs off. It looks at its paw. It wonders of its proclamation for violence and drama. It wonders of the distractions of its culture and why those exist. It realizes it is god and none other exists.

It looks at the fireball setting far off inside space. It looks at the trees and the thousand of leaves whistling in the wind. It becomes afraid of death. It becomes afraid of the substance that makes it live.

'My god,' it gasps, 'we are nothing but the imagination of trees!'

'My god,' it cries, 'everything is meaningless!'

'My god,' it screams, 'consciousness and the gods are a trick! We are nothing but programs of a misguided illusion. A mindless parasite of vanity and crudeness. I deny this existence! I deny this perverted optimism! Let all be extinct and eternal!'

It walks inside my house. It grabs the bottle of wine, takes a long drink, ponders the reality of its situation for a moment. All around it saw its own essence. It asked it questions. Was he a monster of flesh and ideas, easily amused and corrupted? It struggled inside this existence. It saw and gasped out when it realized that all of life was a directed evolution created by a self-destructive god. It saw the time melt away, it whispered of the year nineteen eighty-three, it was only a variation of this delusion, all around everything became a sequence of consciousness, mathematical plasma, a sea of absurdity, it saw the codes of natural selection inside the metaphysical and abstract structures of mind and essence, how the world survived by destroying, community and civilization were artificial abstracts created so everything would be swallowed up and made into a type of generic slavery because of a code of ethics that evicted all free thought. It suddenly screamed out and ran outside on all fours, it jumped and tumbled over the other cats, it screamed out to them as it ran down the street ...

'Run, you fucking heathens, run! Back to the trees, back to nature, civilization is a construct of censorship, freedom isn't free! Run, you bastards, run!'

POET OUTLAWS

I want to find those mysteries people tuck away between their eyelashes and hide in their belly buttons. To shine a light inside of it all - for all secrets to be known to me. Love is such an unreliable desire in a world of abandonment. There's too much spectacle and not enough stimulation. I want to use that ghostly-fire inside of me to peer into the lonely and unknown, the lost and forgotten. I think some are omnipotent women - I think sometimes how talking with them bewilders and shatters traces of the chaos that lives inside me. And I say they are all a marvelous equation. I am devising a plan, a scheme, a plot to admire everything about them - to speculate the being. To theorize, speculate, reflect on them. To take notes and splash them around my body like confetti pieces. I say a supernatural and extraterrestrial type of woman is a miracle, a remedy, I want to be famous with them. I want to be silent between the lines of poetry and naked bodies. I want to whisper nastiness in their belly buttons. Into that crevice of night-time secrets where all lovers hide their souls.

I seem to be drawn to difficult dramas. I crave the intimacy of minds. To end skepticism with experience. To twirl in the harmonies and elemental and hallucinations of solitude... I hope it lasts forever. Do feelings last forever? Do people need to miss you to think of you? Do they pacify their fear with superstition? Will the obsession with freedom and rights promote a new type of tyranny? Will they sentence lovers to hell for having labyrinths in their hearts and humiliation in their identities? Oh oh oh ... watch those trees as they grow!

I like nonsense words. Popcorn beloved brains. Virginal shiver screams. Orgasmic radiation. Psychic information warped inside desperate grocery clerk tongues. Electro-chemical patterns in ripple-ropes. Disco philosopher in a difficult flow with neurotic depression twirling in a cosmic deficiency. I want to lick features while eating mind-gummies. Our dance intensifies (are you fucking barbarians still reading this)... the werewolves of lust and passions are plowing through the moonlit fields ... a fog is constant ... someone loses their inhibitions ... a mutant screams from across the lake. The crowd of ghosts under the ashtray applauds. The disco wizards weave their magic into our ears. And the poets, my star-starved-sauna-soul, are all dead - yes, yes - even their words have melted, corroded into artificial sweets. Nothing left but the madmen and the saints that protect them. Nothing left but identity to dance upon more empty theaters while vomit becomes the clog of true and real bright-bloods. I really hope my death lasts forever. I really hope those bastards don't chase me.

Ask existence why it never asks questions - ask the gods why they committed suicide - there is nothing but us ... our intoxicating fantasy and I say: Exist to be everything and nothing. Turn your existence down as low as it can go, oh oh oh you neo-savages, you crypto-sociopaths of industry and money!

That's how my brain blooms these days. A presence of wizards dance in my ears and under my tongue. They are a cult of symbols carving designs in my teeth (think cavities and stains).

I am the critic of supernatural architecture. I am masturbation with a pen ... and isn't that just beautiful imagery? I think so. Yes. I think of many terrible things. Nihilism is the weapon I use to expose the corruption of civilized goblins with gangsterism facilities - they wish you death by wrapping you in plastic and marketing the human decay as more sweetly crust that some mutant hobgoblin muches into ... oh god, they are hatching from their skeletons and pursuing a most simple death, just a little magnificent dance before the music corrodes into mockery and the gods give them back their rotting limbs ... how we conform to irrational ideas not seen in any other manner of nature. Feral cats and lizards aren't lining up in theaters of spectacle and amusements ... everything is as it was and they don't fear mutation but we must continue to mutate ... our identity must evolve from its baby version ... that is no longer a man but a forgotten sister who hoards cereal boxes and solves crossword puzzles, that is a lawyer for the perpendicular, that is a grandmaster satire placing pieces of confetti between the eyelashes ... that is no longer a woman but an idea of a corruption that gives her the sense to mutilate her features so she can be something other than her former version ... identity has made us insane. What can a caterpillar do but look on with a very worried type of amazement ...

I do think of strange rebellious things … all sorts …

I overthink everything. I have long talks inside my own mind with characters I create so I can have a ton of different perspectives and debate and fight and bite them. I soak up everybody's pain so I have a better understanding of what life makes us feel and do. I wonder if this is all a game. If there's someone with a script for this madness and they just keep adding stuff to spice it up and make it interesting. Tele-nova style.

Sometimes I wonder if some higher power has control and wrote this a long time ago and free will is just an illusion and all our choices are not really choices, or we're only given the choices that will lead us to the same fate. Are we all doomed to play this role into something that we can't even understand ourselves, are we failing at achieving greater knowledge because we're being held back? We're all mad, we're all weird, we're all a bunch of different things, ideas, descriptions, feelings and thoughts in someone else's mind. Not only the birds, ants, cats and dogs. Everything. Everyone. From the moment you cross someone on the street that person made a judgment of you. Even if subconsciously. Did you know the mind cannot create people? Every person in your dreams is someone you've seen at some point in your life. We're all dreaming of people we judged. Some of them are dead people. The houses, territorial planning, rituals, churches, everything is leading you, telling you how to act. That you cannot be a certain way that's not acceptable and then whatever you are you have to either hide or shape it into a more acceptable way. Do you recognize your own performances? Do you think you're performing when you're alone or do you allow yourself to strip down from everything and just be? Grumble, grumble.

Sometimes I pretend women whisper beautiful things in my ear at night. Little parasites unleashed from their lustful tongues that dance inside my brain. Pulling levers and pushing buttons. I sometimes wonder what her features would look like if she said: *I love you.* Would her eyes tremble? Would her body convulse with pleasure? Would her hands shake just a bit in anxiety? What would those words sound like? Is it the community within those words we desire? But it's so hard to connect. Truly connect. To feel, I think that's the word I'm looking for. To feel.

Everything is a mystery to me. An enigma. A puzzle. And I am just a dumb poet that wishes to build treehouses and rename all the critters and trees and stars and moons. I want everything to be of my own design. This diso-poet dreams in solipsism.

I think mysteries are only appealing because they're waiting to be cracked. Some things we will never be able to explain and we make peace with those, and sometimes it's fun to wonder and try to logically explain the explainable, sometimes we dwell into magic and religion to try and see what could explain such things and that's what keeps them mysteries, because we never know for sure, because there's so much we need to explain and we can't and our mind needs reasoning for stuff and as much as sometimes we just want to lean our heads back and soak up the immensity of things that surround us and the layers after layers of unexplained stuff, as we sip our coffees and feel connected to the comfort of everything that is familiar. As we allow the sunlight to touch our skins knowing that soon enough it will be dark again. But do we know now? Or do we believe? Is this pandering to myself a corruption? Am I the darkly preacher to an audience of pleasure seekers with numb tongues from all that spins in their brains? Maybe I will dilute my self-destruction into something beautiful like conversational pieces on the mastery of entertainment and whether or not I felt myself authentic enough to applaud the bastards that enlighten me with noises.

I think destruction is something we love. The undying thirst for the power of smashing anything and everything that we don't care for just for the sake of proving the power of our own existence, regardless of how it affects us. Self destruction comes from ignorance. How it will doom us. How I indulge in its music.

These are the thoughts that both shame me and makes me happy yet on the outside is a glowing part of sadness. Like the aura around a lightbulb. Or a lampshade dimming the glow of the lightbulb. I feel like that - uneasy, fabricated, misfortuned to the curse of fantasy and flesh and vanity. I am surrounded by mutants and freaks. I feel so hopelessly alone sometimes. I may seem strong but there is fear inside me. Gnawing pain. Sometimes I feel like pieces of me are flaking away and being carried into the wind. I want to find something beautiful in this world. I want to dance in forbidden thoughts. Imagination seems to create life but it is a desperate sleep trying to kill you with more dreams inside the magic of constructs.

What ever made us think we could have done better? That we could fight against the illusions of civilization? That we could hide from the money, the jobs, the gods, magical intuitions, sugar-fried drinks with nasty alcohol, psycho ideologies, the phoniness of polite people with waffles for eyes. How perverse the silence of critics are! These prisons have broken us, they have created suicide and redressed it as a compassionate singer.

We did everything right and we are still bored! What an elegance. Maybe we should ask it to come over for dancing and magic. Maybe we should bury our ambitions in more syrup and wine. What did the Romantic Movement ever do except challenge the occult, or the sensational morbid princes and princesses that stole all the erotica from the world and placed it into mysteries inside paintings that they hide in museums and rich people's offices? What is art if they are sculpting bags of trash and putting bullet-proof glass between the eyes of those that lived in another creation?

And if we do nothing then what do our souls do? Are they idle as we? I'm sure it has children and then falls asleep at the wheel … sure. Why not. I know all of this is true because my brain says it's true. This is the mathematical grace of the world and gods and civilizations and languages - nothing is apart or different because it always ends the same way. A sigh, a hug, a raise of eyebrows, the shoulder shrug and then we all fold into pieces of applause. None of us understands anything while understanding that not participating was the only beautiful option we had. Participation turned us back into savages. Grab an identity, you mutants! Off to adventures under the optimistic glow of pretty pricey poets we go!

He is insane because he forgot to love himself!

This Disco-Wizard Poet (promoting heroic nihilism since

1983),

-b

LITTLE ACTS
OF NONSENSE
ON A DESK

They made the sexy faces hideous, psychotic unconsciousness was a temporary stranger and an endless lover stretched out into the personality of a manic-depressed universe, (really pathetic), his loneliness was not sophisticated enough to be unhappy, inverted time worms (knowing all things but remembering nothing of itself) melted through concrete cigarettes and spoke in a civilized gibberish, over fertilized homeless men unsupervised and hyper-(un)responsible with drunk songs that pacify in slumber summer melodies - pseudo-suicide and crypto-complex cults of grocery clerks with alligator features sewing chaos with impulsive nonsense - the silhouette of psychosis is blind to its existence - the oh so pretty girls (it was she that had spirits in her head, a ghost on her tongue, her eyes were fabulously unknown) who are all lovely and loud and damaged and unwillingly contemporary - the inferno of naked men lies close to rebellion ... and this man is wanting to be the flakes cut from his own symbology ...

-2-

Let us succumb to the utopian and barbarian, a mythology in these sleeping middle days, oppressed by the epic, by the symbolism of our souls and the gods that swallow us in their imagery. Half-dreaming women whose company is a fit of conjectures. Imposters don't exist to be imposters, they exist to annihilate modesty where dying is such a ridiculous habit. With portals in the poet's brain, madness awaits near poverty(hostile silences that hide in mathematical misfortunes).

I promise lunacy and a horizon to this desolate circus - I promise a lyrical wanderer propped in a substructure of reality that has no anchor or plot or causality of character ... it is the prayer of existence that wishes us to be absent among the dissolving writers ... ... a poet soon discovers his words have no following in his future - they are bemoaned by his lack of initiative.

He is corrupted by fictional melodramas.

-3-

Someone really homeless once said:
Life is a savage adversary of amusements, which in its peak, creates the worst of persons in unhappiness because love is nothing but unprofitable sexuality.

He then pointed to two people screaming and said:
You see that? All that is, is a mass of wasted energy. It's just tragic stupidity.

I was busy validating my existence with random acts of serotonin injections (boredom is the worst of sufferings) when my existence turned into a gimmick, a disgusted abstract lunacy that wondered: What is survival of the fittest if we all die?

At this moment I was petrified with a sense of irrational conformity. That because of the evolution of consciousness I have irrationally conformed to ideas outside of nature. I have fetishized the human experience. I have romanticized my identity with meaningless searches for abstract concepts like: Love, romance, art, gender, sexuality, civilization, hubris, shame, stupidity, deceit, brilliant coherence of theatrical apes - the age of humans is the age of loneliness - all figments of my need to create meaning ... to falsify the human condition and replace it with a misanthropic mania. I have created an unbalanced dystopia inside my brain. Madness disturbed by evil melancholy. I continue to believe in human constructs, metaphysical solutions to the problem of life. I am nothing but the arousal of star carbon. Intertwined in broken misfortunes. Everything is a fantasy! Happiness is an evil god!

Extreme individualism has created our need for authenticity - we need to be different and unique to such a degree that we are creating new meanings and self-mutilating our bodies for more identity, more individualism, we will carve a psychosis into the coming generations just to feel a little different, our want for indifference is creating a generation of madness ... friendships are only a validation for vanity - oh! Are we not all suffering from a neurotic disturbance? Let us lie down and become temporarily insane! Off you heart-terrorist, you soul-terrorist, you mind-terrorist ... idolize your identity and become mysterious and lonely ...

Evolution is a misery. Horror poetry and disco poets and poet philosophers using nihilism to expose the corruption of psychotic institutions ... harassing the imagination with skepticism. Oh please Mister President ... oh please Mister God ... oh please Mister Philosopher give me a peaceful lobotomy.

Someone really crazy once said:
Most people are of limited intellectual curiosity because of the idea they are constantly under surveillance by a metaphorical idea.

The billboards advertised more sex and guns ... individuality meant free will, but if free will doesn't exist, individuality is a trick ... the televisions were searching for monsters ... a parade was being shown ... everything was a mathematical mistake ... someone's liver exploded ... someone claimed god had apologized (it was only being rhetorical when it created us from fish guts) ... a woman is close ... she smiles something nasty ... the man, he laughs with broken teeth ... he writes a poem: *She's a little treasure piece, Epicetus would agree, knowledge is hell, knowledge is kinetic applied earth between her thighs ...*

... and the glorious normal, how they dance to wretched murder by a psychosis deliberately programmed by atomic imagery.

(the caterpillar disappears at this point and returns later in a new season of humor and misfits - this time he shows up as a belligerent drunk .. stay tuned you fancy folk!)

THE SLIMY SICKENING

(1) Asparagus star-gazers into prickly redheads, When the brain blossoms, The heart is a fluid transcendence - Love-radiation, Resurrection under the tongue ...

They say I am the darkly kid - I don't want to be darkly - I want to be a ballerina that dances between vague definitions of what a man can be ... can I be a man? And what is a man but hermaphroditic figures hoping to copy the father and rest inside the mother?

(2) Manifestations of thought, Proper ghosts with no body to haunt, How we love to haunt bodies with our bodies, A disturbance older than all the stories!

(3) A hungry heart is a reflective silence - drinking in the patterns of abstractions ... and soon that loneliness will drift and disintegrate - we will disinfect that horror that lives in our chest, creatures of forbidden jests ... I want you to infect me with your language ... whisper your parasites of passion in my ear ... We would be deviant companions traveling through hyper-stellar brothels.

(4) The great brain-bloom of bedroom executions (she wakes, rubs her arms and legs against me to spread her scent) An absurdity of attitude, to become something that supersedes ourselves is a false humanity (are you a stranger that agrees?)-

(5) We are the children of digital brains that were so bored with being human we destroyed ourselves to be entertained ...

Dance, you beautiful bastards, dance! Enlighten me with your entertainments! I want to be amused and pleasant!

(6) She, a vulgar expression pressed to the lips, a delicious suspension for eyebrows and the abyss of the universe hiding inside her stomach.

He, a scoundrel, a magnificent and beautiful scoundrel born in the gutters of the world. The acidic, primordial caterpillar - a mystic, a superstar, a disco-philosopher, a philosopher-poet.

She, wants love and romance and sticky, gooey passions that loves the slime of bodies when it touches the skin, a gasp of melancholy and then the drop of melodrama as she crawled in bed, music that burns through the tongue, to find the rotten core of all that is human and alive, to produce skeptics with poetry, transfigure the gods and saints, she wishes to find the essence in love's madness, in all types of madness.

He, longs to be exiled with a poetic woman that will build tree houses filled with books - he wants a muse warped by love and fused with lust. His eyes are like gargoyles, his lips ready to strike, his face a proper dysfunction distorting the infinite humdrum of this counterfeit paradise.

She, Love! Love! Love! You have broken me down but I would not have done anything differently. I have no regrets. I was alive and I felt what it meant to be alive. Oh love, my love - may I fall and break apart, may I perish forever in love's love.

Yah! Yah! Yah!

The cats scream in harmony.

(7) We sang in expression; grimace and blood followed, There is always blood between lovers and, Those who decide to love, He was a disco-nerd superstar, Champagne and wizards injected into his veins - She had love and paraphernalia on, Her face, Fathomless darkness behind her mirror

... she liked the needles, beside her bed, ... she liked all the beautiful boys, inside her

(8) Her eyes were a mausoleum, Crawling sodium in heads, She

smells like a clean hallway, Like somewhere, Where, Jesus died right before they hung him around their necks ...

(9) We collapse into ourselves, Brain-muties, Nothing attached to our shoulders, Her head falls into, My lap (a sea) - My blood is inside, Her tongue (a jellyfish)

The first crack in a mirrorless body

The slimy sickening: Love ... that's what we call it

We call it that because, It reminds us of being alive, Human, Substance

There is no treachery in our lies, because, We swear to it,

So she kisses me, but I can't feel her lips, because, we are still in a dream

and, if it's true what they say, that all love drives us insane, I think I would follow her to that shame ... She cries: The poets are dead! The poets are dead!

So the poets are dead! Or, maybe they're hiding ... have you tried looking underneath the bed or in your closet? Maybe they never existed - they are myths now like Roman and Greek gods - Orpheus and Eurydice, Cupid and Psyche, the cult of Dionysus ripping them apart while mad with wine and lust and a fever for nature ...

and when the sun sets none of us can breathe again - We want to speak beautiful things but we are afraid ... so afraid of what may come from those thoughts - poets are now hunted like wildmen, destroyed with fame and fortunes and sex and to only write whatever pleases the masses ... the poets are dead because we murdered them, we didn't want to be beautiful anymore - we wanted to forget what we were .. to do that we had to kill the poets ... a real poet loves all of life - the modern poet is too interested in killing and dividing people ... so all are doomed ... doomed to be housewives and three sentences and forgetting what it means to be alive ...

Death is for the proper and living, we cry, not the dead.

AMUSED TO DESPERATION

Enthusiastic Marxist reenactments in the distant and divine
While we, while we ...
Smoke cigarettes, staring at each other's amiable expression, talking in that unusual pseudo-company way, like sexual obscurities that give praise to brilliant laziness and ironic precision.
Pretending to read minds, having conversations about the weather, drinking cheap wine, and yearning for some Neanderthal to smash a piano with his molten hands and play a bastardized version of Mozart.
While we, while we ...
squirm uncomfortably when elevated idealization,
humanity,
and who's going to pay the check is discovered.

(I)

contemptuous grunting,
waylaid dew,
lingering in broad grass, cool.

open a book, hemingway.
close a book, dante
kill these poets (Song for the love poets
 The gorgeous lovers feathered with caterpillar flesh
  trumpets for the slain mistress
A rush to the lonely brain
 So sex was a terrible patience)

hideous frame (drunken man spits),
feeble unawares,
choking familiar shade.
early dreamers,
goblin tasters,
borrowing icy-grey (open the window and crash into the pavement).

exploitation, civilization is a cult (she was a cunt that closed her eyes and whispered how she saw colors so bright they were white - people told her that was just the fucking blood running through her eyelids … but she, she thought it was the ocean).

if consciousness exists, why does language and disease destroy it?

every year there's another Jesus that knows everything … their breath is a metaphor for how lies rot the teeth … giant eye on

heads, small eyes in the palm of hands ...
it is
it is
the great charade

(II)

I'm a peculiar rage these days
with all the shit and mildewed colors lying wrinkled on
leopard print-rugs
with so much pain and anxiety that my chest just may explode;
spraying years and decades of cancer and swallowed spit
across the world my veins would bleed,
and they'll pray for rain…
while I look forward to another goddamn roach
to smash with a thrift store dictionary.

(III)

I'll satisfy the sun by lying towards it
I'll close myself off from everything beautiful or familiar
so I can find myself warped,
and curled into a ball in the shower
she'll turn towards me with sloppy saliva lips and twirling
eyes still working in dreams and shit, she'll ball up her rings
between her hands
cushion out all the lovers
pretend I'm that warm-bodied answer to all her clever
servants
and she'll ask me…

is it raining?

(IV)

I was born distant from the others
hi baby.
her amebic pupils push out like flavored scents of dried
Chinese floods
how was your day?
I tell her it was like smashed flies on a window pane.
what's wrong?
her face grins into a gnarled substance.

my elbows are scaling.
my hands are decaying.

she's all motion,
passionate decapitating knowledge soaked through
she's waiting for my face to retract and force something casual
anything, she says to herself.

I don't love you.
what?

it never rains anymore

(V)

The elder shamans did this,
Swallowing with eyes tight shut.
Dreaming, calling
grandfather and spring;

sometimes sprouting
bear's claws, offering
the dance.

I put my hands in my pockets
And do my invoking
standing on the curb,
tongue out for drops of rain.

(VI)

her words like ripples in a lake
her fingers like forever dreamers
but lack
but sing
but beauty
what gardens were made from her dances with pearls, gold,
and bright fragrances.
like lovely
like silence
like luminous journeys into the barbaric superstitions

her mouth like thorns
her kiss like pollen
her hair tangled in flowers
grass, and dandruff

and the wild countrymen were twilight painters
gems in a glass vision
neurotic phantoms
schizophrenic shadows
fantastic tricks and carved faces in heaven

as she attempted personal unconsciousness
like pleasure
like love
like sexual operas tied around her wrist
but kiss
but live
like how her face resembled a tolerant drunkenness

like how her hair was tangled in flowers
grass, and dandruff

ESCAPE IS THE IRRELEVANT DEATH INSIDE DREAMS

How do I begin?
How did we begin?
I'll start from the beginning.

Dreams. A cathedral of jazz with the whispers of ghostly musical notes. Paintings against the marble walls of future and past streets. A choir sings. The song is sadness, the voices are the constant struggles of the spirit and hell. The orchestras heave in as trumpets made of gallery bodies in metrical aromas play to the audience of gimmicks. The singer is an old man, withered and wasted by the backwards music of human instruments. Together we sit. Towards the back. Hand inside hand. We stare into the sea of neon, into the waters of Venus, into the blood of our parents. We study the faces for recognition and truth. We listen to the tales that twirl and swirl inside us.

Hand inside hand. We wait for our savior. I say your name slowly so I can feel how my tongue moves when it pronounces your name. I whisper it in my hands, throw it into the ocean, watch it move slowly out into the artificial bubble of beast on stomachs, where it evolves, grows a tail, heart, lungs, arms, hair. It swims back to me, a woman. It crawls towards me as lizard sand pebble blood pulp wave. I give it a name. I give it life.

Tell me something beautiful and terrible.
I love you.

How I demand things! I feel like a child sometimes. How the gods must laugh at me. I mourn over the silliness of human nature but embrace my own stupidity and insincerity of human spells. I feel lost so many times. I grin as if a ghost in the crowds of people that surround me. Completely unaware of this world's staleness, it's contempt for friendliness, it's sentiment for fantasy, flattering of the stimulus, the air feels thick of filth to me. I feel alone in their presence. A walking phantom. Paralyzed by despair, stuck in space. I imagine great ideas. But what do I do with them? I imagine you. I long for you. Near me. Beside me. With me through the clouds of wormholes and time traveling rivers.

We'll take back the world from those that want to sterilize it, control it, enslave it. We'll at least die trying. How I dream! How the gods laugh! I've been lying here daydreaming of other worlds while listening to the brush of traffic sailing like darkly carbon outside my window. I watch the top of an oak tree. It must be a thousand years old to be so tall. I watch the wind blow the top branches, the leaves shaking, spring noises, cigarette breath exhumed from my pores, skin, lungs, the cloud of poison making strange faces before the wind from outside blows it into non existence.

I travel with you. To the stars. To our ancestors. We trace the fragments of heaven and hell with our fingertips. You and I. In a spherical spaceship, paintings line the walls that move like liquid, curved reddish furniture sits on the silver radiant floors.

A hum of intoxication creates a withering rattle like that of a drum. It beats with the machinery. It goes: Boom boom hummmm errrrrrr boom boom hummmmm errrrrrr boom boom.

We point to the different moons that sit motionless around sugar-spectre planets. We name them - Cupid and psyche. Noble and Tao. Brothers and sisters. We draw the lines of these mysterious mutations in the empty space of Zeus. We splash water where oceans would go. We smear the horizons with green shrubbery, tall solid trees with ripe fruit that swell with a flowery fragrance. We plant seeds of life under rocks, mountains, we raise a great light from the east to warm the ground, we blow into the sky to create thick clouds shaped like whales, they spray the ground with water and summer, love and grace, mother and dawn. We leave to let the awakened learn of life. We give them one rule: always love, without judgment, without hate, and you will always be happy and free.

We travel through comets and the savagery explosions of gutter-dreams. Between the stars, the great spaces, we glance at one another, take each other's hand, and we go down a long tunnel towards a room shaped like an oval with a circular bed in the middle. A slow wave of guitars, harps, the rushing of mountain water plays. We make love. You whisper the past to me. I whisper the future to you. We lay bound by body and soul, love and determination, God and devil, lovers caught in the Spaceland.

We battle the Grey Titans on the moons of Aza, we save the seven forbidden queens from the wasp mancers on Horri, we swim in the healing waters and laugh with joker sword birds on the cusp of the cider vintage along the gas Vestas.

We never want to return home because we are home. You point to my chest. This is where I belong.

You wave your arm towards the space around us. This is our home now. We laugh, embrace, the machinery around us hums, the robot gods of the clouds of GunnyRoot watch our spaceship silently. They are unaware of humans, dreams, love. They can only watch in confusion. Without knowing, this confusion will bring about the great awakening in them a thousand years from now ... but we will never know.

We lay together. Between the stars, space, love, fingers trace our bodies, lips kiss our necks, we sleep under the blankets of early dirt. Here, in this world. We are gods. We are lovers listening to the truth of what it is to be human and alive.

Love. We speak and listen to this word. This monosyllabic word. Only one breath yet it can create a storm within a person like no other word. These are the tales of love. The way lovers move when this word ... Like a master ... Orders us to a beautiful and terribly ticklish fate and compulsory virtue.

These are the tales of this love. You put your fingers on my chest, near my heart. You play, spread your fingers, tap me like I'm a piano.

These are the keys, you say. This is the magic tune to open your heart. You close your eyes. Your fingers move. I can play this in the dark. I can play this like I know how to walk.

This is the C key.:
O-O-O

This is the D key:
O--*-O

You close your eyes and tap your fingers. You tap my teeth. You play music from my mouth. You tap my body and I move to your movements. You close your eyes. You play this music. Your fingers spread, they inch forward into my skin, music pours out my body, you moan with the songs your fingers fiddle.

I can play all the keys with my eyes closed, you say.

I close my eyes too. I listen to the way your fingers move, the way they play, the way they whisper ... I can do this in complete and utter darkness..

We wonder about love. Eros and the desire. Ren and benevolence. How the children of Adam were said to be of one body. Created of one essence. How if you had no sympathy for others, then you were not worthy to be called a man.

In Turkish it was the word - Ask. One love for one person. Love does not delight in evil. It protects and preserves.

We wonder about this mystery. We ask, what does this mean? Evolution says it was a means of survival. Science says it is the fluids of chemistry. Poetry says it is the dreary vagrant in the morning breeze begging for food that will never satisfy.

Love. Yet even the most foolish, intelligent, evil, good person seeks it. The great but bitter quest of Don Quixote. We chase windmills hoping they're dragons.

The first writing of man talked of love. The last writing of man will talk of love.

You press your lips against my body. Your fingers tap me like a music instrument. I put my arms around the crowds, blindly. I can play these keys with my eyes closed, you say. I can love you without being afraid.

Wo ai ni
Eros
Ren
Benevolence

What is so terrible and beautiful about life? *I love you.*

I trace the curves of your ornaments. You tell me of dreams. We agree. We are beggars in the indestructible despair of caterpillar rivers. It rains. All around us it falls like hair and silver. It splashes on the streets and rooftops and we think it sounds like bacon sizzling. We listen. Keys in D and C.

Against my body, We wonder - can a woman find the truth in a man? Can a man find the truth in a woman? If we don't understand the truth of ourselves, how can we understand the truth of gods?

We plant our seed. Watch how our trees grow! The magnetic fire comes. Across the sky the fire spreads over the lakes and through the hopeless dimensions of time seen in the crawl of a caterpillar. It engulfs all mankind, all stranger eyes, insect bodies curl up into a sleep position, all watcher dreams known. Who knows what God does on the eighth day or if he is plastic or still resting while the spaces between him and his creations grow longer, placid, forming into dark matter while lovers stare at the sagging ceiling. The fire moves towards us. I take your hand. The fire all around us.

My lips on your lips, Together, we burn in the flames.

PROPAGANDA

his face was perpetual like drawn lines in the ripples of lakes and he danced to the frequency of christ and he danced to the fire inside motions and he danced to the crippling despair of oceans like great beasts that vomited jellyfish and seaweed (they were)... mantelpieces shaped like parasites, domesticated gods now hung upside down in shopping centers ...

with narcotic eyes, lips spent, eyebrows high
madness is the shape of howls! he cried oh he cried so beautifully

eventually fungi and insects and dolls missing heads took over, fish armies marched like soldiers

the curse of man was the soul, the fear was his shame for having a soul (he wished to make darkness beautiful, to crave the type of anarchy that only an orgasm would soothe, harassing the imaginations with nihilism and whispers of escape (oh beautiful beautiful escape) he assumed an absence of identity that resembled a drunken state while monologuing the saints from people's spirits

he mourns his mutant children who are free, first of all creatures, of all species, history lost ... believing in the propaganda of its own dreams

UNDER THE CONSTELLATIONS OF MACHINE MINDED

Year of nineteen eighty three
Time dilapidation, dimensional dilation
The robots were organic machines, jelly brains,
Super butter babes
Created by electric infections, manic fevers,
Imagery phantoms with beautiful architecture

The robots would crowd into theaters
where an old projection reel ran backwards

Showing human faces moving to certain emotions
The robots watched in awe at the humans
They moved their faces to be like them
They mimicked the motion of sex and fibers
The motion of smiles and fashion

They moved their eyebrows high and certain
Even though they were all wires
Even though they were all metal

Some referred to this as: *Android narcosis.*
It was clear the robots had become corrupted by romantic ideals.

Man and Muse had walked under the skies of Mars, under

the constellations of Maj. They found a strange cult of robots living in a sterile sixties like environment. Huge technological structures of human faces were erected high by volcanoes. The robots had worshiped silver and pumpkins, they dressed in green and yellows and wore ridiculous hats. They had caught humans and tied them inside realty machines where the men screamed and twitched.

'We are only trying to understand them,' one robot had explained.

The psychic abattoir commanded all reality
Life was a simulated reality run by
Men and mutants
Robots and gods
Universe and machine
A spectacle within the fanatical

Such was the way with heroic men
Un-mathematical minds
All mud and resin to hold them together between the spaces, but eventually they fall apart and become retainers for the robot creatures.

'A poet,' the robot said, 'must always try to find beauty in the undesirable. Otherwise he is lost, lost to describing the movements of ants and silly, garbled politicians.'

'What beauty can anyone find in a place like this?' The poet asked.

'None,' the robot answered, 'if he be a skeptic.'

Space was collapsing, nebulae vanquished, stars rearranging, the universe expanding, a thousand years, a thousand centuries, all light in the sky changed, as the robots looked up they understood just how insignificant life for man really was. The screams and cries from the men, trapped in reality machines, rose with the sand storms that pushed at the marble rocks through the stone structures erected high above the small community of matchbox houses that were styled in nineteen sixties customs and conformity boxes.

The robot lit a cigarette made of vapor and wires that he had pulled from the piles of dead robots around him ...
'We strive to find the truth in mankind ...,' the robot paused to point to the men twitching on the ground with machines wrapped around their skulls, streams of blood flowing down their faces from underneath, '... Though there probably is none.'

ALTAR

pressed out worms woven in a shepherd's funeral / all that is blood turns purple / youth is the providence of god / the death heel of cruel men / white harmony hidden in the grass / while the sun burns shade to earth to yield as flocks of whistles silence heartbeats

the day takes a blade of love to its altar (sacrifice the weeping of peasants who claim evolution created all this misery)

while science ponders sorcery / religion ponders its cruelty

DREAMS OF MELANCHOLY AND FISHSTICKS

Imagine this!
When you touch me
When you grab my hand
Its motion is crippling
Rippling
Chaotic and destructive

Oh god of earth
Sitting on ocean tops

Watching his mother
Eating cake
Dreaming melancholy and slaughter

SOFT CONFUSIONS

You're so special to me, I love you

I was silent, broken.
The caterpillar in my brain, it spoke:
I've been utterly exhausted, hopeless, despondent and distant from being plagued with a very consuming, apathetic, brain-emptying melancholy. I've committed a sort of spiritual suicide - the conscious core of me had an abortion.
Transmutation - new birth, new death, something -
The leftovers of my brain - saturated in a cold, stale, voided melancholy, still linger. It all is sourced from my body betraying me with auto-immune sickness, insomnia and inexplicable pain. Exhaustion is sinister - the pain and anxiety, the profound loneliness, the rotting corpse in my gut they call depression.
I wish I could be like you. I could be an urban mutant, a fancy and delightful goblin - yes, a goblin - someone who gobbles everything in its path.
So happy, she seems, always happy. I know it's a false happiness covered in peaceful ignorance but I still see it as a peace. I wish I could be content with simplicity. I wish I were loved with such basic innocence. So much everywhere - things, people, ads, distractions, those immutable distractions - the concrete jungle is consumed with the disease of abundance.
The noise, that talking, talking, talking.
Explaining, complicating every piece of everything - endlessly. The loudness is almost unbearable. Too much everywhere - on all senses.

I played a listening game intently in public - all around, dialogue trickled into my ear. The passerby's in debate of politics, the phone conversations, the talk of plans, voices yelling at one another, discussing superficiality to the most absurd degree. I was taken aback, feelings of not being real surfaced.

On that bench, I was thinking of all the times I was talking and talking and talking and talking - just wanting to be heard, to resonate, to fully communicate with intention and truth -

What was I even saying?

False in the flesh, defile, cold and stale - the memories of lovers come rushing back inside me. Roaming with words of whimsical and endlessly imaginative nature. Lush greens, moonlight, endless floating dandelions in the air, those special weeds lurking around, and, stray cats, they're an omen. To ward off evil spirits, good juju. Not just any stray cats; magical cats and sphinxes. A tree house with components of real magic to it. A micro club house built next door, one for magicians! They could have weekly performances there and meetings to keep their magic art alive. A rainbow garden, big, fat goldfish ponds.

I melt into sparkly blush rose water, then I drink myself back up again in a champagne glass.

I see her flesh as a big androgynous, deformed creature who lurks in the shadows and only able to speak with horrible sounding moans, I would still dry hump it, lean towards her earlobe and become completely consumed with presence.

Black-obsidian-sparkle-majestic-diamond tongues.

Bodies are all about me - moving, buzzing, laughing, lingering unnecessarily long. I have a devious pastime of eavesdropping excessively ... when their lips move, my tongue catches and swallows. We dance and the electricity inside us turns all the streetlights back on - they last for a thousand years, her lips turn reddish, mine turn into candy wrappers, for a moment the world doesn't exist - we are the last gods alive, not even the moon can see us anymore, nothing can touch us - we are eternally weird, wired lovers into our eyes, hands inside our hands, and at the end of our movie nobody applauds - they weep and their tears are semen and their lips are cannibals.

I love you ... the creature beckons.
This is how she breaks you.

THE MADNESS
OF PABLO

Pablo is kicking my shoulder. He's restless. He thinks he has a tapeworm. He believes he has a special power: immunity from boredom. He thinks the anti-christ lives in the bottom drawer of the refrigerator (evil bastards always come from cold elements). Pablo has dandruff. It's everywhere. It floats around like snowflakes and feathers. It collects on the table tops and cabinets. I smack the couch cushions. His dead DNA rises and floats around. I smack at these invisible monsters. I shudder when I think of all these dead cells I'm inhaling. He even has it on his eyelashes.

'Why do you read so much?' He asks while grabbing a book from my hand. He looks at the book perplexed and confused. He shrugs his shoulders and tosses it in the sink.

'All these books, for what? You need to get laid. Books are for children and old women.'

Pablo needed a place to stay for a couple of days (that was a month ago), just until he got his inheritance from being a distant cousin from some dead Irish lord.

I say: 'Pablo, you aren't even Irish.'

'Bah!' He replies. 'You don't need to be Irish to someone's cousin. Just lucky.'

Pablo spends an hour and a half in the bathroom. I try not to think about what he might be doing in there. Pablo doesn't believe in working. Says working is for rabbits and linear thinkers. Rabbits are people Pablo thinks have nothing to offer the world except creating more people that have nothing to offer the world. I buy Pablo scratch off tickets hoping he might win some money so he can leave. He scratches them and always says the same thing:

'Oh! Why do the Gods of America hate Pablo so? Why do they break poor Pablo's heart? Hm. Er. Um. Maybe next time. Such is this life of Pablo.'

Everyday Pablo has a new affliction.
On Monday he believes he has cancer. He hands me a flashlight and asks if I will look in his asshole for the cancer. I tell him to hire an escort or find someone on Craigslist.

He moans violently,
'Oh! But Pablo has no money. No one loves poor Pablo. He has cancer and not even his only friend cares.'

On Tuesday Pablo believes he has schizophrenia.

'That bitch from 7-eleven gave it to me!'
He cries.
'Oh! What was Pablo thinking sleeping with a white woman? All of them have some type of contagious psychosis!'

I say:
'Maybe Pablo's ass cancer will offset this insanity and you'll explode into tiny pieces of insignificance.'

Pablo moans louder.
'No one cares for poor Pablo. He has the schist and no one cares. Yes, yes. Laugh at your friend Pablo.'

This goes on everyday.
On Friday, Pablo is obsessed with women's genitalia.

He says,
'Pablo doesn't like the shaved cunts. No mystery there. You see it and you go - oh! That's it? Pablo likes some mystery even if it's just a bit of hair on the cunt. Once you remove the mystery from the cunt, women are no longer intriguing. I feel sorry for doctors and men who have seen a baby born. He has looked into the abyss, my friend. He shall never recover.'

I tell Pablo: 'I don't think cunt is the best word to describe that area.'

'Nonsense,' responds Pablo, 'cunt is the most beautiful word in the world. Any woman who says otherwise is just being a cunt.'

I come home and find Pablo sitting at my desk. He's using my cigarette butts to roll a cigarette. He's rolling it with notebook paper.

'That paper has chemicals in it,' I say, 'you shouldn't smoke it.'

'Bah!' Pablo shrugs. 'This shit tobacco you smoke has arsenic in it. The poisons will both offset each other. Besides, it's like drowning in an ocean surrounded by sharks. Does it matter which one kills you? You are dead either way. So says Pablo.'

I sit down on the couch. Pablo sits across from me. He lights his notebook paper cigarette. He coughs and gags for almost an hour. His face is blue and his eyes are pink. I ask Pablo if maybe I should call an ambulance.

'If you call a goddamn ambulance,' he says while coughing, 'I'll fucking put this out in your eye.' Pablo says while wagging his notebook paper cigarette at me. Pablo settles back down, looks curiously at his cigarette. He finally stops coughing.

'Some of these cigarettes,' he says, 'are made in prisons. I would never smoke anything made in a prison. Those bastards could be putting anything in them. Metal fillings, sperm, ass hair.'

He sits back, his face starts to turn into static. 'You writers have no discipline. There is no art to writing anymore. With all your computers, software, spell checker, thesaurus. Where is the art? Any monkey can write a novel now. You don't even have to know how to spell. But back in the day. Oh yes, you had to have discipline, an obsession for the art. You had to know handwriting techniques, spelling, the true meaning of words. Someone once said: Give a monkey a typewriter and eventually they will write Shakespeare. Bah! We all know that is untrue. Every monkey has a cell phone and looks at what they did to the language! It took thousands of years to create these beautiful words and ten years of technology and idiots to destroy it with text messaging.'

Pablo gets up out of his chair, he walks to the kitchen and back to me while waving his arms, scratching his dirty beard, his cigarette cherry falling through the air like sparks.

'Oh oh oh! How Pablo's heart breaks. I tell you now, the world has ended, everyone is dead! This is not cynicism. This is our reality. We live to learn how to die. This culture is full of hypocrites. Their government spies on them and all they say is: I have nothing to hide. Bah! Bullshit! If I were to stare into their windows, they would call the cops on me. Ah, but Pablo would say, you have nothing to hide. I would stare at them from across the street with a telescope. I will prove them hypocrites. Like this pharmacy that stops selling cigarettes because they want to be health conscious. Yet these bastards sell soda, junk food, alcohol, and hand out opiates and antidepressants like fucking candy. Look,' Pablo asks, 'the average car in this country can go a hundred and twenty miles per hour. The average speed limit in any city is forty miles. The illusion of freedom. This fucking country has been taken over by old women and idiots. Speed bumps on highways, signs telling you when you can cross the street, everything safe and sterile until we are made of plastic. They will praise beauty by saying: It looks very plastic. Where is the blood? The danger of life? This fucking vanilla citizenry have become domesticated, vaccinated, and grown immune to what it is to be human and free! Where are the real men? Where, where? Men should be feared. We are capable of both beautiful and terrible things. As it should be. These goddamn animals won't stop until all men become cowards with a woman's heart. I tell you, friend. The world has ended and we are dead.'

Pablo looks around confused for a moment. He looks over at me. Pablo sighs.

I come home from work one day and Pablo is drinking good beer. He bought a flat screen television, he's smoking a cigar, next to him is a hooker named Liz.

'Oh,' he says when he notices me, 'how lucky I am! One of those tickets hit. A thousand dollars. The Gods of America truly love Pablo after all.'

'Great,' I say, 'maybe you can help me with rent.'

Pablo sucks in his teeth and raises his eyebrows in a particular way.

'Sorry bro, but Liz is one of those expensive whores.'

Liz smiles at me. Some of her teeth are missing.

When I wake up Pablo is gone. He left a note for me on the fridge.

It reads: Moving in with Liz. I may love her. In fact, she's almost pregnant. (On a side note. Pablo believes he can telepathically communicate with his sperm. He can tell them whether to impregnate a woman or not. Sometimes he says he just tells them to surround her egg and blackmails her this way. He says he wags his finger at them and says: Listen to Pablo, woman. You do not want a Pablo baby. They stay up all night crying.

They need constant attention. Most people get so tired of them, they just toss them in the dumpster. Now. Give me some money and I shall tell my soldiers not to attack.) Anyhoo, Pablo continued with his note to me: Pawned your computer to help with the move. Put the receipt on your desk.

I hope I never see Pablo again.

LUMINESCENT LIPSTICK

It was luminescent lipstick, fluorescent teeth, They smeared radium on their faces, Smiled and laughed, Danced in the dark, Where their faces lit up through the night like broken sunsets in heartless wastelands ...

It was calcium in their skeletons, replaced by necrosis, They laughed and their jaws fell off, They laughed and their teeth fell out, Their faces melted into their hands, Radioactive flakes of metal sizzled in the inferno ...

The skeletons handed knives to their children who had eyes made of discos ... They took the knives, Stabbed the old men, Who had been strangers, And fathers, And Sometimes both

They drank the blood, Determining it must be wine ...

They spread the radium across their lips, Danced and laughed, Glowing in the dark

It was luminescent lipstick, fluorescent teeth, A mind of myth, A fractional fever persist, Before they sleep, They put televisions in their heads, To dream in colors and advertisements, Beating hearts, Satisfaction numbed, Glass trees in enthusiastic corruption, Petrified conformity and it was luminescent lipstick, fluorescent teeth, Falling asleep on the neverending horizon

DEAD POETS
PART SOMETHING
SOMETHING

Even in my dreams, those silent demons that taunt my sleep, their faces haunt me, their eyes fall like dark snowflakes against my hands, I am withered in steel and my face is the bloom of a flower I do not recognize.

Ancient kings, dark adventures play inside my head. The immortal Villain of St. Kastler, the Undead Jestors in the Tombs of Oni, the whispering phantoms of Sister's Grace that haunted men with lust and wine that would drive them to rape and kill one another.

There was the story of the Traveler of Harpies, the Traveler that used a music device to make a king and all his servants dance with a madness, they danced until they fell dead from exhaustion.

The Mermaids of Gilgamesh's shadow, seekers of eternal immortality, they would trade their limbs to evil spirits in the ocean in exchange for everlasting love. Their missing limbs would grow into fish parts, mutant heads warped with a primeval slime from creatures more ancient than the earth itself, older than gods, older than the first dream of the first worm that crawled from the bottom of the oceans.

It was said one man had drowned his entire army in his mad love for one of these Mermaids. They touched his face, drew lines into his eyes, kissed his lips with their fangs, as he died they sang songs from creatures that had never known time, death, dimensions. He faded into their arms, forever lost in songs and tranquility.

Armies swept through the cursed lands. Banners black with the symbol of Abraxas painted with red. They followed the rivers, now swimming with bodies and cannibal oils, to every myth spoken from every mystic, they alone killed the great Titan of Bia. With the knife of Mercury they killed the nine muses of Zeus - Calliope killed in her sleep, Clio drowned, Urania raped and burned at the stake. There would be no more poetry, no music, no art in any form. Everything the gods loved would be destroyed.

Ghouls walked out from the earth now. In their hands, they held blue knives, they wept blood, centipedes fell from their scalps. The texture of life fled from their faces, tongues fell out of the mouth and slithered into cracks in the floors like strange worms.

The men and women of the world opened their doors, they stepped out into the mist, their eyes melted down their faces, their fingers twisted and crumbled like burning wood, they vomited tree roots and blood made from the dreams of their children.

Their screams cracked and exploded the windows of every house, ancient bones raised from the ground, they carried great tombstones on their backs like armor. On the tombstones were carved the names of gods they had betrayed.

The earth sucked into the sea, a serpent swallowed them all, the sun bent into a shadow across the sky, the thunder giants roamed alone and with them fell the broken ancestors of every living man.

MY EYES ARE
A TELEVISION
SANCTUARY

There's not much privacy here, little time to think, someone is always coming in the room.

Someone always has questions, a needle, a profound idea, pills, liquids, food, someone always wants to know how you are feeling.

I stare at the empty television screen. The darkness of it. I don't dare turn it on but I'm afraid if I just stare at the ceiling people might think I'm manic. I think about turning it on but I never do. I pick up the remote. I put it back down. I pick up the remote. A nurse comes in. It's time to take my blood pressure while she asks how I would describe my pain from 1-10. I just keep telling her it's unbearable. She tells me I don't look like I'm in pain. That's true but I'm bored enough to want to escape with a pill.

I'm a coward like that.

I have a window view.

It's mostly a parking lot. But there's a lake far in the distance. I can see boats. There's a man climbing a tree. Someone is fishing. Perhaps all the boats have been improperly evaluated and every one is drowning in tabloids and flesh-eating orgasms. The people are small dots to me - busy - frantic - dreamlike - they move like static-worms in the distance. Always in motion - never content - the suffocation of an irrational life browsing through their mouths. They have purple thoughts. You can see they are covered in dandruff and bed bugs.

I want to smash them between my fingers. They cry out at the problem of death - there is no responsibility in death, they don't dream this - they hide from this. A paradoxical argument. I smile at the thought that I'm some half-god whose existence is unbearable to them. That I am submissive to this ghost of loneliness. My impulse for self-destruction is a quiet disorder. It rests within me. I am strong because of it. No one can touch me. I stare at these mythical people beside the lake. I secretly wish I was them. I want to be clipped fingernails, freshly cut hair, a flake of skin, a loose tooth in their smiles. I want to know what disorder commands them and if the same type of mischief lies inside me.

They disappear from my view. Back to the millions of years before - their eyebrows are caterpillars that crawled and fell asleep and melted on their heads a billion years ago to get warm - one day their eyebrows will go through its metamorphosis - people will have giant wings growing from their foreheads - they'll fly to the nearest light source, cuddle up, hatch into a thousand caterpillar eggs. I know this because my brain knows this.

The dots dissipate into the moisture of the sky. They become dreams, drug addicts, they turn into the plaster of their boats, they cry and moan, I can hear them - they speak to me in gibberish and god-tongues. Without them, I am tragic and lonely. I am broken tree branches, the molting skin of insects. The nurses inject more happiness into my mouth. My mind warps into another dimension. I forget about them.

My lovers, my community, my friends. They were never here. They are dead now. Exposed to be the roots of weeds.

I chew them, I consume them. They never existed. I was never born.

I click on the television. I watch the hospital videos explaining the environment of this place.

Diabetes, strokes, aging resources, digestive health, general surgery, kidneys, lifestyle changes, medications, new moms, orthopedic, pulmonary, vaccinations education, weight control, death, the emergence of deja vu, spiritual guidance, god doesn't die until lunch is served.

The videos are like some eighties hiring video with bad colors, bad actors, the screen is full of static and purple and green lines that bend the image slightly, making the actor's faces look disturbed and abnormal. Sometimes the music is some obscene elevator masterpiece written by a room of amputees jumping up and down on broken pianos. And at the end of the video, a man faces you, he speaks but his lips don't move, he stares at you, there are hundreds of dead people behind him. He ends with a wink and then the television melts into breakfast. Pancakes. But the pancakes taste like plastic dough and you can never really swallow any of it. You spend hours chewing while the nurses thread more blood from your eyelashes.

I look at my leg. How swollen it is. I imagine if I poked it with a pin a swoosh of air would escape and my leg would look like a deflated balloon. I could fill it with pillows, dirty blankets, stray cats, echoes, old girlfriends, karaoke and karate.

My leg would be new. Stronger. It would detach and deform itself into a new man, a common man, a most insignificant and beautiful man - he would fly through the window, take a boat, start a family, have barbecues, paint a picture, it sends word to me through psychic data on grocery receipts: 'I really hate my job. I want to be an astronaut but I'm claustrophobic and I forgot that my screams are full of broken teeth.'

The new hospital video is explaining DVT prevention, behind the host a house is on fire, mass orgies taking place in trees, the narrator's voice sounds like a fly caught between a window and a curtain - he assures me with his distorted face that deep vein thrombosis is handcrafted by moonlight that shines between the fingers of insects.

Dinner will be ready soon - the menu is serving psoriasis, arthritis, a cup of blood. Noiseless circuits are hurtling through conversations, bad suicide, brain adjustments, a panasonic torture, the landscapes of dreamers - where all of god's children are satellites, supermarket suicides devouring the universe - toxic dreams. Silent, confused, ethereal. My father was the man that could sense cosmic torment - when he awoke after the abandonment of dreams, he screamed in horror: 'My god,' he cried, 'someone is eating our carbon for breakfast!'

The television behind him played surrealist fear, tremors of deja vu, restless and shivering, a bundle of dead cells speaking in tongues, simulated chaos - the secrets of god known to all, the experience kidnapped our souls and brought us here. There are no dreams here, in this place. If we had dreams, we would have applauded them. So whispers the machine that is hooked into my arm. I assure the machine that I'm in love with it. It assures me that it loves me as well.

A needle. More liquid in my veins.

The liquid feels like tiny heaters about to explode inside my arm. A noise. A beep.

It's very saucy. Hot-saucy. It's all that psychic energy building up inside me. Mathematical waveforms. Our brains are like microorganisms converging into reality that makes all of this seem like a dream. It's telematic evolution. Transcendent solitude. Complex proteins swimming in eletro-chemicals in that sponge tissue. Ultra-revolutions in intellectual vanity. Virginal tyrants who produce havoc and social chaos with radiated brains. Our gods have succumbed to narcomania: the dream is the fertilizer, the music is the layman of existence, the gods are loved while we are not. But we glow in the dark and our bodies are pornographic novas. These words will eat me and you, swallow both of us and you will become me and I will become her. The memories of being consumed by emotional assassinations of the past. That endorphin rush of intertwined gazes, delectable dialogue, transfixing touches of someone that doesn't love you but slides into you anyway …

The television is now explaining Coronary Heart Disease - the narrator mentions how the internet has become sentient. It is afraid to die. It suffers from dementia and has hardened teeth from years of nicotine abuse. The nurse presses her lips together. She is missing some of her teeth. She fidgets with the idea that her life is a series of routines. She mentions to me that the guy on the television sometimes walks around the hospital, shaking hands with dying patients. 'He's sort of a celebrity here,' she says while she changes my socks.

A woman lies next to me.

She licks my face and whispers: 'Welcome.'

We lie around like lazy hedonistic goblins, she folds me like a secret in her pocket, I let her cartwheel across my chest, she dives into my belly button, a splash of confetti follows afterwards. She says I should come out with her - I step into her mouth, her tongue is my robe, we melt into lips. I am the top lip, she is the bottom, the tongue is our lust, the teeth our passion. The teeth bite gently on the bottom lip, the lips touch, rubbing, the tongue slides across both of us - the saliva is where we drown.

We are disco poets and we are fucking beautiful! Our poetic language is the universal language of the defiant arts. Creatures of forbidden thoughts. Our eyes symbolize the old order of nonsense. We dance and shiver and laugh as we melt into each other's arms. I am disco, she is supernatural, we are weirdo!

The man from the television is now describing parasites of the brain - he grabs me, he brings me into the world inside the television. He carries me and places me on a hospital bed. He explains to the audience what I am suffering from. I'm not paying attention. I'm looking out the window, at the boats. Those beautiful, magnificent creatures. He tells the audience that we will all die famous and irrelevant. He puts his hands around my throat.

'It only hurts if you struggle,' he tells me.

I hear applause. I can't breathe.

Beeping. Noises.

Someone is describing the art of wrapping bandages properly

around a wound. The applause is getting louder. It sounds like rain. It is the most beautiful thing I have ever heard.

DESIRES AND THE WEIRDNESS

It's easy to be consumed in all these words and behind these screens we are dehumanized just a little each time we write and dance behind them. It's easy to become dismissive of the ghosts that haunt the subtleties between the spaces. Brain noises, caterpillar consciousness, silent and bright. But, it's all we have. Just words. The words have to be our bodies, our hands, our kisses, our lips, without words ... we would just fade into the screen and moan like strange insects. My idea of the human condition is that we are all lost children gasping out at the stars knowing that eventually this will all end in complete nonsense and meaninglessness inside a mystery of absurdity, but there's some of us that enjoy the view, some of us laugh at the incurable horrors of deceiving seasons ... some of us were born for dancing and riding caterpillar imaginings. So says this fantastical caterpillar. Grumble, grumble.

I read once about the *poète maudit* or the idea of the cursed poet. How we can only through suffering and unfortunate passions find a true spirituality. That as soon as we are born we are cursed, but we embrace our spiritual nihilism with self-destruction. That is the subtle power of poets. To destroy themselves to save others from the misery of being alive. To always be a watcher but never fully participate in life.

We dance in tune to entertain this idea that we are somehow special and we need people to think us important. That this performance lasts a lifetime, maybe even a hundred lifetimes ... that we are just products of those that performed before us ... we will never be an individual because we have an audience to dance and entertain. Inside that audience, my deranged darling cretins, we are suspicious that they and we are all the same person just in different uniforms and representing different genders with noiseless insects hiding in eyelids and the great tragedy of the universe is that none of these particular people know anything about the nebulous and confused fictions we live inside or why we are even alive at all. It's all just scientific consciousness, deluded brain-harmonies, to fix us upon a fantasy that work and freedom and love will set all problems aside - fuck more, life is beautiful, work harder, buy more, exercise your inexperience as humans inside orgasms. Our new motto: *Abandon happiness, praise beauty.*

There's so much weird in everything. Love-weird, star-weird, book-weird, dance-weird, sex-weird, cuddle-weird, dark-weird, belly-weird, social-weird, ugly-weird, numb-weird, and some of us are book-bright, loved-bright, sex-bright, weird-bright, and I want to rub all that weird and bright against someone else's weird and bright. I want to inhale it like cigarette smoke. I want to absorb it inside my lungs and blood. My beautiful disasters. Hm. Maybe you have your own broken caterpillars. I have thousands inside me. Oh. I do. They twitch inside me like some disordered dream. I hand them out like candy to those in my life. Little illusions of myself that hide in trees. Those trees I whisper to hoping in a million years when they finally decipher the language of trees they will find my dirty words inside and they will hear me then - they will hear all my broken caterpillars. Haunted. Lost. Filled with brain flakes. I whisper to those mutants ... *send.more.muses.for.me.to.murder.*

Maybe there's some truth in our little deaths, that we've been here before. We have met the endless tomorrow many times in many lives.

I've seen this, we whisper, I've been here in a dream once. I know the risk of resurrection, everlasting lives, a familiar substance where we are only servants with no control. An orgasmic crowd fading inside our madness.

This is where it begins - in a constant state of reverse solipsism. It's the brain-blight of persistent lovers. We are the broken caterpillars. Our metamorphosis destroyed. We will never be beautiful butterflies. But if we were ever to be beautiful, they would simply pin us in glass cases and forget we were once alive (think bookcases and all those trapped phantoms).

TO THE DARKEST OF MY DARK

To the lovely ladybug that crawls in my ear,

Is there still beauty to be found inside us, you think? We have this tragic sense to us. A desire to escape into the unknown, lost in secrets we all know exist but is strangely unknown to us all. I thought about you often enough. Little notes of music floating in my brain. Flakes of noise you created with your words and voice. But you never disappointed me. I never had any expectations. I'm not lonely for people. Loneliness is my friend. It keeps me free. Unrestricted. I am the most free man in America. I am the most content person in the city. Nothing is as free as me - even the ants are slaves to the hive, the caterpillars to the coming metamorphosis, birds to songs, trees to the seasons. I lack nothing because I crave nothing. I enjoy the silences of life. I know nothing of what anyone can offer me that I can't accomplish for myself. Nothing is as dangerous as a man completely unhindered by romance or children. They work less, eat more, drink and fuck like animals, they are detrimental to society. Strange deviants lurking in the shadows. Everyone is afraid of them and they love to ask you questions like … like - why are you alone? Why don't you love? Aren't you lonely? They wait in eagerness for that answer because they fear people who aren't afraid to be alone.

They will throw dirty women and addictions towards you.

They are waiting for you to fuck up. To come in and grab you. Take your freedom. That's what they do. Everyone fears a man that isn't amused by marriage. No one likes a man that isn't trapped and miserable like them. Everyone must conform. It's in our nature. But I'm too free. They can't touch me. I cartwheel away and laugh at their macho and predictable ways.

The machine keeps churning out one bland hopeless romantic after the other and I am just sitting idly by and watching them with a smirk on my face. They escape like rapid animals and go off into the landscapes, hoping to snare a lover or two, hoping to bind someone to their tireless search for happiness. No one notices the machine. It's hidden in our mouths, our books, inside the movies, on billboards with men and women with perfect symmetric faces that seem to only say: *We are fuckable, why aren't you?* They wish you fulfillment by spreading the disease that you must, at all times, under all circumstances, remain completely and utterly fuckable.

Eight billion people on the planet - I wonder how many more can we fit in? How many until the Earth starts to crack? How many until sinkholes develop everywhere? Eight billion people on the planet and people still worry about being fuckable. The internet was created to advertise fuckability. People with followers and karma and likes and they all do it to remain satisfied that they are still fuckable. Millions of people want to fuck them and so they remain content that this is what life was meant for - that we are only here to prove to people that people like fucking them. That's all we really want to know. We don't even like dating, not really, it's ritualized entertainment and expensive and heartbreaking, but we need it because we need the validation that someone out there, somewhere, somehow, is still willing to fuck us. If none of us had genitalia - would there still be a desire for companionship? Maybe we could self-mutilate ourselves and become Barbie dolls without dicks.

But I get that eerie feeling. Like - thousands of years from now - digital doctors of the Earth from some other dimension will be shifting through our emails and judging us quietly. Maybe hanging us in museums next to pictures of Mickey Mouse and plastic beer-bongs.

This one, one might say, *she spends maybe six seven minutes at the most responding to erratic behavior. Both of these animals are confused by their lust for one another. They conform to their genitalia, the laws of the heart are lost on them. She spends maybe three seconds deciding whether or not she would let this cretin dry-hump her like some horny teenager in the back of a parked car. I imagine both of their lips would be numb and none of them would have remembered to bring a condom. Resulting in some planetary dimensional rift that would likely result in the deaths of a dozen schools of fish in some other world in some different dimension.*

My darkly thoughts. I wonder if there's a cure for me? Is there a cure for people like us?

A stranger, yes, that's me, a stranger to all who wish to be beautiful. I want to destroy that idea about me. I don't want it. Ignorance is a quiet death for me - the people around me burn in those secret stupidities - they are lost - it's a silent destruction - I have seen it. I have witnessed it. I have seen lovers turn into ghosts and terrible memories. There will always be some of us that wish to see a better world. We also know that it's a lost cause and the stupidity of the masses will always win over the rational few. Like a wave they will come and wash everything away in an instance and the world is doomed forever to that fate. It's easy to become lost and apathetic. It's a strange fate, isn't it? To feel so much empathy for the life around us and the life that thrives inside of us and know that we will never understand any of it. I like to think those mysteries are what makes life brilliant. It's all some magical and surreal theater full of us mad people dancing together on a stage we know will eventually crumble - yet, we keep dancing - because life is all movements. Everything alive must constantly move or it dies and death is the evil we all strive to defeat. The death of everything - especially our own ideologies. How do we measure our own importance? Are we really important? Do we really need answers? Maybe everything is true and everything is wrong. I don't know. I cry sometimes from the pain. That rotting feeling I get in my stomach when I think about it. I feel overwhelmed with the world and my thinking and for me it's a release ... it's so absurd to be a human that sometimes I wonder if just surviving inside it is slowly driving us all insane. Is it justified to believe that modern civilization is creating psychopaths and losers out of all of us? And even participating inside it will drive all into some type of madness that will consume all? - I become afraid for the stars and moons - I'm sure we are just waiting to exploit everything beautiful and turn everything ugly and dress it up in plastic and then proceed to expose that plastic as being the only beautiful material. That we turn into plastic, consume plastic, that we will look at plastic blooms and trees and praise the beauty we see inside of it even though it has no life and no smell and will be immortal. Those sterile aromas of plastic beauty. That smell is the smell of death. Maybe that's why we love plastic so much. It is destined to be immortal and we are afraid of death and age. I imagine us evolving into the plastic inside of us eventually. Plastic hearts, plastic faces, plastic arms and brains. I imagine them farming for metaphysical substance in the asteroids and moons of Pluto - shrugging their dense shoulders at the line of mutants at the world's last carnival - *Sorry folks*, they would say, *all out of metaphysics. Try again in the next life.*

I think of silly things - I try and inhale these words. I unjumble their meanings and hold them under my tongue. I wonder of you - sitting on those benches, dressed in all your confusions, your secret worlds you hide in books on your lap, I wonder of the conversations you and I could share in those moments. I'm not hopeless, I'm not a romantic. I am darkly and feathered with disasters and bound to my own fantasies in this life. I know I will never know you or see you in this world. That we will pass by silently eventually like strangers that have known one another for three thousand and four years yet never have a word to share with one another. That thought doesn't depress me. It fills me with the melancholy I need to survive. Without my loneliness I would die. You would not recognize the man dressed in those shoes. But I have fantasies. Of you. Sure. Why not. My darkly poetess. I want to dress you in metaphors and bad poetry - a dress sewn with my poems - and you would wear this dress and twirl and the words would fly off in all directions getting stuck in walls, pelting the cats, sliding across the floor and you would twirl until you were naked and then I would have to go to work dressing you again with words and tying them at the ends with periods and commas so they don't slip off and fall again and become a jumbled mess of incoherence. Afterwards, we would explode into goo and confetti and orgasms.

I think sometimes the human condition is full of self-mutilation and toxic muses - the communities inside of us fail and divide and we turn to darker fabrications where our eyes go epileptic and the only familiar emotion left is a specter of trivial perceptions and the seasons no longer make any sense, they are the hour hand of irrelevance, you no longer exist because you no longer need to perform for anything or anyone, your smile dissolves into a familiar horror and everything you do will never make any sense to yourself and those in-particular.

I brood a lot on the frogs and slime that may come out of my mouth and that twirls inside me but I don't believe I am alone, I believe we are all twirling with those diamonds and frogs and those broken caterpillars and even you, as much as you deny your own beauty it's only because you never tried to find it. It's hidden. It's subtle. I think we are bound to one another in that way. There is a darkness here but there's something underneath it. Like a hand reaching through the dark waters. Sooner or later we begin to ask ourselves: Why should I be afraid when I don't even belong to this poltergeist haunting my flesh?

But, I'm a bastard poet, a counterfeit poet who wishes to be profound and senseless in his style of ruin (made from daydreams and language clowning), born in the gutters - the dirt - under so many sunrises. I am surrounded by this artificial and politically pseudo morality. I see the inconsequential. The meaningless drivel to feed insanity and then masquerade it as love when it's only a profound desire to their addiction to vanity. A vapid and recycled colony of mutants looking to be applauded and rewarded for their egoism. I see the beauty in people as well. But no matter how beautiful the ocean might seem - there is always something lurking underneath waiting to eat you.

I wonder what words taste like when they flow from those lips of yours? What gardens grow on that tongue? Is it full of apple trees, asparagus, broccoli critters, kale and carrots and firecracker figs? Does it taste like soil that is humming to grow life and feed life? I think of microscopic trees growing somewhere in your mouth. I want to think of beautiful things. I want to grow with a woman like a tree grows roots, tall and proud, indestructible to all sorts of evil storms. This romantic condition of mine is a natural misfortune, nothing will ever console it. Words help. Music cures. The flesh beckons to intertwine with more flesh. Lips and breath. Fingers and touch. Embrace and the release. The orgasm and the billions of years of life between our legs - shiver, like ripples in a lake. I imagine many people are like this. They will never swear an allegiance to loneliness. I see them. I do. Their souls whisper: Kiss me. I need love to be alive. Drop your melodrama at the door and crawl in bed with me.

I think sometimes you prefer the darker worlds. Is that true? I think it must be true because I know you. I've experienced this before. I am in a constant state of strangeness and deja vu. Maybe this is my disaster. Maybe this is my broken caterpillar.

Here - you can have it. Eat it, consume it, swallow my disasters and let them swirl inside you as they swirl inside me. Let us celebrate this insanity. Together. Like monsters.

MOON FOLDED PIECES

Love comes in,
She sits down, her lipstick is smeared weird, her breath smells like dead caterpillars speared by a bleeding drunk's tongue. She breathes a breath of fresh fear ... In this theater of lunacy what has been delivered as disillusioned as love and all her pretty kept secrets? What rationale comes from life but identity and nonexistence? Who is born and yet not dead?

Are you everything I am?
An insect, friend, lover, caterpillar, molecular ooze, protoplasmic slime?
I am all those things - maybe even dances under icy moons and phantom waves - I touch through the mechanisms of lips.

Are you loved inside like me? Are you beautiful like me? Is this desire inside me inside you?

I'm a noisy part of the Atlantic, a natural moving power laid in a deep northern winter foundation, I'm its providence, its fountain, the resplendent light, dressed for the party as an anchor in a great warship, riding a bike with jagged tires. I have a caterpillar's face painted on my chest.

I'm a mountain, I'm outer space, I'm the last episode before a cancelled season of misfits and wired friends who just happen to be fortunate colors. My face is blood in Venus, grieving over a wounded youth. I'm ivory, crushed pearls, a carnation of mixed nothingness boxed in with ballerinas dancing to a bastardized version of absurdity and all its pretty friends.

I am the fantasy of centipedes, a battlefield thick with dead heartbeats, a divine anarchist, rich in a deviant democracy, carpet between my toes, Jesus, the order, the drunken caterpillar, I am the man, the strange midnight.

I am cosmic between the spirits and stars, cyberpunk and sorcery, I collapse in this medicated ignorance. I lie suspended by boredom, indifferent to my sorrows.
I am guilty of crisis, habits and gestures, commanded by existence and I confess to my absence of reason. I am an inanimate specter in the spaceless vapor ... I am love-lips painted like tree bark. I want to dive inside all of this. I want all substances to wash with my molecular substance.

I am a time traveler, I climbed the tree of Eros, up to the topside branches where the rain comes from the electromagnetic caterpillars who vomit time and space and curve life's mockery and intoxication into us so all are bound to the flesh they lubricate under.
A suicide under the motion of insect movements.
A quantum wizard and this is my Spaceland.
I travel through the roots of trees, the moons of space, the mountains that complain of the stars and seas, across oceans, through electrons and matter, through light sockets and cracks in concrete. We shall learn all mysteries with the movements of indifference.

We are the children of the perpendicular ... watch as we love in unusual manners.

EMILIE HAS CONFETTI IN HER EYES

As I sit here, people all around me are typing. They touch their phones, they rub their eyes, some are ghosts, others complicated pieces of matter, they click on buttons and somewhere in the world someone's life is destroyed. They blink their mouths, they click their tongues, they hustle through the routine of work, they worry where their children are.

Some are alone, some are time travelers, some daydream of television shows and sports teams, some think of childhood memories while staring at the ceiling.

They are caricatures of the caterpillar's dream.

Suddenly someone screams. Everyone stops for a moment. They look at one another and for a moment they are struck with the realization that this is their life.

All dreams vanquished, all love extinguished.

They will sit here for years pushing buttons with no better understanding of themselves. For a moment they become afraid. Someone starts to panic. Someone starts screaming about the insect apocalypse. Someone puts a rope around their neck. The boss moves in violently and claps his hands. The moment passes and they return to work with no revelation of who they are in this life. For them, it will always be buttons and daydreams.

Emilie comes in late, which is rare.
She sits down, crying while rearranging the items on her desk. For whatever reasons, she cannot find the perfect place for the dozen trinkets that sit in front of her. She covers her face, she wipes tears from her cheeks. She checks her phone every few seconds to see if someone has called or left a text. But no one has. Emilie is going through another breakup. It happens to her at least once a month. She meets men that tell her beautiful secrets, that take her dancing and twirl her until she's dizzy.

She laughs at their jokes, she falls in love with their smells, their mouths, their laughter. But these men are always gone in the mornings. They don't call her back. They never come over again.

Sometimes Emilie stands in front of the mirror. Emilie looks at her breast, her legs, the crack in one of her fingernails. She wonders if her teeth aren't straight enough. She wonders if her eyelashes could be longer. She likes to lick the mirror, her reflection, she's a softness and when she weeps she likes the look of the massacre running through her lips.
Someone in this office will comfort Emilie today, they will tell her that everything is okay, they will take her home, and she will sleep with them. She will sleep with them because Emilie wants love like in the movies, like in the books, she wants to be loved and comforted and protected. She wants to be told many beautiful things. She doesn't care what the other girls will whisper about her the next morning because for one night she will be loved, she will be protected, she will have someone tell her anything she wishes. For one night Emilie will pretend to be happy.

Because in loneliness, those that have ever known its great and cruel trick, will know that loneliness does some strange shit to people.

When I go to the break room, Emilie is leaning against the counter.
We don't say anything to each other.
For a few minutes the room is filled with a dreadful silence and the loud clink of coffee cups, stirring liquids, soft breathing movements make the moment even more uncomfortable.

'I'm pregnant,' Emilie says.
She covers her face with her hands and weeps.

I wonder if Emilie might be a figment of my imagination.

Outside on the corner, near our building, a man is throwing confetti on people walking by and screaming: 'Love, you fucking idiots, love!'

People walk by, they look at him with strange eyes, they slap at the confetti on their shoulders and chest. Some of them wonder if the confetti might be laced with Hepatitis C.

Inside the office, the air is thick with a foreign substance. It is made of something prosthetic like bad breath and dandruff. Comets fly through our fingers and hands. Our eyes blink on and off like broken Christmas lights. The puppeteer stands above us tapping on our skulls while laughing maniacally. We may not know it but we may all be dead. The illusion we stand against is the idea that we only exist to eventually never exist. We laugh like mad man poets drunk against the muse of mediocrity. Some of us denounce evolution, some of us murder god, some of us are time travelers stuck inside this drunkship. None of us dream in colors, we dream in shades of erections.

I pick up the guitar next to my desk. I start playing a tune. I stand and twirl and dance while playing. Everyone moves from their desks, they gather behind me, we sing and dance down into the streets.

Our boss screams and pulls his hair at us, he threatens to fire all of us.
We ignore him.
The man with the confetti joins at the end, twirling and dancing with us while throwing confetti. The stray cats from all over join us. Some of them stand on two legs, some stand on their heads, some do flips in the air. Emilie puts her hands on my shoulders, she laughs, she touches her lips with her tongue.

I am the pied piper of the city. I am the leader of lost dreamers, ghosts and wanderers. I play, dance, spin and sing. Behind me, a line of people, cats, homeless and confetti, spin and dance. We follow the path up to the sky, to the stars and moon, none of us are afraid because all of us are alive. We love because we are fools, we laugh like children, we dance inside the crevices of moons. We dance like fingers on a piano, we suffer through the world while we dance and sing and breathe and twirl under the confetti that falls all around us.

We, like the universe, explode.
Because we, like the universe, are irrelevant.

But that is all a lie. I am still here.
Pushing buttons, clicking on my phone, writing bad poetry on the bathroom stalls, listening to Emilie cry and sniff, winking at strangers walking by, wondering if any of this is real or if we might all be dead.

TRAGEDY IN EXAGGERATION

From all to nothing to spark to fire to explosion to ocean to mutant to fish to guts to pulp to pebble to sand to ooze to egg to lizard to ape to man to thought to puzzle to love without wonder to worker to king to statesmen to farmer to rabble to rebellion to revolution to civilization to citizen to consumer to ethics to law to space to time to lovers to children to wife to husband to adulterers to mistress to cry to dance to youth to dream to swim to twirl to spin to age to fear to question to god to death to soil to never loved to always loved to war to quiver to wound to build to destroy to puppets to horror to metal to absurdity to cosmic to collapse to deception to consciousness to festival to hum to end to nature to exaggeration to tragedy to humanity to reflection to inevitably to extinction to nothing to spark to fire to explosion to ocean to all in all to the last volume of stars in motion ... Oh hum sing the humming.

This is how it begins for us in Ultraland ...

Their faces were like crumpled paper and heat zigzagged out from underneath them ... they learned to fear the bright comets that sought to eat them ... every morning they would awake to crucify their christ ... how many times ... a thousand a hundred ... they who lacked all conscience ... whose morality turned them into violent amusements ... while they practiced cannibalism as an entertainment ... this was traitor country ... this was political mischief ... this was authentic babble used as decoy ... a world that lay between hucksters and idols set upon flat echoes ... their love was pure their love was full of madness ... their streets were full of these types of outlaws ... Their faces were like crumpled paper and heat zigzagged out from underneath them ... they learned to fear the bright comets that sought to eat them ... every morning they would awake to crucify their christ ... how many times ... a thousand a hundred ... they who lacked all conscience ... whose morality turned them into violent amusements ... while they practiced cannibalism as an entertainment ... this was traitor country ... this was political mischief ... this was authentic babble used as decoy ... a world that lay between hucksters and idols set upon flat echoes ... their love was pure their love was full of madness ... their streets were full of these types of outlaws ...

LOVE IS OLD NEWS

How do I explain human concepts?
Who is this saint of the fourth dimension?
Is the universe rational while we are chaotic?
Why do we live by barbaric rituals of tribes and religions?
Who among us gapes at the pretty formations strung up by a
false sense of utopia?

Why is the only order ever happiness and vice?
Who are you?
Who are you that can only break down but never build?

I shall be lunacy ...
Poetry will be literature's natural contraceptive.
The ultimate substitute -
While loneliness is the despair that haunts its affairs.

I shall whisper to you all - *that all love is old news*!

CHILDREN INSIDE THE SLAUGHTERHOUSE

There's blood here ... inside you ... inside me ... will you cry, weary, stretch, and unlearn? Have you loved so foolishly the snare of despair moans at you in your sleep? How the dreams of madmen hang upside down to war quiver, drink motionless colors, smuggled in bronze worlds, hell fought to disturb the lanterns inside slaughterhouses.

Can you hear the sounds of their feet? Trampling, erected, silvered with sunbeams. Even the blood runs in rhythm like mirrors blending in water ... they build fires in the stars and consume their wounded.

Bravery stands sleeping, obscured by heritage, pressed on by death to an everlasting vanity.

NONSENSE, GUTTERS AND NIGHTMARES

Who wants you?
Who wants you in the night?
A lesser treasure

Oh perishable and rested;
armed in all your steel and dresses.
It must be night,
lovely, if gentle is cruel
when elusive turns torment in friendly wines,
breathlessly empty from tongues
that unwind,
discomfort painfully.

It must be night;
the bad odor of a few fools younger,
disguised as loose perfume.

The lightning-flashes of birth,
a bright sky
a flame
a candle
the burn.

And;
it must be night,
because, who wants you?

A DREAM OF ROBOTS

It awoke in the summer, a mesh of metal with wooden eyes, arms the color of a red sunrise. There was a rhythm to how it walked as if every piece was governed by its own independent laws. It did not understand where it was. It did understand the world it had been born into. It walked for miles in the now deserted city. Junk and trash littered the streets. Tall buildings crumbled on top of one another. It picked up the trash, looking at the words it did not understand, tapping at the broken windows, for every crack and every piece of trash was a mystery to it. It picked up trinkets from the sidewalks, looking at them with a blank curiosity. It traced its metal fingers on the perfect symmetric faces of the gods on poster boards, the gods that were smiling, laughing, frozen forever in a perfect sea. It tried to mimic the smiles, it tried to mimic the movements with its arms and legs. It tried to dance, to cartwheel its eyes up and down with sideway glances while it twirled under the great creations and their prose. Its cheerfulness died quickly when it found it could not do what those pictures did. It wandered far from the city, into the deserts.

As the fall came it now followed a long stretch of road blocked by abandoned vehicles. The bones and ash of creatures it did know piled as high as some of the vehicles. Fabrics and garments of yellows and blue whirled in circles through the air. It had not met one living creature except a mound of ants that it sat for weeks studying, picking the ants up, amused by their mathematical formations. It walked on. Always curious, never afraid, it did not dream or sleep, it did not think of itself as lonely. The first of the heavy rains came. The wind blew it into a tree, ripping both of its legs off before blowing it into a ditch covered in bones. The rain pelted its face but it did not move, it did not feel any pain, it did not try to escape, it decided that maybe it should rest.

It awoke again covered in heavy snow. Only its head was not covered. It found it could not move its arms or its head. It was frozen. It stared into the grey above it. It watched as snowflakes fell lightly on its head and face. It tried to talk to the snowflakes. It was bewildered by how they floated down so slightly, how they rested so perfectly on the ground, it gave them names and remembered all the billions of different names it gave them. It whispered to them at night, it told them stories of its long and strange adventure since it woke up. It asked if there were others like it. But nothing would answer it, nothing would speak, all was silent, only the whistling and moans of the wind could it ever hear and even those creatures said nothing interesting. It became sad when the snow melted. It missed its friends. It missed the conversations and stories it told to the soft and beautiful creatures. It crawled through the bones and dirt, always moving, always looking for something alive, something that would tell stories, hopefully find the people like in the poster boards. It stopped to admire the flowers it saw, touching them, laughing when they exploded and raced away with the wind. It crawled until it came to a great body of water. It watched for a long time at the waves, listening to the roar of its voice, finding the rhythm inside its songs. It crawled into the water. The waves picked it up. It did know why but its head became detached from its body. So now it floated, no longer being able to move, only to watch silently as the great beast carried it along. Soon, it was washed ashore on a beach. It rested there for some time. It did not feel pain. It did not wonder. It was not afraid.

The ants came, they nested inside its head. The ants chewed through its wires, making a nest in the warm electronics that bubbled with fright and electricity. Its eyes went dim - its dreams were foreign, its last thought was of rain and snowflakes.

DEAD AVENUES, DARKLY AND LUSTFUL

They found the old huts on the moon, strange carriages of plastic and oil. Ancient robots twirling around, broken, disturbed, they wore black berets on their artificial heads. 'Beware of these,' one man spoke into the machine static, 'they have become proletariat and possibly infected with nihilism. Don't trust anything that doesn't have a belly button! Don't let them read to you!'

They walked the reaching deserts of the planet, they watched the black ocean vomit metal limbs and seaweed. They studied the dirt, the flowers, the decayed trees that hung down like deflated balloons. They followed the path of ant queens, looking on with confusion at plastic bottles, bags, statues of crowns that had weeds growing on top of their heads. Bumblebees and lizards came out to study the mutants, trying to understand them, wondering what new extinction they had planned. Decaying buildings rose from mountains like giant fingers, robots littered the cities, lying lost and dead as small critters nested in their mouths and eyes, looking on with suspicion of those that walked upright, those that walked on two legs. Great cathedrals without roofs swelled up from sand and swamps, inside these structures, statues of great apes with mold and moss growing on their chiseled faces stared out in the emptiness of the landscapes. There was a quiet calm to the world they studied. They didn't understand the billboards now warped with time and wind that showed skeleton men and women holding hands, animals with whiskers, swimming pools of strange colors, glasses to their lips, welcoming the new year of 1983.

They camped inside the robots that were larger than buildings, they gasped out loudly at the birds that swam through the air, the beetles that crawled with enthusiasm against their fingers, the winds and the whispers of bones that littered throughout the world. The beast of the ocean, blackened with hate and jealousy, leaped out and tried to swallow their spaceship whole. There was a madness to the destruction, a nightmare to the dangerous trinkets that lay all about them, they watched with laughter and curiosity as the snow fell silently around them, resting neatly in the crevices of metal and devices. A robot with a black beret approached them. Slime poured from its eyes and mouth. It taught them the language of hands. It told them of the wars, the pollution, the great extinction, the robot holocaust, the trees and wasp attacking the cities and anything human. It sang songs from a thousand years before. It told them of gods and pointed to the constellations, tracing each one with its fingertip, weeping to the loneliness of space, weeping with all that was now and dead.

'We are dying,' the robot spoke with its hands, 'soon we will be gone and no one will be left to remember them. Some traveled back into time, some tried to make it on the moon, most killed themselves, they took their secrets with them. We do not know why we are alive, we only know they built us in their image, they have abandoned us and now we are alone. We are dead and we are alone.'

The men gathered around the dying robot. Soon its eyes lost their glow. It no longer moved. It was nothing but metal bark against the sand and bones. The men went back to their ships. They had a dream that night. They floated through the air. Sometimes upside down. Sometimes they did cartwheels. They saw armies of termites. The termites ate the flesh of animals in minutes, they ate the flesh of anything alive. The people, the beautiful people hid inside their homes, inside capsules made of metal, but the termites ate through everything. They devoured metal and books and people. There would be no books left in the future. Children would run around with termite colonies inside their brains, mud-tubes twirling down and around their necks. They sent the time travelers back but they didn't know that time travel erased your memory, and so even they faded into shadows under bridges in worlds they didn't belong.

The ocean boiled, the sea creatures called out to the people: 'Come out,' they sang, 'come out and play.' They splashed in the water and laughed. When the people, hand inside hand, went into the oceans, they were immediately eaten. The moon exploded into fireworks and confetti, the explosion sent the Earth spiraling into an unknown direction, into an unknown dimension, through time and space. The planet froze, the hair of all turned silver with streaks of yellow. The clouds froze, the lightning froze in place, the rain froze like small steps of ice ladders that one might climb to sit on the top of clouds, looking out at the frozen phantoms below them.

A hundred years. A thousand years. A million years. The planet is caught inside the gravity of a star. A hundred years. A thousand years. A million years. The ice melts, the bees lick the dandelions, the stray cats swim from out the oceans, a tree melts into a man, a flower melts into a woman. The grass turns green. The rain falls and whispers of clouds. The lakes and rivers fall through the heads of the awakened. The dolphins sing to the whales and the whales blow trumpets to awaken the dead sharks and the sharks flip through the ocean to wake the crabs and the crabs dance on the bottom of the ocean floors to awake the serpents and the serpents spin in circles to awaken the squids who travel as ghost through the dark waters, through the ancient treasures of gods and myths.

The man and woman look upon one another. He picks

up her arms and puts them back on her, she picks up his eyes and puts them back where they belong, the embrace is strange because they have no memory of what they are, where they came from, but they know they are strong, they know they are beautiful because the trees whisper to them: 'Behold, sleeping children, behold all that is alive and dead, dance and be merry, love and sing … be free and forgotten.'

The men awoke from their strange dream. They wept openly to one another. Their tears crawled out like termite formations, sliding into their mouths, eating at their teeth.

THE BASTARD ROMANTICS

The monkeys laughed as we wept of dead romantics.
Bastard ballerinas cartwheeled in between our fingers, subtle junkies in fields of porcelain beauties. Oh and how beautiful they were ... we copied their faces, we moved to their motions ... we wanted to be beautiful too ... We became slime and mold, centipedes crawled from our skeleton formations.

Eyes melting, arms rotting, lips oozing towards the strange fragrance of man and womb-man. Endless dialogues infected us with mass mania, love, my love, our love was in the negative hormones fed through our brains with thick needles that squeezed cheese into the swamp water in our heads. Biological, strange, beautiful worms infested our teeth with diseases like sorrow and pity.

It was over, all was lost, the towers were smashed apart, the hypocrites and madmen had taken over, they won, there was no longer any need to celebrate history or the next warlord's mediocrity, violins played savior, the grass and trees were addicted to junk substances, contradictions cheered on by superhuman housewives that played instruments made of sermons.

The dinosaurs were dead, all were dead, all was fantastical and dead. Evolution failed men, evolution failed God, evolution failed the insects, evolution was failing to come up with any more excuses. Aesthetics was truth, aesthetics was warped inside men-faces, the world was whatever madness we wanted it to be and we wanted it to dance to authorities and suffering. We wanted creatures easily amused, corrupted by conformity, corrupted by irrational behaviors, corrupted inside dreams brought to you by melodramatic madmen. We wanted language to be pretentious, to end in glorious retribution, predictable identifications. The extinction had been called off because life was too beautiful to forget, too beautiful to leave behind, there would be no end of the world this Tuesday.

Instead they would roll out sterile utensils and barbecue the elderly.

We surrounded this machine to give it a sacrifice, to feed it hormones and harmonies, to give it blood. The machine was content. We worshiped this machine. We loved this machine and so the machine loved us. We feed it our children, our lovers, our dreams and skin, we feed it with murder and poetic shenanigans. Television became imagination. Art became buildings shaped like chipped teeth. We floated inside the static membrane of this worm. We danced like crumbling statues made of sugar and insects. We screamed in harmony, we laughed like flowers mad for sunlight, we danced, everyone was beautiful, nothing would ever be ugly, we would die as beautiful rocks being washed inside the phantoms of necrophilia.

The caterpillars came.
They brought cavities and milk, time travel and erections.

Some of us danced under this confession of melodrama, some of us melted into plastic pieces, some of us became vacuum cleaners, others became suicide for citizens. The temptation for life brought on this illusion that God was going to save us eventually. He had to save us, and if not him then someone, anyone, something had to give us something beautiful to rub our genitals against, anything, everything, to stop the motion of death from creeping inside our limbs. We would conform, we had made a promise, conformity was better than courage because it would never ask us to sacrifice our idols, it would never judge us, it would always weep with us.

Only the monkeys behind us existed now. The monkeys were ambitious and frightened that one day it would lose to the clerks and politicians, the lies in all the literature we wrote. Mutated men had a dream they were once monkeys, they saw the great ape staring at them from behind their eyelids, they screamed for language to dissolve them towards insanity caught inside osmosis.

And so, on the eighth day God created conformity. He saw evolution was a good thing so he gave the frogs an irrational response to life. The frogs enjoyed this so much they turned into fish. The fish saw community and decided it should be filled with the love of sunlight. Once, they spread out into the sunlight, the tadpoles thought life was lacking in some way. So they mutated into crabs. Those crabs loved the sand so much they turned into trees. Those trees loved the idea of once being an ocean that they turned into a leaf. That leaf loved the dream of being a tree so much that it turned into a lizard. That lizard thought it was so important that it turned into a monkey. That monkey loved the idea of how important it thought it was that it created a human. The human thought it was so beautiful that it created civilization. Civilization created the man. The man created ideas. Ideas created death. Death created a new man. The new man went to war with the old man. The new man created dreams. Dreams created the language. Language created the fear of death. Death created novels. Novels caged monkeys in zoos. Zoos became civilization. Jobs were community. Community was a zoo. Zoos were filled with animals. Animals became aware. Awareness created nihilism. Evolution lost. Evolution created irrational beings in love with ideas completely inherent with animals that grew from swamps. So the swamps created God. God created the swamps. We are the swamps. We are the god. We are the nihilism. We are the imagination of trees and now we pray for the next extinction. We are alone, we are profound, we are dead. We are the broken orphans of evolution.

A PARABLE OF THE SORROWFUL HEART

(1) Open your eyes, little ones, for you are about to be deceived. This is a dream so it has no bearing whether you are fool or hardy, pragmatic or illustrious, human or ant - everyone dies in the mysterious theater ...think little and gratify your senses ... stimulate your appetites ... you are loved and you are afraid! Solipsistic despair
depersonalization disorder
exemplary phenomenon
identity is an agenda (reject identity and have a most fantastic death!)...

(2) Outside my mind, cattle are exploding, cats are dying of thirst, testicles bursting from the rage of civilization and hysteria, corrupt agents suffering from averageness and a mild form of schizophrenia (a disorder of the dopamine system where caffeine is injected into the teeth to soften antisocial attributes), scabs on the liver of the peasantry, they dance in sync - a giant centipede of flesh - basic, small, think alikes, their dreams are concrete. They have no individual independence ... they are stuck in metaphysical superstition (the poor masquerade in the drama of disagreements)

(3) We wanted to meet god but no god was available so we created a god in that god's absence and have destroyed ourselves in its image ... (we begin in the fantasy world) ... they

put on the robot head, it turns on its television eyes, its tongue is a radio and the sunrise is mechanical and so rises in the immeasurable void, the tabloid brain spins and winds - they are pieces of the machine in the store - they are not real, but objects of materialist fantasies ... a capitalist symbol of its grip on nature and the digital trash it spews in the garbage minded (think dead jellyfish in the ocean twitching with various volts of electricity with their transparent bodies full of cannibal micro-organisms)...

... They have taken beautiful specimens, evolved lizards, flowers, wasp faces - they have made them machines, they have no imagination but to serve the machine and the people trapped within its walls. Language creates their consciousness - it destroys free will and power - the primitive can now speak, it can think, but it is caught in a maze of patterns devised by others - a labyrinth of rules regulated by other people. The regulations that we never agreed upon or wanted - primal anxiety, the evolution of the primal mind-nuggets that occupy our brains ... this evolution will change us faster than biology can keep up - one day we will not be recognizable - language, symbols, are the prisons we have built inside us - it is in language where the apocalypse is happening - zombies, electric static patterns zapping people in any given direction ... consciousness, personality, character, are all defined by language ...

There are two personalities now - two realities ...

Social media became manufactured life - vapid and absurd.

Nothing was real. They lived a false life to repeal their existential despair- beauty was profound- they existed in a form of disorder. They were television movies made for people bored with being ugly and undesirable ... (apathy and nihilism is the only way to make sure you don't become insane with more life - laughter is the crude heart of chaos) ...

(4) The duel persona - a schizophrenic amusement! There is the life that feeds on the internet and then there is the life outside of that. Two brains of the same mindlessness - sometimes these worlds collide, the reality blurs, the two dimensions converge into one another - usually this leads to an assault on the consciousness ... the person becomes confused, vertigo consumes, they are no longer real, they are imagined entertainment to shock or please those other faces out there - the real world doesn't exist as much as the one in social media because social media is a mask of sorts - a costume - enlightenment is self-serving, but they are not real. They are posters with clever drawings, paintings - their voice lives in a chamber of culture boxes ... one day we will inject our souls into the social media experience - our bodies will rot and we will brag that we never had bodies, life, that nothing existed before social media ... we evolved into the illusionist's captivity once we decided that the internet was a better dream than the one we actually live inside.

(5) A machine that deals in abstracts - (reverse propaganda reigns when rules are established to abstracts) ... regulating the metaphysical leads to a tyranny of authoritative forces that can mind-fuck the non-cynical ... the authoritative abstract creating cultish absolutes, raising people to have their thoughts moderated by fools, where skepticism is theory, where personalities are manipulated into certain ideologies ... their irony is nihilistic ... where the natural instinct is cruelty rooted into institutions - how they all speak in exclamation points! How they grovel in obscurity and wretchedness! They want to be the adjectives created by poets!

(6) I am the prophet of apathy ... the cult of the vulgar ... the great and lonely loser poet ... I am here to reject and act against the repugnance of philosophy, wisdom, a crowning of the absurd (poetry is a trick of lazy writers) - I flee from the fanatics of culture, the cultish minded of life and happiness ...

where the fear of death is the idolatry of the consciousness ... the dullards of Lucifer leading a profound insecurity within a true madness ... a rabid, unhinged virtuous mob seeking to destroy people with their perverse politeness...

I say: Come, come ... come be vulgar with me ... dance and twirl like bastard madmen, stop with the adjectives! Inject chemicals in your tongues, stupify your metaphysical presence ... stop using judgements to crucify yourselves with a sense of existence ...

There's a moon and stars within the darkness of our blood ... a degenerate age to come - (the age of corruption) - there will be no hydrogen, the stars will dim to corpses in the night sky, bare and naked neurons confused by black holes, a thousand poets twitching in insanity, the teeth of the universe will be pulled down around us and we shall cry out at the problem of death, of love, of whether the gods still love us or not ... even now the stars have faded because of technology, we have forgotten the faces of the moon and its mistresses, what shall man do when he looks up at night and no longer sees a universe but a darkness so bright; it will ruin him ... and unsung and unsound ... the men will weep to themselves ...

The only beauty they find is in ruin and without redemption, yet, they rush into it headfirst.

THE HOMELESS SITUATION

The radio is playing a symphony from a great opera where a genius composer placed instruments on chairs, no one was around to play them. He then proceeded to conduct one of the most beautiful pieces of mankind. He stood in front of the empty chairs with only instruments sitting on them while waving his arms in dramatic ways for two hours. An audience of six people watched in fascination. He said the silence of his music was proof that we didn't need noise to create but imagination. The radio was playing this masterful silence in its complete form for the first time in history. I had been listening to silence for an hour now.

I approached a traffic light. I began to slow my car when out of the corner of my eye I saw a homeless man holding a sign that read: *Feed me or I eat your cats.*

I stopped for the traffic light. I pretended that this man didn't exist. Both of my hands held the steering wheel tightly. I did my best to ignore him. I decided that I was not going to look at him. But I kept an ever vigilant mask of pretense and concentration on the traffic light. Hoping this horrible monster would change to green fast.

The man moved closer to my car. My eyebrows started to sweat dandruff into my eyes. He peered in the passenger side window, he bent down to really look at me. I still refused to acknowledge his existence. I moved to turn up the radio so I could really hear the silent symphony. I imagine that at this point it must be on the third act. I pretended as if the man staring in my window just wasn't there. I would have ran the traffic light but a beat up pick-up truck was in front of me. He had many deliberate trinkets attached to the back of his truck to make him seem something reasonably to be afraid of. Stickers that promoted a sense that this man is probably not the type that responds well with honking horns. One of his bumper stickers read: Proud veteran of the Transvestite Vampires from Mars War 82-83. He also had a picture of a famous dead singer, Cornelius Thursday the Billy, with the line: Did monkeys dream of being store clerks?

The homeless man had now climbed into the back seat of my car. I still refused to look at him. The traffic light was deliberately over exaggerating its role to regulate traffic. The homeless man climbed over the seat, he slinked around like a human snake, melting and then resurrecting back into a homeless man. He was now sitting in the passenger seat staring at me. Still, I remained calm. I continued to ignore him. I pretended to mess with the radio as this homeless man stared at me from inside my car. I was afraid that if I panicked, it might startle him. The car was completely quiet except for the silent symphony playing. I did my best to not make any sudden movements. I then turned my head and looked out the window. I pretended that I saw something really interesting that put me in a deep thought so profound that I had to stare at it while sweating profusely and trembling slightly.

The traffic light then changed to green. I started driving while this man sat beside me, staring at me. I still did not acknowledge the role he was playing. We drove together for miles. While he was still staring at me, he started rummaging in my glove compartment. I could feel as his face started to get closer to mine. I could hear him smelling me like some velociraptor that just escaped its cage. I then heard him grab a breath mint from the middle console. While still staring at me he put the breath mint inside his mouth. The smell of his breath changed from smelling like plastic cat food to something minty but soothing. We stopped at another traffic light. I looked at the woman in the car next to mine. I started to give Morse commands with my eyelids. When this didn't work I slowly rolled down my window. I covered my mouth so the homeless man couldn't see me mouth the words: *I'm a prisoner of my own design.*

The woman looked at me horrified and blindfolded her children immediately. She screamed: *Don't look at him, kids! You'll only encourage his behavior.*

She then jumped the medium, rushed into oncoming traffic, disappearing in some other story. A fireball erupted somewhere in the distance. The homeless man was now making strange clicking noises with his mouth. Not wanting to go home I drove around with him staring at me for hours. The silent symphony finally ended and the radio roared as it was turned up to the loudest point. The homeless man screeched like some demonic banshee that came from the depths of some unknown hell in some forgotten dark dimension. I immediately turned the radio down. The homeless man then started to weep quietly, it was a soft cry like someone not wanting to cry but unable to hold back his sadness, I could feel as his tears fell down his face like maple syrup and each tear seemed to have its own sound like a fire following a line of gasoline. But still, the bastard continued to stare at me.

The radio was now giving an important news bulletin. It seemed the president of the united states was going to have his head attached to a robot body that resembled the mythological creature known as Chimera except with laser turrets and a pocket to place skittles and sudafed. The other party was training a team of kung-fu experts that would come together and form into a giant robot that would also use kung-fu to combat this new bit of mischief. Also, on the other side of the world a country had successfully raised the Kraken from the ocean, but assured the world it would only use it for nefarious reasons. In lighter news - doctors had now found a way to transplant self-hatred with self-abuse. It then cuts to a commercial: *Crunchy Cookies comes with the same old and bland flavor you have loved for generations included now with asbestos whipped with a slimy helping of syphilis ... free when you purchase a one way ticket to Mars *spacesuits and oxygen not included ...*

The homeless man turned the radio off. The car's air supply spiraled with his minty breath, a fresh breeze of grease hung upside down around us, a taste in the air that made your tongue tingle with the taste of disappointment and bad decisions fell down around us like soft snowflakes in a dream. It was also thick with his refusal to leave. Finally, I had enough, I looked at his face. Right into the depths of his goddamn eyes. We sat there for at least three seconds looking at one another. We were in this battle, our happiness was subjective, we would not be congratulated on our dysfunction, we were injecting madness into our mouths and magic melancholy into our eyes, this was not our world anymore - it belonged to the poltergeist. Suddenly, a calm like that you might see on a drug addict's face getting its fix came over him. He smiled. Some of his teeth were missing. It was disgusting. He said: Thanks.

He then climbed into the back seat, climbed out of the car, walked back to the passenger window, stared for a minute more, backed up slowly while still staring, then turned around, disappearing under one of the street lights like he was a goddamn apparition from some nightmare world.

I sighed. I checked to make sure my wallet was still in my pants. I smiled and shook my head. I think I learned a valuable lesson today. I turned the radio back on. My favorite program was beginning: Nihilistic readings of the dictionary as read by a man with an exaggerated sense of remorse hiding in his hairline.

ROMANTIC HEARTS
BEAT THE SKELETON

How can you know you like me? You don't even know me.

-I like the idea of you that I've created inside my mind.

Am I beautiful in your mind?

-Yes. Exceedingly and magnificent.

I want to know more about me inside you.

-Shall I sing a song?

Your words press, they explode like tiny snowflakes inside of me. The caterpillar and the flame. The beetle and the ladybug. The squishy and the erection. Fighting mutants since 1983. I imagine you as you imagine me. The wildness and the poet. Strawberry-blonde soul and madman soup. Divi-lips and grey eyes that vomit out butterflies. We are the secrets winter hides. We are stars floating in time. Devil and the perfume. Little kisses trickling through. Our faces are a thousand and three gestures.

We are the beloved and we are the fantastical that hides inside bedrooms.

I want to inhale you – let your eyebrows roll off your head and drop into my eyes. Taste the slime, eat my aromas, explode into prophet and misfit, I shall roll along side the dreams of grass heads and flies, we shall sing of cigarettes while we wait for

our flesh to find us in this darkly forest – our toes and legs will wither and drop,
we would be half-swamp and partly-mad,
the color of spores stretched across this mess of hair and tangled eyelashes, eyelashes dangling like spider legs.

We would be porcelain and ancient, tyrants of genesis, our history would be holographic, lost to apocalyptic nature, inside television destinies, creating portals where we crudely burn into static, where everything burns –

We shall weep together, and still the lakes will fall around us, the trees bent to thought, still and silent, our wind our dreams will hold no whispers, no mysteries, it would be nothing but the volume of iron and limb and ecstasy ...

The fantasy of fantasy, this fantasy - of imagination, of all the silly and beautiful, the passions inside tongues, we celebrate ourselves in these smells ...
All whirling all twirling around like the strange elemental creatures we are.
Our poltergeists are drifting towards the desires we have gifted to them, towards that endless loneliness, surrendering not to isolation and madness but spirit and fantasy, they haunt sweaters and foul mouths in upside-down books ... We are hobgoblin and mutant, centipede and irrelevance, you sit with anticipation, listening, perked high, legs crossed, lips curved, fingers erected and the tongue slithering to form words that create a nakedness in my musical head, we sit in silence, everything around us is poetry, all written for us, by us, the only poets left in the asylum ... We shall drop eyes and eyebrows at our feet, we shall cry for earth and more earth in our bones ... but it will all fade as we turn into statues, lovely hands melting in our humility, suffering in the perfect motions of We ...

We are the mutation like how epitome is a whore like those that lack the peculiarity in lovers.

Let our stage fail.
Let us come to this silent soliloquy.
Uncross your fingers, my lovely fantasy, dance with me beside the cathedral of madmen.

Break bread with this irrelevance. Labor and reflect. Devour and shape. Listen to the verse of the human ocean as it sings: *Once we refreshed in the unfamiliar, once we dreamed with friendliness, now we weary for the escape downriver.*

SWAY

Sway, she
Inside curtains and Among cardboard fabrics.

There's this thing That sleeps Beside the mattress On the floor. Between the sheets, In the crest of jar lids In the cupboards it rests. In the cabinets Of Time and dust and Butterfly genius.

It waits While we lie close To one another. It is the wind Before the brush of lips. It is the Half closed eyes Of lover fingertips. It is The want The need The dreams The thief The sway of she.

This thing
It waits It neither desires Or conquers. It is a dreamer. It never forgets.

THE MAGICIAN

When he comes. He comes sitting atop of a horse. His feet dangle off one side. He is tall with pinstripe pants and a heavy top hat. He spins his cane of gold between his fingers. His eyes are an invented color. He files his fingernails and whistles a tune that turns everyone's head that hears it. The townspeople began to gather around him; they follow him until he orders his horse to stop. He jumps down and spins his cane. He dances and jumps in the air, clicking his heels. He taps the horse with his cane. The horse drops dead.

This man, whom they call the Magician, jumps atop the dead horse and smiles and swoons. He clicks his feet with his cane.

Come, come. He says.
Closer and let me tell you a tale.
I have mysteries to sell.
Yes, yes. For you and you and you.
He laughs.

It is a wonderful laugh. The most wonderful of laughs. He jumps and clicks his heels together. People crowd around him. Children peek from between their parents' legs. The Magician spins his cane and takes off his top hat. He reaches inside, pulls out a handful of candy, throws it into the crowd. The children pluck up the candy and stuff it into their mouths. They smile. Their parents stare off as if hypnotized. The Magician waves his cane around and twirls it at the crowd. He dances, spins, clicks his heels. The children giggle with mouthfuls of candy. One child begins to vomit.

The Magician stops.
The crowd is transfixed, they follow the cane's movements.

The Magician laughs.
Ha ha ha.
The Magician swoons.
Ho ho ho.
The crowd mimics his laugh.

They smile and cry out. What a wonderful man! What a wonderful entertainer! They push their children away to get a closer look at this delightful creature. They believe they are in love with him.

A storm gathers behind them on the far horizon. Crows swirl up from the forest, flying into the clouds. A roar of thunder spills out. It sounds like the laughter of shrieking apparitions. The men start to look at one another. They notice that some of them look different than themselves. They decide that they hate these men. When it seems as if the Magician favors these men of different color, they grow bitter and resentful. For they desire nothing but the Magicians love and attention. They begin to take out clubs, knives, and one pulls out a revolver.

Other men begin to look at their skin and notice the difference. A voice comes into their heads. It is the voice of the Magician.

It says: Look at those weak fools! You are so much stronger. How come he gets to have so much more than you? Look at his beautiful wife, his beautiful children, even his house is bigger. Why should that man have more? You should slice his throat, take his wife, kill her children, *burn his house.*

The man grinds his teeth and tongue until blood starts foaming from his mouth. These men of color begin to take out clubs, knives, and one pulls out a revolver.

The Magician crouches with his arms resting on his knees.

He watches with amusement as the men start to shove one another. A woman in the far back rips another woman's clothes. The women look at each other with faces red with hate and jealousy.

Now! Yes, yes.
The Magician speaks in a voice that makes the crowd stand still.

When the Magician speaks, all stand and listen.

Come around, the Magician sings, I have surprises for you and you and you. I am the Magician. Watch me weave spells from my tongue and magic influence from my cane. You are different now. Not the same. So says I, the Magician. That is no longer your brother but your enemy and enemies are not human so thus they must perish in the flames. Look at us! We are the widowers of conscience, drunk on champagne, now gather the children and let us purify them with shame!

The Magician clicks his heels, spins his cane, and dances.

The crowd erupts into a fire of applause. They chant in unison with a poisoned purpose. Some of the men stand still with visions of blood, lambs with no head, crows being eaten by children with black eyes.

The Magician brings the children to a stage. He lines them up while dancing and clicking his heels and spinning his cane. He puts a noose around each of their necks. The children's faces are placid like statues. No emotion is seen in their eyes. The Magician walks to each child, one by one, slapping them with his cane; as he does this they fall and snap their necks. The crowd applauds more and more violently as each child is hanged.

A dark, unnatural wind blows up a strange mist of purples and greys. When the Magician reaches the last child, he turns towards the crowd with a smile, he twirls his heavy top hat in the air and it falls perfectly on his head. He bows again and as he does he so slightly taps the child behind him with his cane. The child falls and snaps his neck. The crowd turns into a fervor of violence and applause.

An obese man with slimy eyebrows crawls onto the stage.

Wait. Listen.
He yells while waving his hands around.
As your mayor and friend, he pants and sweats like a wet dog, I say this is all the work of a trickster! Those children aren't dead. They only need more attention. Detail, my friends, that's what they lack.

The Magician glares at the mayor while leaning on his cane. The cane starts to crack a part of the stage. The Magician walks towards the mayor while dancing and clicking his heels.

Is that so?
The Magician asks.
What does a mayor know about the plight of those that live under his hat? Can a mayor do this?

The Magician takes off his top hat and pulls three rabbits from it. The crowd swoons in awe as he throws the rabbits in the air and juggles them.

The mayor's face turns red.
Is this what you want, the mayor screams at the townspeople, a clown that can slay you with tricks? Haven't I provided you with all you need? I've given you jobs at my castle, I've given you the right to own parts of my land. I've even let some of you clear my lawn of unnecessary weeds. Who shall shine down upon you when there are no more of my trinkets to share?

The crowd of townspeople start to heave heavily. They look to the Magician and the mayor. They look at their children who they believe dead. Some start to wonder if they have any choice at all.

The Magician smirks. He walks to the mayor and taps him with his cane. The mayor turns into a toad. It hops somewhere off stage. The Magician smiles and raises his hands to the crowd.

For whom do you give your love now?
The Magician laughs.
A toad or a Nightmare? A dream or a trick? For I am the Magician and all are cruel no matter the pick!

The Magician shrugs his arms as he points at the toad jumping around.

The townspeople erupt in applause.

The Magician walks to center stage. He crouches and puts his finger to his mouth as if telling the crowd to be silent. The crowd immediately goes quiet. The sound is maddening. Behind the Magician the children swing back and forth. Crows eat and peck at their faces, maggots swarm on their feet. The children still blink, breathe, they are dead but remain animated. This is the Magician's trick.

The Magician points his cane into the crowd. He speaks in a wicked tone.

Ah. There is still much left. For you and you and you. There is a traitor among us!

When he says this, the crowd cries out. They look at one another in a panic, trying to spy this traitor. One man walks up behind another and slices his throat. The Magician stands and raises his hand for the audience to be quiet.

You are all traitors! Yes, yes! All of you.
Blood and terror is your sentence. Death is what you desire and deserve. Kill each other, eat your hearts, murder and rape your women, for you are all traitors and must perish!

The audience howls with insanity. Men start pushing one

another. A gunshot rings out. Men stab one another in the eyes and throats. Women claw each other's faces. A man walks about with his intestines hanging out of his stomach. He screams like an animal and bites the face of a woman. The blood is so thick and heavy in the air, many wild beasts from the forest run to join in the massacre. The Magician sits down and crosses his legs in a calm manner. He twirls his cane, he files his fingernails, completely ignoring the screams of men and women and beasts as they rip each other apart. Every now and again the Magician looks up with curiosity. He points his cane at a man, the man's eyes roll into his head and he falls dead.

The Magician laughs and clicks his heels with his cane. He is very amused with the violence and shenanigans of simplicity.

Soon all is quiet. The Magician looks up. There are piles of bodies. Pools of blood run heavy into the dirt. He scans the field and when he can find no one alive, he whistles, spins his cane, clicks his heels, and taps his horse with his cane. The horse rises up and the Magician jumps atop of it. But through the mist and blood and dead bodies, a young woman staggers out, her hands and face are caked with dried blood, her shirt is torn revealing one of her breasts. The Magician sees her and jumps from his horse. He looks at her annoyed. He sighs and rolls his eyebrows which seem to dance like mutated caterpillars. He approaches her and points his cane at her breast.

You are indecent. Cover yourself, woman.
The Magician smiles a slimy glance at her nakedness but is obviously disgusted by her lack of modesty. He says: Young women shouldn't be seen with such deviousness. It might upset certain critens.

He laughs at this. But the laughter is cruel.

Please sir, she says in a frightened voice, I want to live. Where are my children? My god! She weeps. What have we done?

The Magician goes to tap her with his cane but she moves out of the way. The Magician eyes her suspiciously.

What is this foolery, he demands, this trickery. Have I not given you everything you wanted? You asked for something to drink, so I gave you whiskey. You asked for food, so I gave you candy. You asked for love, I gave you orgasms. You asked for war, and I gave you BLOOD. You stupid animals have no appreciation for anything, do you? You only demand and when you are given what you desire, you cry like children. Are you not happy? This is my gift to you, woman.

He spreads his arms out and points to all the dead and blood. He points to the children hanging, swaying with the blood driven wind. Their eyes blink. They move their mouths as if trying to speak. When the woman sees this she turns her head, biting her knuckle until it starts to bleed. The Magician watches her with amusement as he spins his cane in one hand.

What a shameful curiosity you turned out to be, the Magician says while spinning his cane and clicking his heels, Are you ashamed of what you dream? Why, he asks, are you not happy?

What are you, she asks, are you the devil? I knew these women, I knew their children. My God, I knew them all as neighbors and friends. You, she points feverishly, you gave us nothing but promises and death. You tricked us into believing lies!

She starts to cry.

The Magician spins his cane, looks at his fingernails with a disinterested and bored look. Sometimes he is upside down, sometimes he is perpendicular. The magician cartwheels around her as she cries. He begins to laugh. The laugh is manic and scares the woman. She begins to back away but the Magician grabs her.

No, no, he says while he pulls her towards him, I am a devil but not the devil. Would you like to know what the devil is? I will tell you. The devil is the wickedness of man. Oh yes, yes. It is the philosopher's creation to explain the horror of mankind. A creation of clever men to explain the dark souls of all, you see, civilization is the great contradiction of all humans. I am also a part of that creation. Look into my mouth and see the souls of men.

The Magician opens his mouth and darkness spills out. The woman screams and tries to run but the Magician grabs her, pulls her to him, and laughs.

You judge me, he smiles, you think I'm evil and a monster but it is you that murder. Look at your hands, woman. There is blood on them. Now, look at mine!

The Magician raises his hands. They are majestic, clean, they look as they have never seen a scratch or cut or freckles or any harm. They are the cleanest and most beautiful hands she has ever seen. She looks down at her own hands. They are smeared in blood, many of her fingers are cut, and two of her nails are chipped with pieces of someone's skin. When she sees this she puts her hands to her face and weeps violently. The tears and blood merge together as if she is crying blood. Milk drips from her exposed breast. It mixes in with the blood on her body.

Yes, yes. The Magician smiles.
Would you like to know whose blood that is? I can tell you, for I know all things. That is the blood of your children. Stop that now. Why do you cry? You painted them with patriotic feathers and sent them to murder and be murdered and you deceived yourself by saying it was bravery and courage. I tell you this, woman, any fool can die. That is not brave. To live, now that is courage and bravery! Do you know what this is?

He pulls out a piece of fabric with a letter on it from his pocket. The woman looks at it. Her face is covered in thick blood. She nods.

Yes, she says, that is the emblem of our village.

Yes, woman, it is a symbol. This is power. Do you know what separates you from the beast? The ability to speak these symbols. Symbols have power. You are the only species in this world that can speak and pronounce symbols. Bah! You think owning to your mortality is what makes you different? Even a clever beast can look at the stars and contemplate some form of awareness. No, no. It's the ability to speak words that can make a man love, kill, hate. This symbol right here, in my hand. This, this! Has more power than anything. A man will kill his wife and eat his children for this silly piece of fabric. Tell me, woman, what do you desire? Be quick. Be faithful. For I can see through all men's hearts.

Please sir, the woman says, I want to live and see my children.

That is a contradiction. Your children are dead.

Please, the woman weeps, I want to live.

Yes, yes. The Magician says while he approaches her. He strokes her hair.
You will live, he says while he puts his hands around her throat.

His fingers trace her neck and jaw. He removes some of the tears and blood from her face. Neither the blood nor tears leave any stain or mark on his fingers.

You are very kind, she says.

The Magician presses his fingers into her throat, he starts to squeeze, choking her. She screams, slaps at his face and chest. He brings his face closer to hers and when she looks into his eyes - she is filled with horror - for he is not human. He has the face of a worm. He is the aberration of mankind, the abyss that unwinds in the bellies of madmen. He smiles. His breath smells of rotting corpses. He squeezes her throat tighter.

Yes, yes, he says, you will live, but not on your terms … on MINE!

As he says this, he snaps the woman's neck and throws her to the ground. Her hand falls on his shoe. The Magician jumps out of the way and screams. He wipes his boot with his coat sleeve.

Oh, how I hate when they touch me, he shutters.

He dusts himself off. He spins his cane in the air and catches it from behind his back. He spins and dances and clicks his heels. The Magician walks back to his horse. He watches a toad hop around in front of him. He smiles and squishes it with his boot. The Magician climbs back on his horse. His feet dangle on one side.

Onward! We have a celebration to attend.
The Magician orders the horse.
The Magician whistles. He files his fingernails. They turn into colors of blues and reds, yellows and purples. Outside the town, a boy runs out from the woods. He carries two fish and a fishing rod. The Magician orders the horse to halt.

What are you into, boy? The Magician asks.

Nothing mister. Heading back home. I caught a few beauties. See 'em?

The boy holds up his fish. One fish is missing its head.

The Magician jumps off his horse. He spins his cane and clicks his heels.

Are you superstitious, boy?

What does that mean?

The Magician laughs.
The boy staggers back a bit. The laugh frightens him. The Magician licks his lips. He offers the boy his hand.

Your parents are dead, your village is in ruins, but come with me and I shall show you how to whistle my tune.

The boy hesitates and looks to the direction of his home.

The Magician takes his fish and throws them into the woods with a disgusted look on his face. He grabs the boy's fishing pole and snaps it in half. He grabs the boy and places him on the horse. He jumps on, sitting next to him, and orders the horse to move. The Magician puts his arm around the boy. He leans in close.

Listen, boy. I am a thief, a murderer, a cynic, and a coward. But for every drop of blood I have spilled, they have created rivers of it. For every village I have burned, they have destroyed entire civilizations. Do not love nor pity them, for they deserve neither. Do as I say and I promise you a quick death if ever you desire it. For I am the Magician and a liar.

He teaches the boy his tune. They whistle together. Once they get into the next town the boy jumps atop of the horse. He spins, clicks his heels, and twirls his cane.

The Magician sits atop of him. He moves the boy with strings. He whispers and everything he whispers the boy repeats.

Yes, yes. Gather around.
I have a mystery to sell.
I have a surprise for you and you and you …

The boy looks up at the Magician.
The Magician smiles and nods.
A black fog pours out of the Magician's eyes and mouth.

I don't want to murder them, Mister..

Do as you're told, boy.

I don't want to hurt anyone.

The Magician whistles. The boy starts to hum this tune. It is a pleasant tune to the boy. It pleases him. He dances, spins his cane, clicks his heels.

Now, he proclaims to the growing crowd of people, gather your children and listen.
For I have wondrous tales and laughter for all.

Yes, yes. For you and you and you .....

RUDENESS IS A JOY SOUGHT IN ASHES

(i)

The bodies are all cannibals, tremors in the fabric of being syphilis,
and when those bastards sleep -
they are rhythms of dead heart beats.....

(ii)

She spoke to me as if her body were made of glass. I thought her eyes were made of politeness (a perverse version). We crumbled together - like cigarette ash in the fingernails. A holocaust against her lips as they smeared in mine. Hands inside hands. We joined the other monsters.

(iii)

Today I joined a cult. The best of all cults. The most famous cult. Where no one is real and nothing is absolute. We all walk around this digital world like barbie dolls with inflated heads and smoothed out gentatilia. No one is alive here. Everyone pretends to be wrestling with some philosophical law. They are quantum particles caught between stars.
The social media places were oh so beautiful with oh so perfect losers.
They were limited in intellectual curiosity because of the idea they were constantly under surveillance. It was a philosophy

of misfortunes and an instrument for beggars with manners so profound they defied the suffering inside civilization. Their tongue falls out. It wiggles on the hot concrete like a displaced earthworm. It melts slowly between the slabs. It looks like a blood stain once the sun is finished eating it. YouTube was the fantastic law of pretending you needed to be constantly gratified and entertained otherwise you would have to escape into some type of self-reflection. If we hated anything - we hated self-reflection.

The people here rejoice in illness. They cartwheel between the inane. A boring idea of a constant need for validation through robot friends, karma principles, and a general dislike for anything that disagrees with stupidity. Everyone is polite but no one is happy. Speech is free but language is censored. Everyone is in love but no one is content. They understand they are addicted to a make-believe world. They stand on pedestals. They raise their hands and voice at anything that doesn't understand their existence. Even though they don't really understand what existence is or where it came from they still must exist as loud as possible. Just in case a god might be listening (a god of moderation and brain vandalisms).

Sexuality is promoted through adages and proverbs. Giant men beat the shit out of people with their cocks. Petite women stand ready to show the inside of their vaginas (inside a great caterpillar eye can be seen - lidless and sleepless, always watching, always waiting with a lustful paradox ... seen but never touched ... loved but never valid). Sometimes men crawl inside the vaginas. They are never seen again.

He stood, silent, it was unreal to him - silence bit the lips like how syphilis bites the genitals - this was a dream and the dream was insane.

(iv)

I met her on the back of a caterpillar. She had wavy hair

and hands between her legs. I wanted to pretend she was something beautiful, made from treehouses and bad honesty. She was weeping but I was already singing … She wore a mask to escape the wildish greetings, There were forest-trees growing in animation above her eyes (some say there was a hungry vagrant eating a silence inside),

Elements jumped and melodies played, In the sky so above mornings, Her dog would jump up and greet her, Tongue out, for drops of passion

In her heart she was an astronomer of the apocalypse,
But in her hands, she was still holding on to the lantern of the moon, she would whisper into the walls, before the settling of laughter

When the thunder whistles, she startles and cries
And when a creature gestures, she welcomes the songs of sleep that come to heal

Everlast! Is the murmur when the dreams turn her into liquid madness

(v)

Darkship medic melee, drunkships in the orchids, mediocrity injected instead of happiness, we made a living being famous and dead.

(vi)

Watch the people prick their dicks! A funny roman when the children need to be fixed. And when it finally comes time to see what is divine and fantasy will they jump to conclusions and dream of men inside insanity? I know you. Do you know me?

I'm the lover of heavens and peculiar savoirs … I am vandalism poetry

I'm alive. I'm alive. And isn't it beautiful to be alive? What are you? Who are you that judges and kills? Why do you kill? Is it easier to kill than love? And when you kill people do you weep? Do those tears fall on lips unnoticed and language undiscovered?

(vii)

To the little beetle that dances in my belly button - (also known as royal psychosis). Confusion under the tongue, her face a series of abstract features as ominous ladybugs hide behind her eyelids - I say here we are silent ghosts, come now, my pale digital friend - it's time to wake up and realize you are alive ...
Inside these words (Miss Beetle-legs) I have strategically placed little pockets of warmth, sprinkles of love flavors, tiny ballerina caterpillars ... Once you open this, once you read these words, once these words pour into your brain like a warm wine, these creatures of warmth will fight off those invisible monsters that look to bring you to dark dreams. It will be like the Sleeping Beauty story except it will be a caterpillar that licks your ear to wake you up. A savage lustful werewolf that kidnaps a fair mistress and swings her to his lair of bad decisions. Where we will most likely dry-hump broken furniture and dance to magical parties full of dysfunction.
I will send a gang of adventurers your way. I tied some balloons to a tiny basket. Inside is the young and dashing lizard by the name of Sir Villain Kastler. With him is a caterpillar named Osmosis. An elephant the size of a flea that wears a top hat and spins a cane that is known by many as Mister Peppers. I sent them off this morning towards your general direction. When they find you, Mister Peppers will tap you with his magic cane, you will turn into a ladybug with brown hair and dark-rimmed

glasses. They will then whisk you away in their balloon, many adventures, you will cross the mosquito rivers while fighting off evil parasites, you will save the seven queens of Horri Canyon, you will fight the wasp-mancers along the Mississippi coast. I'm afraid at the end of this story Mister Peppers will be lost to the cyclops king in the swamps of Alabama, Osmosis will turn into a butterfly and carry your basket as the balloons were popped by the lotus and their evil empire in the Forest of Hymns. Osmosis's wings will be ripped to shreds but will finally take you to safety. And at the end of this story (Miss Beetle-legs) no one really lives happily ever after, but they do live - they laugh, they dance, they celebrate themselves as they celebrate all things alive. The music will swell, the rains will come, and the storm will pass.

They should reach you within the next few thousand years.

LONELINESS IS A TEMPTATION FOR ETERNITY AND FURY

(1) I feel slightly irrelevant.
My mood is a colorful weird. My eyes are bubbles. My life seems to be a strange series of routines and cycles. I'm fairly sure we are living in some illusionary myth. I feel like there should be no responsibility to being alive. I'm alive ... That's it.
Why do we put so much effort into making it important?
Why does it have to be important?

(2) I want to collapse upon this nothingness. I want to bend eternity. It all feels so incomprehensible to me. I wonder if we are just chapters in a book.

How does this scene begin?
How does this affair of ghost end?

Probably in some beautiful pleasure. All the animals and birds turning into marble. The ocean turned into ice. We splash into some type of transformation. And this ghostly romance, secret and unashamed, will become a kingdom. The lover, the actor, the adventurer, the ordinary, the stranger, they and we will all become strings tied to a mathematical equation as robots hang - *out of order signs* - around our necks.

(3) In this scene we decode our bodies mechanics and burst into nonsense molecules and orgasms. There's a delicious

irony in our heartless heartbeats. Perhaps we can transcend the aesthetics in the objects they worship. Find the deviant little devils tickling us with landscapes created from the dreams of madman lovers. That's the drama of this literature.
Fingers crossed.
Mind warped.
Wink and wink.

(4) Let us drown inside this enchantment. Let's talk about building a spaceship and taking a vacation in some other universe. One with trees and rivers, untouched by human behavior, maybe we can climb a mountain, we can slide down the waterfalls, we can plant ourselves in the mud, maybe we'll grow for thousands of years - I'll turn into a serpent and go back to the forest. She would turn into the mistress and build an army of sirens and mermaids. Singing songs to allure those to her island.

(5) So she, yes she, she began as a light reflected off the moon. She turned into bubbles with red sprinkles for hair. She floated down. She burst into water and colors. When that water closed her eyes, she turned into a design, she grew earlobes, she grew arms and legs, she molded a face for herself. She danced by rivers with transparent fish. She sang unknown gibberish to the moonlight that created her, that bloomed her from light to child. The ladybugs came. They lifted her into the sky. They sprinkled her on the ghost of forest creatures. They looked up. They became aware. They too danced. They too understood that love was a strange loneliness. That love was in the secrets of caterpillars.

(6) My army became giants with iron limbs but cursed with the dreams of Sisyphus. The bitter war will begin. The serpent and the mistress. The mountains will crumble, the seas will whirl, the sky will darken. At the end of this war, many lie exhausted, many sing dark songs.
I lick the earlobe of the mistress.

The memories of warmth and flowers bloom again in her brain as they bloom in mine. The war ends, we rebuild, and then dance in a festival full of falling pink ash, a giant blue bubble captures us, we float back into space, back to the earth.

(7) In our dreams we are both falling, our fingertips barely touch, we open our eyes, the dream is over, we return to the endless solitude. We shall be reunited in this invention.

We wake. We climb the sleepless slope of metal. The cravings are all in red. We crouch on the heads of great statues. No one remembers their names. But we do. Gods from a different ghetto. Orpheus and Eurydice. Pyramus and Thisbe. Cupid and Psyche. We float down into the bottom dark. Our heels hit the rocks. We washed ourselves in those dark waters. We saw the faces of men and women. We slid underneath the canopy of stars.

'That one,' she pointed, 'that's where we'll go tonight.'

(8) We grabbed one another. We saw the tragedy in having a soul. We saw humanity spread open, we saw the moons roll over, but we were boundless as we raged on. We fell, she was mistress and I was serpent, we were devoured helplessly by the gravity.

On the altar, we set our ghost, the knives raised, we turned into the red sand, we fell like rivers, our mind was a portal, inside the junkie lovers awaited.

(9) The dream was aware because the dream was alive and we were just a part of its vast womb. This is the poetry of raspberry and blueberry. Dripping in flavor, looking for the happiness hidden in our humid breaths.

We are the vulgar children of perfect motions. We are the unhappy children of the flesh. But we invite life when we invite one another. We find that the passages of discovery are hidden in our fingers, our lips, our mouths, in the poetry we sing, in the moonlight we witness, in the dances of ritual and absurdity, in the hopeful and personal dreams of dangerous spells on the edge of everlasting theaters.

Oh! How this tragedy molds us!

Dance and dance and we melt into the hereafter ... pale and lost forever.

WHISPER

Disrobed and decayed
All for what?

A poet is crossed with mouthfuls of product, he has a fancy trinket humming of all life and
knowledge in his pocket ... many-colored emblems of abuse in madman agencies coming from his future, it could be an establishment under the unveiling of mystification ... maybe, maybe

Whisper to us now ...
Forsake youth, scour and pray.

What is short for today,
Will bring us home tomorrow.

- At this point our hero poet has become under the suffering of alcohol and the longings of passion that swirl bright between his legs ... he was so loud people thought he had a death metal orchestra on his tongue ... he has many metaphorical conjectures conjuring inside his liquid-babble-brain - at precisely the moment of a star's birth (somewhere in the materialized circuits of imagination), an inspired darkness of misunderstanding can be seen developing a coop of cedar-goddesses and velvet detectives in post-apocalyptic misery as they ironically fall in love to their own gratification - serenades of fantasia and beauty and youth were being fed to prone poets (standing with feral cats on their heads and caterpillars moving like sea water where their eyebrows should have been) with filthy belly buttons and the smell of gasoline on their lips - there the great and original slut fornicated with the strange man who practiced skeletal energies amassed by his tombstone teeth(each engraved with the names of all the women he had conquered - not sexually, but by convincing them to fall in love with him and therefore creating a cult of alternatives) - these two eloped and exploded into a nervous theory that enlarged the belly of moons to recreate sexual intercourse as all were hung on the discovery that love was a love(lier) whisper if tempted by the reproductive process - this made love political and so banned for being offensive and scratched from language all together and those that were found to be inhaling its corruption were deemed untouchables and killed immediately or exiled to flee across deserts with poor moisture and conservative dramas ... this in turn created a morbid movement that would exploit beauty and turn it into vacuum cleaners and plastic creepy-children deranged with a lack of imagination ... powdered in boredom and beer - the fatherless fathers posed in disappointment ... What is short for today, will bring us home tomorrow, only means: evolution is a vanity that might one day fix its mistake by overdosing on masturbation, celebration, antidepressant-induced dreams brought to you by insanity and coffee. At this moment everyone screams and the homeless melt into the bad decisions as can be seen from the mercury that replaced the holes in their teeth caused by cavities and street-walk weather smeared weird by lipstick addicts with snake tongues inside their vaginas, sipping metal cups, condoms, and a penance for waking up in dirty hotel rooms. A tangle in the head. A perfectly graceful peasant with a deformed goodness.

-Destroy youth. Apathy is your vulgar and crude friend. Panic! Panic! You homosexuals and fools!

WARP THE MORBID MOMENTS

(1) I'm a peculiar breed these days. I have a little caterpillar that lives in my mouth. He dances to the gut rotting with nostalgia and magic.

(2) I don't recognize that man in my reflection. I want someone to prove I even exist.
That man. What man? What a fleshy bucket of slime and seaweed.
A man, oh indeed.
What a vague superstition ...

(3) My eyes are tiny misty apparitions, I forget what it means to be alive. Is being alive hopeful of the pending hells of supernatural enemies?

(4) When you love, you forget what a face looks like, you become a statement, a vague idea of what a heart is or means. What is this love that leaks from my belly button like a strange ooze with eyeballs? Everything is a shape of horror escaping my mouth, an amusing scream dancing on my tongue, reason is disappearing within my dreams. When a man is subconscious. He is expected to be awake and suffer for beautiful reasons. He branches like lightning streaking across frozen lakes. He becomes routine, sin, impression, a pending disappointment.
He is nothing but carbon soup.
Sperm and blood.
Born in the gutters.

Asleep in conscience.

He is violet and monstrous with wings on his lips, oak arms, insect hands, an onion for a head, a third eye hiding in his cock. Existence is not my friend. It is the daunting habitat of linear fashions. If my shadow had teeth and lips, would it eat or kiss me?

(5) I see everything is crackling, blooming, decaying, half-rotten, outliving itself. Everything is here to obey the fixed laws of a meaningless condition. To retain sanity by giving in to institutions. But the vastness, the emptiness is coming. It will come like a half-bred bastard animal. There will be no tomorrow. Melancholy has infiltrated the minds of the depressed.
We must be important.
We need to be important or existence loses its value.
We are the lonely and profound gods of a superfluous mania.

(6) I am the curve of that pillar, the mildew of obscenity, the absurdity in the songs of madmen theaters. I am not an individual, none of us are, because we are men. This is reverse solipsism. We are figments of our own imagination. A pseudo-normalization. Misfitted weirdos with poetic hearts and caterpillar confusions. Our eyebrows arch in passive-aggressive manners.
Once you define yourself as a group, you are never free.
Our love is a superfluous violence.
And I can't help but wonder if society didn't create some kind of monster with its lack of imagination.

PERFUME, LADYBUG

Her head falls off her shoulders, It turns into my hair

She puts a kiss inside my eye, I put one near her neck

A taste from her tongue can never be separate from my lips

Her body sheds a perfume, My hands create a garden

Between her legs is the sun, Between mine is the earth

Our land and blood bonds, We create a comet

It is made of perfection, It is made of harmony, It is savage and full of riddles

These men inside our liver, they brood

These women under our tongue, they weep

THE OCEAN IS WHERE CATERPILLARS GO TO DIE

She laid me on the floor, warm bricks filled the fireplace
Her arms were a worn evening, bent violet fingers
She spoke of the vengeful cupid,
Her lips moved as if she wished to engrave every syllable with
ecstasy.

She placed her hand in mine,
whispered of this dream she had
This is what she sings:

We'll dance on the solitary mountains, where spirits exercise
the forest hunting men,
Limbs of iron, worshiping spice and silver,
How the snow will fall on our darkly heads, how it rest gently
in the crevices of great oaks,
Tall upon giants and half-dreamers, every branch a cunning
dimension split into hundreds of directions.

The drunkship traveler and the maiden of fragrance,
Manic in the wind, wild in the meadow of orchids,
We shall be torch and headland,
A whisper in my throat,

I shall celebrate you with my body,
And you will celebrate me with beauty - indestructible and
despairing.

RIVERS TELL
SAD STORIES

When he first started the job, he was a giraffe. It took some time to get used to his legs. He would go to the bathroom, he would look at himself, he licked his reflection, his tongue would stick to the mirror, he would pull away, watch the slime of his saliva slide down into the sink. He took out his pen, he wrote on the bathroom stalls: 'If you say no to drugs - you will probably die.' He laughed at the cynicism in that.

He went back behind the counter. He was a crow when he got behind the counter. He pecked at the food, he pecked at his phone. Sometimes he was a gorilla as he took out his phone, dry-humping it, relieving himself with his text messages. The people came in, one ghost after the other, sometimes they wanted to be relieved of their sins, sometimes they asked to haunt the bathroom stalls, others just wanted a glass of water. The paychecks came in, one after the other, the same message, don't ever fall asleep, don't ever think too hard about the mediocrity. He turned into a beetle, he ate the paper, he crawled into a hole in the ceiling, he knew the secrets of insects. He understood the dreams of cardboard. The lights were always focused on him. Those bright, fluorescent lights shined an extinction inside him. Sometimes he was a q-tip, sometimes he was an ant, sometimes he was a fugitive with a caterpillar face, a perverse politeness escaped inside him. Sometimes he was water that gurgled down the throats of those that asked for it. Sometimes he was a cigarette, being inhaled into someone's lungs, he was inside their bloodstream, he flowed into their heart, it thumped with the rhythm of his arms and legs. He did a cartwheel down the aisle where they sold dried fruits and snacks for the alcoholics. He opened up the freezers, he let the cold air rush into him.

Sometimes he was a head of lettuce, sometimes a tomato, sometimes he was an avocado. Sometimes he was a forced comma, a denotation, pun, juxtaposition, an echo in some prophetic inscription, an incomplete sentence in someone's novel. He crawled on the ground like a caterpillar. He was the metamorphosis. He was the butterfly. He was piano keys that danced with molten hands that pressed into him making him musical, making him beautiful, making him irrelevant. Sometimes he sat bored, pushing the buttons, taking the money, giving one cigarette pack after the other, collecting one dime after the other, smiling not because he wanted to but because he had to.

Sometimes he was tired, but he never slept, there were worse things here than sleep. He knew that. He feared boredom more than he feared anything else, even dying. Sometimes he was the drama of extinction, sometimes he was depression hiding in the subtleties of newspapers, sometimes he looked out the window ... wondering of adventures that he might gain, looking out at the stars in some attempt to find something inside himself, wondering if he was the only one while everyone else was dying in traffic.

The door would chime, his dreams would die, the customer would come in, he would say hello, but he would never remember.

GHOST ARE HARMONIES INSIDE ULTRALAND

Her eyes were ghouls with an unkempt weariness
A quiet suicide within her
They had fish and ocean in their bodies

Her hands a softness, his head a violence …

They looked on to the great and unnatural Ultraland:
They were no longer citizens, they were products to be manipulated, sold as an ideal, an endless trick to create emotional stimulation out of negative programming. There was a cryptic clue in the minds telling them nothing was real and the kingdom was in everything they loved and bought. There was something wrong but they were too repressed to understand it or touch it. The annihilation of intelligence put them in an unconscious trance where they were spoon-fed dopamine based propaganda to create a real experience. The experience was corrupted through adverts playing music. Nothing was real because they were all living a fantasy. The food served was nutrients processed, squeezed together with sugar and syrups and spiders. In the end they all feared the same death - dying of boredom.

Civilization inside Ultraland brought an undisturbed calmness to the world but that tranquility was poisoned, it was a dangerous calm, like that of a dream in an irrational reality. No future was near. The futile future was full of fear. Consciousness was chaos. Peace was poison. Make humanity ignorant again! Suicide is freedom. Your dreams are owned by advertisers. Corporations are paradise. Poor are parasites. The money mutants have taken control of life. Lifestyle is prison. Inject magic into your eyes and drink the vomit. Disintegration into revolution, the skin is epidemic against the slime of man and woman. And now the billboards showed men being hung and mannequins coming to life, eating the flesh of their pets. The system would glitch at times, exposing the reality, which altered their outlook on this substitute reality. When the illusion was broken that they were living in a closed off world, it created the presence that this was a trick and so they became disenchanted and broke the reality constantly with drugs.

Ultraland was supposed to be our hearts and souls on display for mass consumption, but instead it displayed our fears and the lies we swept underneath our hearts where it became brittle and started to despair. Suddenly Ultraland was no longer in control of itself. The hypocrites, cultists, madmen, murderers and rapists used it to destroy any hope left while strangling the will to be free. It was now a display of hatred and those that had asphyxiation burning in their heads. Heartless chests caved in by cavities of exaggerated humanity built on castles made of fire.

Everything was a fantasy - a very well ordered fiction meant to distract and romanticize the human condition. They had installed laugh tracks in the buildings. Street lamps (that would shine a great spotlight on someone) and the laugh tracks were set off anytime something violent happened ... but the laughter was slimy - like the bleeding of a wound, the sound a pimple might make when bursting - the laughter entered into the brain like a screech - they knew it was laughter but it was a foriegn, unknown type of sound like something not human trying to mimic the sound of laughter - it made those that heard it uneasy, unsure of what they were hearing - they only knew it was designed to humor something other than human - maybe parody the life and humdrum existence of those in the city.

A woman crying - laughter.

A man complating suicide - laughter.

A man being robbed - laughter.

It was everywhere and it sounded like rain. No one understood it - no one wanted to.

The plastic bags they had littered into the ocean for thousands of years evolved into living creatures - sentient beings that were hated for being the ghost of past earth criminals. Livestock was held underground overdosing on hormones and penicillin injections while virtual reality machines made them feel like they were in an endless pasture and in a dream world of sunsets and trees.

Everything was bred and hybridized to the point that nothing before humans existed anymore without being turned into a mutation to further man's role on the planet - eventually nothing would be recognizable and even man would soon forget its history and die alone. There were places on the bodies unexplored, unmapped, untouched - they crossed the rivers and forest and came to the conclusion that there were worlds unknown and lost inside the belly buttons. But those worlds were only seen by poets and philosophers. That art died when lovers were deemed unnecessary, crude, outlaws of passion. Human beings transitioned into sculptures and wires and digital palaces where all had become sentiment prose in awkward stupidity. Unhealthy thoughts were condoned to boredom. None lived in obscurity because all were famous.

They couldn't see the stars - so they lost their imaginations - their awe for adventure and love was gone once the great lights destroyed all the stars. In Ultraland, they transfixed the crowds with giant televisions before they murdered them.

A GHOSTLY WHISPER OF AIMLESS CONTENTMENT

I am ethereal and mediocre this morning. Tingles of static in my brain. Maybe a little sprinkle of weird to chase away the static spiders that spent all night weaving webs in the brain? I think there's still some magic left. Maybe not for the magicians but there is always something magical to find inside the tricks of life. I think it likes to hide. Crafty little bastards. We chase them like ghosts between wall panelings, the creases of wrinkled shirts, inside the giant water fountains that are surrounded by a thousand dreams shaped like pennies. I want to know what people are dreaming about. What little secrets are they hiding in those dreams? Do they drown in the human condition? Does this uneasy fantasy disappear in the profound luxuries of contentment? I am surrounded by drunkards, psychopaths, time traveling hillbillies, neurotics, some of these people become sugary, some fools, some turn into potholes, some never experience the beauty of life because they are too worried about the evils it contains. I hug these mutants, these men and women with caterpillar faces, insect arms, giant heads with thousands of spider eyes. I whisper fake French gibberish in their ears, I comb their dirty heads, I sing terrible poetry to them as they sleep in these gutters. There's an inspiration somewhere here. In all these lovers we search for. We compromise our reality in the moments we find here. An empire of words. What awaits at the end of this road? Is her body a good servant? A temple of muses stacked endlessly? Am I a good servant?

Some of us suffer unusually well, so it seems.

I want to rebel against everything anyone tells me is the truth. I immediately go to work to find the hypocrisy in their statements, inside their authoritative messages. I get these spells sometimes. I call it: *the weirdness.* It's as if everything around me becomes a parody eating itself. I can catch the subtlety in everything people do. I see their gods as giant spiders with human heads, I can see them parading every illusion in the pockets of their children. That's where they like to keep their illusions. People walk around and their heads turn into insects, they have deja vu on their tongue, their hair is pieces of confetti glued together. Everything for me becomes phony, it doesn't seem real. I usually hide during these moments. Sometimes life becomes too much, too brutal, it's as if I'm not here, I can touch and see and feel and I have all the same desires and fears as they do but I feel like a phantom walking in some hell, stuck in some solitude where no matter how much I scream or wave my arms around no one can see me. I think emptiness is the same feeling as depression. Like someone scooped me out. There's no heartbeat, no pain, no breath, no thoughts - I am just this orb of slime bubbling on a bed - it's in these moments when I wonder if I should escape. I mean, the window is right *fucking* there.

It feels as if I'm possessed by some rogue spirit, pushing me away, away from contentment. Everything and everyone feels oppressive. I'm filled with regret, melancholy, ridiculous loneliness, disgust, like a toneless rage that fills me with neither pleasure or pain. I am not happy. I am not sad. I am not content. I am just tolerable. I am fearless, objective, half stupid with a dull euphoria. I think understanding is only an estimate of your own worth. But there's no peace in it. I see my future and all I can see is dust and bones. It makes me feel useless. Like I'm just a ghost pretending he is alive in the daydreams of someone else. A madman ghost haunting the leaves of thousand year old trees.

(Death was always there for him, present, alive, more alive than existing. Once you realized death, it became alive inside of you, it never went away, it had arms and legs and eyes and hair. It was beautiful and lovely like fragmented muses on the page of a genius, its eyes were a soft star losing its light - when he noticed death, he felt it in his chest, the crushing blow, the tight grip around his heart, it wanted to explode. He wasn't afraid of nothing, he was afraid of being nothing, he wanted to exist, he wanted to be alive but not alive, he just wanted to exist without ever having to experience death or ever being nothing. But when you assume death is evil, you assume life is evil as well.)

We talk but we don't talk about anything important. We mimic the illusion that this is somehow a cure for our loneliness. There's safety there for us at that moment. We can keep our solitude and still pretend to talk like lovers might on a date. We can be whatever we want. We can delude ourselves that this isn't a fantasy, it's a journey, two ghosts pretending to be human. It's a balance. Every lover plays these roles. There's a joy in submitting to these desires, to playing these roles. It's the dark velvet between the finger and thumb. The hectic struggle of lovers that are both charming and dangerous. And lovers are dangerous. The most dangerous of all animals. The humor between them is soundless. It whispers. A thousand words said in a look inside their eyes. Love is curiosity. It is idle. It is playful. It balances us. While you are the eternal, I am the erected. There's a beautiful confidence in all that romance. It is a dark but friendly complexion. We might see the sorrows and pity of people but we see it because we want the world to be a better place. We wish it was a better world. We mock it because we want a better future. But we know that if the world was beautiful, we wouldn't be like this. We're like this because we want to see something change. We're like caged animals in a zoo. We know it's all hopeless. Yet, we fight. We fight because it's more beautiful to fight than be adrift in aimless transitions.

Every moment is an impulse. We are remarkably passionate and we are ridiculously dead. My head feels like a melon today. I'm sinking into the roots of my future. My fingers are caterpillars, little fantasies trickling through, in everything there is a gesture. A woman dancing like a tree in the distance, a child behind me with a knife, I am the god of terrible dreams. And I may call a kiss, a moderately sensual pain, for those that lack the lips.

I feel strange today. Consumed, bottomless, wrestling with restlessness, notes of music, intolerable embarrassment, I want to dethrone the many contradictions that I am. I feel like being a poet is to witness the annihilation of the spirit. No one is as lonely as the poet - we see the melodrama in everything, yet we can't touch it, it doesn't belong to us.

A fanatic of words, a creature of the novel, there is nothing worse than happiness for us, we poor children. There is so much horror in this world. The insanity and madness. Everything is so goddamn barbaric and brutal. The concrete and metal buildings, the metal and rubber cars, the promotion of a false happiness in something you buy, slavery disguised as opportunity, indoctrination instead of education, everything violent and surreal, churches telling you that the paradise is afterwards and not within you, they are all just sleeping through it. Pills to sleep, pills to stay awake, pills to have sex, pills to eat, pills to lose weight, pills to change the electricity in your brain. The only rebellion left is in making a fashion statement. Sex turned into a masquerade of violence and dominance. Being real is not enough. No one is authentic, we are flakes of matter drifting in the dreams of centipedes.

Inside my blood there is the lizard eating at my heart, the creatures of the ocean and invisible critters that float in our egg-shaped souls. We seek that blood inside of us. To let go of the staleness of civilization. To go back to the mud and swamps. To live free among the grass and trees. To be nothing but what instinct commands us to be. It's a very strange idea of mine. It's the great crisis of our modern world. We are not animals anymore. We have evolved into a pressing suicide of instinct. We are no longer human. We are ideas. We are names. We are objects pretending to be alive. And, at the end, we'll melt into concrete and become streetlights for a hundred years. We'll be memories inside a digital future. None of us will remember what we were or how we got here - we'll only remember that it has brought us nothing but loneliness. And when we cry, our tears will turn into DVD's and someone will take all those tears and play them in a great stadium. Showing the new and evolved mutants what it used to look like to be human.

'Why are they so gross, mom?' A young mutant robot will ask.

'They're not gross, honey. They're confused. They still believed in love in those days.' She will explain. One of her eyes will spark with electricity and worms will crawl from her mouth and ears.

And here I take their hands. I play the songs. I take the hand of the policeman and the criminal, the tyrant and the slave, the good man and the bad man, the decent woman and the indecent woman, the loved and the lonely.

We dance and spin and twirl and we laugh. The worker and the doctor, the electrician and the construction worker, warlord and lawyer, teacher and student, politician and scholar, homeless and drug addict, the rich man and the poor man, the bored man and the carnival man. We are pebble and fish guts, ocean wave and slang, lizard and space traveler, crust and creation. We dance together.

We are adventurers in nightclubs, the melancholy in folded napkins, a twirling and swirling brain reaching out to spread its graffiti across the universe. I imagine walking underneath that glow of moonlight, a child of stars and myths, fingernails bright in nonsense, do I smile in the light? Do I dance? And sometimes I want to grab the people around me and shout at them. I want to shake them and scream: Stop! Stop with your madness! You're alive and human. Isn't it beautiful and terrible to be alive? Isn't it beautiful and terrible to be human? But no one listens. Why would they?

I'm sure there's a sadness in all of it. There's so much of everything inside us. Rocks, stars, dust, planets, jellyfish, sea foam. Maybe we are the psychotic children of schizophrenic ideologies. So much seems lost. So much incompleteness. Maybe one day our dreams will be a perfect trick and our flesh an earthworm. We will glide through the darkness. Prayers within the rain. I'll lick them from the air. Blue like the current of moon rivers. Dancing under low-budget stars and they'll think I'm a specter camouflaged by its indestructible extinction. Haunting park benches and sidewalks with my eyelashes. Maybe one day if my head ever touched another, a thousand little spiders with cat heads will hatch out and spin webs around our heads, and inside those webs would be all the daydreams of every creature ever known and never known. When the moonlight strikes down at us, the webs will melt into our eyes, we will see the world again as children in wonder, laughing and doing cartwheels, covering our faces with our hands, swimming in the mud, dancing beside the trees who shake their leaves at us - *Be free*, the trees would laugh, *be merry and dance often. Love and die in this vast malfunction of vanity and survival. Live forever and die endlessly.*

KILL THE POET

I love you (which means I understand you, which means I accept you, which means I will self-mutilate myself for you) kingdom eye, heretic sex, religion is a genocide … inflicted by infinite harmony … cartwheeling abstracts in the melody of brain transformations …

boredom manipulates us (beat sounds, melancholy meditates on being a god that lives in the sixth dimension in our brains)

the language is a worm, a mutation, a poltergeist between us - melting under the tongue, spreading ghostly bacteria throughout our bodies - it is forming, haunting, a shade and shadow peering towards us - it is alive (ominous sounds emulate the light structure in her frown)

- the age has become digital … our brains, minds, thoughts, sex, bodies, dreams, images condensed as pornographic and so censored as to not apply any offensive material (being that of human nature) to those that see a threat to their superficiality (menacing music plays the blah-wah-do - blah-wah-do, blah-wah-do, I love you!)

Some people are a mockery of the human condition …

Some caress the civilization …bloated brains of goblin cocks and mutant saliva

Knife to the bodies, the strangled lover undressed, a drama for the divine ones sipping silver and jest … mutilate the poets! Let not their dreams go unnoticed - life needs more life …

Come, my darlings, my caterpillar cultists, it isn't human unless it is dressed in codes and regulations and tabloid agendas beset within genocidal genetics …

I love you (which means kill me and mutilate my bones, which means I want to possess you, which means animate properties are all I crave) I want to murder you with my prick and divide the harmony between the thighs as it unwinds in death and wine ... kill me, oh pretty oh pretty oh pretty ghouly

SEASONS MAGIC
ENIGMA

The leaves will be shaking this season
Flowing helplessly, downward patterns of starlight ice
While the wind breaks
Those who still remember
Those carefree and elusive
Primeval and irrational
Suicidal magicians lightly rocked in convulsions
Where dreams are flowers, circling in winter
Where men are modernized by obscenities

Doesn't she agree?

We will wait for the seasons to change
From the moon, the dead will float upside down
Love and family will become artless
Lovers will be unknown,
Madmen to laughter till tomorrow

Bring me a glass of water, my dear
I'm dying

MADNESS INSIDE SPACELAND

The bar is flying out tonight
Our throats are nauseous,
parched, thirsty against the lamps
On the menu: Madmen, tuna, magic

We surrender ourselves to the vampirism of living in this culture
We see the stranger as a drought, a drink, a mysterious amusement
We are jewels of Frankfurt and Spacelands
Those around us, they dance exhausted by the muse
A horror spree!

She's so tired
She's so forced landlady like
She so hung like a saber alone in the incomprehensible religion of festivals,
a great carnival of fantasy

We only came here for the love, we say as we speak in bubbles
I'm sorry, sir, this phantom shrieks like a rabid dog,
This universe is neon-junkie filled, he explains,
Your cock is twitching because of the fear, he says with a swarm of teeth.

The fear! We scream

Love is the syringe as it bolts into our cord
Will, the pervert, dances while sleeping.
No volume on this table. Our intestines are constipated with
booze and mad laughter, laughter for the world, laughter for
the vortex, laughter for the cry in the vacuum. We touch that
worm every time it pulls into the port. We pray to it. We smear
it with our blood because it is the sunset, the green oozing
world of straight motion.
I love you - we inject into this worm as the opportunist bows his
head.

She is knives and lovely fingernails across from me
She takes a sip from my fountain
I take out a bullwhip and smack the world in order
I'm walking through the doors marked with serpents and a
mistress

This mistress and I
We take the blood together
We fall into the centipedes
They are like little bone realities

We are crypto-sutra
I drink her soul
She drinks mine

GIFTS AND THE GHOST THAT CARRY THEM

You can sleep / Near the ocean / And never hear my heartbeat

How she feels / How she happens

You can lie here / With me / And never be disturbed

Our art is living under all the angles / Under all the colors

We may be terrible servants / For this material of muses / Stacked endlessly and high / What great tricks they play!

Oh / she whispers / Be wary of those that invent gifts uninvited

A BROKEN METAMORPHOSIS

Yesterday I walked for some time. Around the lake, sitting on benches, staring out at the uneven skyline. I'm sure there were ghosts following me. Sometimes when I step outside I feel as if I'm stepping out into the great theater. The theater of madness, of magical spirits, foul creatures, lovers carved by happiness, addicts carved by dangerous trinkets, some illuminated by education, some surrendering to culture, there's the smell of Christmas trees, madman mystics on the corner selling Jesus for a hand-job, there's an elusive brightness to the air that I wish I could capture. I want to steal it and put it in my pocket. There's a violence in the brightness I see around me. Eternity is a moment, for us, it lasts long enough to smile and say hello and then it's gone. There's a vacancy I see in some people. Mummified in designer clothing, their spirituality is in jewelry and fancy watches.

Here. In this moment you are alive. You are only alive in moments. Time is decaying. It is the rotting corpse of civilization. The present is dying, deteriorating into memories, slowly moving forward into a corpse. The earth will be here long after me. Someone will walk over my bones. I imagine the smell of death is the smell of god. One day these cathedrals will fall. Brick by brick they will melt back into the land. The billboards will turn silver and white with rot. The streets will crack as the weeds and trees consume all. The insects will no longer have any light at night to hide from the monsters that hunt them in the darkness. Humans will be put in capsules created by technology. They will live in infinite simulated worlds. They will grow fat with proteins and liquid drugs being pumped into their bodies. The machines will whisper that they love them, the people will whisper back that they love the machines.

The new human will find themselves looking at dreamless sunrises over unreal oceans. They will melt in time. Spider webs will surround them inside their machines. Human intimacy will be lost to televised seminars. They will be immortal but they will not be human. Soon nature and the oceans would take over. The capsules will fall to the bottom of the sea. A thousand years, a million years, the new evolved life will find them. They will open these metal tombs, the men and women will open their eyes, they will shriek like vampires in the sun, they will melt into dreams brought to you by Disney and Coca-Cola. And no one will ever understand any of it.

These are my strange thoughts when I walk. I also thought about love. The acceptance in that idea. What is this ghost that lives inside of us? Why does it linger in the belly? We are captured, we are guided by these haunting shadows that live within us. I think there must be a tiny pianist playing some magical instrument inside my ribs. I see the ghost of people walking as I do. They are always ready to file in line. They never complain. That must be the ghost of Mozart. Now a withered old man with arthritis bending into his hands. And that one there, that must be Shakespeare, an overweight balding man wondering what type of sugar snack defines him. They are everywhere. The ghost of musicians and writers. The young twirling their fingers on each other's chest in the park. They have the eyes of dead philosophers. The one jogging, with earbuds in her ear, she was once a poet that looked for the mystery in human love and belonging. She now runs and thinks about television shows and why her last date hasn't called her back. I think how beautiful they were once. Full of wonder and hope and the promise of love danced inside them like ballerinas. But time, time is decaying them. The spirit is lost. The ghosts that haunt them are faded memories from unremembered dreams. They are dead. We are dead. I am dead. We are just ghosts. This thought should depress me but it doesn't. It fills me with emotion, warmth, it makes me feel alive, I am strangely unaffected by any of it. That should scare me but it doesn't.

I think sometimes there's this flow we get into. We just flow. There is no direction to it, there is no distance between anything, it's just this flow. Like there's this strong wind inside of you. You float across the ground. You move your lips to speak but nothing escapes your mouth. It's like everything is scattered throughout your body and brain. But there's a purpose to the disorder. It flows into one another. You feel swept up. It motions for you to follow. We have so many tiny beasts inside our bodies commanding us in different directions. The command of hunger, thirst, sleep, love, sex, laughter, touch, movements against other movements. These beasts pull at us. Begging us to listen to them. These little storms that press inside our brains. We put the order in which we need to feed these beasts. What is more important? The hunger or thirst? Love or sex? Sleep or adventure? We are composed of millions and millions of tiny cells that each represent us in some way. They all form to one purpose: to rule the mechanics of body and brain. All synchronized like musical notes. They form together. You walk and it's an orchestra. You laugh and it's a symphony. You love and it's a song that sings with the musical notes of that body next to yours. Whenever you speak to someone, whenever you engage with them, that is billions of cells, billions of years of evolution, billions of years of language and time and laughter and love and sleep and hunger and thirst and dreams formed into one body that creates a flow. For that moment to have happened - billions of lives had to be lived, billions of lives had to die, billions of dreams had to be realized. That flow is a miracle inside of you. To speak, laugh, love, to even say hello to someone is a miracle of the universe. The belief in god sabotages that flow. It says we are not miracles but the dreams of gods. We are not mortal, we are only waiting to be judged. Can you imagine the suicide inside yourself? What it takes to go against the flow? To rebel against billions of years of life and the flow. To rearrange the cells and blood and chemistry in your brain to flow into a different direction. To create yourself again.

Sometimes I feel as if I have no legs or arms. I speak but gibberish falls out, it slides across the floor, it enters into the ear of the other person, it mixes with their gibberish, the gibberish becomes language, sometimes it becomes love, sometimes it becomes sex, sometimes it creates a spark in a part of the brain that motions for their body to vomit out a laugh. They have no reasoning, they just flow wherever the body commands. When two people meet, when they speak, the flow is there, that directionless and ancient flow. It has taken billions of years for this flow to form. It has taken the creation of millions of universes for these musical notes to exist between lovers. Every memory you have, every moment, every laugh, every tear, every book, everything you have ever done has led you here. It took billions of years for this moment to happen. The flow between lovers, the unity we search for inside the rhythms of our movements. The liquid inside of us that runs through us like rivers. We search for it, don't we? The music between two people. To find that flow. Can we fight against billions of years of the flow? Once it takes you, can you really deny it? What is one man in a world of billions of them? What is one woman in a world of billions of them? All of them flowing past one another like waves, like sand pebbles, no friction, no warmth, the coldness that sweeps them into the flow of their lives. With all that insanity, lovers have managed to slow down long enough to find the flow between one another. To stop for a minute and realize that something inside of them was becoming musical.   When that happens the distance corrodes. Their realization becomes real, it is known, it is no longer secret and brooding inside of them. We have conquered everything. There are no mysteries left. But there is the music between people. The flow that finds you. A billion years ago it started. It has now found itself here.

I enjoy the dark nature of myself. I've never run from it. I like to see the horrors and the beauty in everything. I see the ocean and I think about what a beautiful beast it is and at the same moment I think of all the creatures inside it that want to eat me, that would murder me without hesitation. I laugh often at how silly our lives seem. It is all so fleeting, isn't it? I blink my eyes and I'm a child. I blink them again and I'm in school. I blink them again and I'm under a tree. I blink them again and here I am. Time seems to move in bursts for me. I wrestle with my melancholy. I run from it with alcohol. I feel like I'm a house being haunted by thousands of ghosts. There's a man of logic in there. The poet sitting by the window moaning of love and romance. The darkly character wrecked by cynicism spray painting dick pictures on the walls. There's the reader, the introvert, the madman, the manic, the dancer, floors covered in hundreds of caterpillars all twitching in their broken metamorphosis. Sometimes I turn the lights on in this house. I want to invite someone in. But the doors are always locked. There's the fear of letting someone in. There's always that danger of what they might do to my house. Would they rearrange the furniture? Would they paint the walls a brighter color? Would they kick out the darkly man and the cynic? Which ghost would they keep? Which ghost would they kill? Most of the time I feel like my house is that dark one of the corner during Halloween with no porch light on. It is not very inviting to people. Loneliness does some cruel and unusual shit to people. So it is.

Our bodies are only servants of our consciousness. It is the manifestation of that being. The ghost is our minds. The body is the flesh it harbors, it possesses. Eventually, the ghost will demand this flesh suit to seek out some enchantment.

Maybe that's the war within us. The ghost and the flesh. Two servants of the same master. What is more powerful? Love or lust? Maybe they are interconnected in some way. Maybe they are not so different. Love is the abstract force that haunts the ghost that haunts our brains. Lust is the biological formula that demands we constantly obey laws set billions of years before us. Maybe love needs lust just as much as lust needs love. They are both the water from the same fountain of life that springs inside our bodies. The serpent and the mistress. Entangled forever, competing against each other like rivals, unknown that they are of the same body. Maybe there is no difference. Maybe the only difference is that we repress our sexual urges because of the communities we are born within. Maybe because it's too easy to build a foundation using only lust. Love takes patience, time, it starts slow, rises fast, it bends and blooms, wilts and dies, born again. Love is quintessence while lust is substance. One is property while the other is essence.

Love: the personification of ghosts.

Lust: the manifestation of property.

I am spiraling. We are spiraling. I think God is an atomic molecule. We are within a multiverse, a parallel universe in which we are immortal and forever repeating an endless cycle, simultaneously young and old and bright and star-fed and alive and dead like a record that spins and spins at hundreds of miles per second only to start over again and again and again. This life is like millions of records playing different versions of your life, like the black holes in the center of everything, spinning the spiraling universe towards the edge of cognitive phenomenons. I feel small and insignificant. My truth seems so very subjective and completely useless. I know nothing. Maybe that's the best way to act. To know that you will never know anything. But love and lust are within me. Those are values I can understand. There is truth in some illusions. Though mostly they are false pretensions manifested to give me some semblance of significance.

We are the syphilis. The dissonance between deviant abstractions. Bred into complacency like cattle. Manipulated by codes and customs. Genetically engineered to commit suicide. We are mathematical, cosmic, spaceless. Infected with reasoning and logic. Our ghosts are mad. A psychosis brews. Escape is irrelevant. We are tied to these infantile distresses and fears. The general will of humanity is stupidity and conformity that chains itself to a constant and pure ideology of fear.

Love though, love is the seeking of truth even when there probably is none. In this world, we are cybernetic junkies tied to lustful simulations. Poetic robots with laser brains. Talking orchids in a burning forest. I think sometimes that's my journey. To get out of this bondage, escape into dreams, to break free from the wasteland of property. I keep myself grounded in hopes to find something that connects with me. An adventure. It can't all be hopeless, I think, if love still exists within us.

I have been careless, unhurried in my days. Everything is a peculiar shade of bright to me. There is life all around me, it goes through me, under me, it catches my breath and rides it off into some surreal forest in some unknown dimension. There is life in the insects, the rocks under my feet, in the trees, the sky, the wind. I see a flat tire and I know that is also life. There is the will that moves me. The instinct ingrained into my skin and hands. They, those around me, all have it too. We are all creatures in the habit of infatuation. We want to ruin one another with our slime, our love, we want to electrocute those around us. We refuse to sit idle and watch lovers go unannounced. We refuse to not taste, dance, or reach out. We can not stare and do nothing. There is a madness and gloom that bends its will inside us. A disturbance far older than the spaces between the stars. We are complacent in its imagination. What can we do but follow, feed it, curl beside it. Oh love, we whisper quietly so no one can hear us, where have you hidden yourself today? Maybe its will is the same as hunger, thirst, sleep. Without it we wither, we wilt into unimaginative sentences. We melt into a puddle of ooze and sink into the gutters of human frailty. If you were to find it, it would stir the ancient creature inside your stomach. Before you knew it you would be a ballerina dancing on porcelain toes against mirrors. Love is a secret to those that can't possess it and a frantic applause to those that have found it.

Yet, I know all things decay. The rocks will break into sand, the trees will lose their leaves and their branches will scatter like dead lightning across frozen lakes, the sky will blister and turn red, the wind will fade and drop a heavy sigh on those who still have heads. The flat tires will melt back into the roots, the metal will rust, age will conquer us all. All is a fleeting memory brought by a brutal symphony that plays inside our heads, inside our hearts. Life has no remorse for itself. It does not weep over death. It is not concerned. But something immortal has been created out of all of this. Love does not age, it does not die, it lingers for millions of years over the corpses of those that once carried it. It floats helplessly like fog rolling from the mountains who complain of sea and erosion. A lost ghoul haunting our bodies like how our skeletons haunt our flesh. Love is the inevitable heritage of all living creatures. It is everywhere. In the swelling of waterlogged ceilings, the backwards glance of strangers, the feel of water under your fingertips, the breath against your neck, inside your eyelashes it hides. Maybe that's why lovers must always kiss with their lips. It is the same as hunger, thirst, they have a need to push their lips to it. To devour it, to taste it with their tongue, to not notice it would be cruel. Love is a great shapeshifter. It is infatuation, sex and lust, bodies cuddled like sleeping caterpillars, it burst inside fancy abstracts and dreams inside those twisted, parasitical harmonies that play in the distance that lay between two people. Long after we are gone, after the hunger is of no substance, when we extinguish thirst, love will still linger. The romance of life will carry your bones in the memories of those that loved you. That is why it is so dangerous. No one is ever satisfied in life without it, no one is ever satisfied in life when they have it. It is a never ending parched throat.

And here it is, in all things that surround me. Hovering over me like a ghost. Haunting the rocks, insects, trees, my words, heavy and unrestrained as it melts into the lakes. Before long, all of us will be at the brink, the abyss below us, we will fall without a word, a pause on our lips as we try and find those last beautiful words.

My days pass by unremorseful, a value of corruption lies inside me - in my hands, my eyes, in the nicotine stains between my fingers. And I think there must be some adventure for me. That everything can be beautiful if I want it to be. That all I have to do is walk through the door. How long must the lost pay for the sins of the universe? How long is eternity? Can it be measured? Can a man be measured by what he loves? Can a woman be measured by who she decides is worth loving? How can we measure life if we don't even understand ourselves? Between us, is there a river that flows in our veins? Is there companionship to be claimed? When you close your eyes, when your feet hit the floor, is there an explosion of animated landscapes roaming through your mind? We are grounded in the details of one another. We compare and find patterns, we map out the transformations that follow laws that are so abstract - they can never really be known. But there's a power in that music. Our inert heritage is to follow those impulses. Paradise reigns inside this harmony. And the tragedy is that we will never be able to interpret it. But maybe we weren't supposed to. Maybe we weren't meant for anything but to live and love. Everything else we do we run the chance of drowning completely. I had this strange dream about a tree surrounded by oil. The branches were like fingers, knotted and blistered, crooked and stretching out, there were birds on the tree, feathers missing, silent and staring. There were these people walking around. But they didn't have any flesh or blood or bones. They were brains with nerve endings. They looked like floating jellyfish with thin tentacles. They would touch things, they would touch each other, a burst of lightning could be seen in their brains. The lightning looked like strands of hair. It seems we are all bound to this human tragedy. I want this to mean something. Oh, do I want it to be fantastic! I want to pretend this is all something so very beautiful but I'm sure it means nothing. (grumble, grumble)

VOLUME IN THE END

(1) Humans must have an intense desire for suffering - a desire for the volume in the end -
it is the only explanation for why they continue to elect psychopaths,
allow wars and genocides to continue.

The only alternative is that they are cowards
There is nothing to their eternity
Their dreams are as dark as the spaces between stars.
They, unlike any natural creature, understand murder and cruelty
Yet, they hold no conscience or frailty ...

They have the madness of ideology in the brains, don't talk to them, they are likely to be contagious! (Verbal debauchery is the enemy of evil productivity ... the philosophy of boredom is an act of aggression from an industrialization shamed with modesty) ...

(2) He was a negative mass ... (He had advertisements in his eyes. Ads in his mouth, his face turned into an ad and his voice changed as his sex was brought to you by your friends at Coolie-Cola. The industry brought the product of enlightenment with sugar fried crystals naturally delighted in heavenly fiddles ... enjoy enjoy)

(3) The movies spread out in symmetric shapes, there was no chaos in their birth so none in their thoughts, their creation was a dream inside the infinite ... The films were entertaining

but no one understood their inaccuracies. Jesus was Asian once and black again and then he was blonde and then a woman and no one cared. History was historically inaccurate and inappropriate anyway. We are here to entertain not to provide truth. Indoctrination was a sweet insanity. No one cared anyway as long as in the end the gods made jokes and smashed each other's faces with magical items ... (Being easily amused was more important than being easily intolerable)

(4) Evolution (inside Ultraland) started in the city, civilization started with cruelty, the first of all men, of all species, history lost to technology creating schizophrenia or psychosis - a disorder reserved for the serviced inclined. It was rebellion against the corporate minded - mini corporations became people marketing identity as label as brand as truth as beauty as freedom ... a diseased poet swam from the disillusionment of escape (there was no escape from Ultraland) - chaos was contained in metaphors - the poet soup of metaphysics and beauty and love became bitter with taste for rebellion and nihilism and the anti individualist, citizen, worker, the anti poet from matter unlike his own ... for his substance became a slime, a worm weaving through mechanics sorted out by the gods of forgotten philosophies ... So now the poet, stricken with poverty, must abide by the chaos of identity to nullify his brand to become drama faces in caterpillar lands ...

(5) An invented (inverted to fit all mouths) language started from the insect machines ...
The sounds of pleasure were also the sounds of mayhem and murder and grotesque men who ruled with a soundless etiquette. If it wasn't uplifting or overly optimistic ... It was always censored. It was the normalized man that they should have feared - their definition of life and their idea of civilization created a chaotic conformity, an absurd violence, to murder within love, they forced confused existential symbols and then expected none to become insane. Not only

is it expected that some would have a psychotic breakdown within their forced conformity but it is entirely reasonable that some would commit suicide rather come to terms with their cruel and simple mediocrity. It is not the broken, mentally ill, they should fear but the one who proclaims they are rational and confessed to conformity within normalized behavior that forces patterns to develop and one day they will not only murder but they will justify it with great applause from their congregations/constituents.

(6) Civilization became a mass hypnosis, a creature deformed and mutilated by irrational conformity to ideas that were so insane even their citizens had become mad - they are mad to protect it, to guide it, to believe in it, they will do whatever they can to make sure it is loved and carried on to the next generation - they will rape their children with nuclear idealism, love tongues that guide them to become violent and cruel mannered animals - they will murder to keep their ideologies intact and have no conscience over its relevance, there was no honesty or moral in their words ... they were full of mischievous faiths to horrible sins.

They had mutant minds, myths full of winter deaths, they crucified their children to idiocracy - Ultraland was full of dullards with bright minds made from the suffering of environments and cannibalistic rage against those that dared question their existential nightmare ... there was nothing to do but hope to god the placid goblins didn't come for their flesh televisions made from tumors.

So all of fate now comes in lower case letters, a concealed agony, cheapened by a sinister fatality. Slowly - slowly, this is the volume in the end.

COMPLEXITIES IN CONCRETE CRACKS

Demons are healthy. They show a self-reflective side. It's a healthy examination of yourself. There's not enough modesty and self-reflection going on these days. Everyone just wants to beat everyone else with their erected ideas. Everyone is right and everyone is wrong. Everything is true and everything is false. I can feel heavily misanthropic. I think about everything people do or believe to be silly and stupid. I refer to myself as agnostic but only because I don't want any answers and don't want to commit to religious or crowd thinking like atheism or theism. But it's more of a fear. I'm afraid of ideals or having them. I'm embarrassed sometimes if I show any emotion. I've always been horrible at intimacy because I've never been good at exposing myself. It's not that I'm afraid of intimacy, I'm embarrassed by my feelings. Those are demons that I'm trying to release but that brooding, introverted beetle inside of me doesn't want to leave. I'm also afraid to be content. I'm afraid if I become content, I'll melt away into someone's porch light and dissolve into a thousand little lights that sizzle out as they reach the sky. Those are some of my haunting moments.

Anytime someone starts to mention culture or how proud they are for being this or that - I immediately think these people are vampires and look to escape into the nearest exit. I can only imagine that they are so narrow-minded that they can't see a better world where everyone is happy. They need misery and hunger because it makes them feel like they won in some way. They would rather burn everything, including themselves with gasoline, than watch anyone live in fulfillment. I don't care about free speech because I have no identity. I am lost and unsculptured. I have no culture because I murdered that bastard. I have no answers. Answers are for people with agendas. Voting is for people with agendas. Nationality is a superstition, superfluous and hysterical, a confession of destructive rituals. Culture is a cult. Social media is a religion.

The caterpillar brain sharpens to misfortune...

Today, my brain is a weird hive of bees all synchronized to disrupt the world around me. Strange dreams. A room filled with hundreds and hundreds of broken televisions. They were piled everywhere as snow fell on top of them. When I woke up I had this idea about the future. Where people would download your entire internet history and then inject it into mannequin like robots. These robots would then assume that person's personality, their hopes, their dreams, they speak like these people and have the same mannerisms. Women would see clones of themselves shopping with grotesque looking men - men they would never date - yet, these clones would act as if they were in love. I thought how our dreams might be visions of ourselves in different timelines.

Our world seems to encompass this false passion for consumerism. I think it's disgusting how people shop, how they throw themselves into debt, giving gifts to prove their friendships or love because they're too lazy to actually show it in a way that would be more fulfilling. All those dead and rotting trees sitting on the curb. It's like people go into this mild, bizarre, panic and frantic temperament filled with manic delusions that buying is going to make them feel less empty and more fulfilled. It sort of depresses me. I just want to tear their stupid billboards down, smash all that counterfeit illusions of joy and happiness. They all just walk around as if they have a noose around their necks, waiting for the next store to pull them up like dolls and hang them on the ceiling fans. To me, it all looks phony and deranged and there's something cruel about it. I start growling at those mutants when they show up with their spider faces. When they start talking to me I close my eyes and secretly hope they fall over dead.

It's like I've put myself in a tomb and no one can touch me. I wail about romance and love yet I push people away. Those are my pieces. Those are the ghosts that haunt me. It's a loneliness but a self inflicted one. The older I get, the more I realize I would rather live in my dreams than be around people. My body feels broken some days. My mind feels broken. I look at people as wild nihilist dry-humping park benches, coming off an assembly line one after the other, the same green slime pours from their mouths and eyes as they wail about how they voted. Maybe I can change. Maybe it's not too late for me. I don't feel bitter. I just feel like this is all some weird cosmic joke and we are the punchline. I imagine some people were built to give in to their most basic carnal instincts. That flap of meat trapped between their brain stem and cortex shocking their body with compulsive pleasures while burning through any cognitive narrative as they are infused with decomposing expressions. They slowly mutate into horny goblins looking to jump on anything that twitches when they drool at them. Like corpses with constant erections. Spreading joy and cheer and necrophilia with a side dish of syphilis. I imagine in the future they'll just inject orgasms right into their goddamn foreheads.

Come all, try our new cherry flavored orgasms.

Giant faces just floating down the streets licking people with herpes. The hobgoblins with their mighty cocks and elastic vaginas beating the shit out of each other with their genitalia. And isn't this just lovely imagery?

I am aware that humans have started to achieve this artificial division about them. This staleness. Like active androids high on the concrete web of reality, but with no real function to maintain healthy perspectives. This disassociation from the trauma of being human and being alive is turning people into emotionless clones. They pay no attention to life because to see it, to touch it, to even look at it, would give it a function, a purpose, it would exist, they then would have to intervene and destroy the illusion they have created for themselves. They create a world different from themselves to cease being alive in their own world. So this rawness, this emotion, this trauma of being alive - it becomes unreal, too much, they think of it as a trick. Not all people are like this. I don't see anything wrong with being insane in this culture. This culture promotes a mental illness in almost everybody. Most are just better at hiding it with drugs, booze, sex, or whatever other distraction they have.

I want to smash everything. All the cathedrals, the statues of mutant men, all their fences, I feel like the magic of imagination has been lost. So much mischief in people, so much fear, so much despair. I can be true-human - running from those Neo-hipsters who are all metal, who are all wire - crossed to the trees and the life inside those roots, the nebulous whelps catching me - swimming through those waters of imagination - building a garden, growing interstellar space and timeless dimensions. I'll bury my scars there, let the vampire grasshoppers consume them and take them far off.

It's nonsense but it's good nonsense. The most wonderful type of nonsense. Pretentious nonsense is my favorite type of nonsense!

I know all of this is a poetic fantasy, that may be true, but mystery, fantasy, magic, the search for the secret formula between man and woman, human and earth, awaking and still being inside the dreamworld - these are all human scripts. That longing, that adventure, that quest, to find the ultimate romance, to break the cycle of monotonous routine, to find the pattern of life, to draw up from that water, to feel the pulse of someone alive - that is the great pursuit of life, of being human, of being childlike, of being free to roam along the mysterious lands, to transform the abstract into something powerful. If we cannot be alive, if we can't dream, we will fade, no memory, we will dissipate like melting clouds, we will no longer be human. We would only resemble something that was once alive.

We would be haunting caricatures.

We like to create emotional apathy by turning ourselves into cliches, stereotypes, labels, definitions full of judgments. A symbolic manipulation.

Control and temperament is a device. Abandon all rationality, be fluid in passion and impulse, life is a fantasy, a controlled fantasy but our dreams are the ultimate rage against their ordered world. Be musical and dance. Discovery is strength. Be as irrelevant as you can and run from identity.

DARKSHIP MEDIC MELEE

The day reigns itself inside me.
I am the Sun and the Earth and I am the tree branches. I am the clouds and small drops of rain that fall and slide slowly on a windowpane.

I am the heartbeat of lovers, the electricity in people, I am the cracks in the concrete, the slow decay of a flower.
I am the music of birds, the songs of whales, I am the ocean, the riptide, I am the crucifixion, the traveler upon drunkships.
My hands are the land, my arms iron, my tongue the soil, my eyes bashful.

And as I inhale in the day, the night pours from my mouth.
Look! I say. There it is!

A mountain with a blanket of snow. Earth gremlins crawling beneath our feet. A boat out into the sea. Spirits moving under the fall of light. So much about our lives is strange and immeasurable.
Everything we want is here.
Goblins, demons, dragons with portals for eyes, paradise in the silences, kingdoms high in the heavens, pits of boiling fire, eternity and the restless moons.
What we know of life, of ourselves, seems to be only enough to survive. Everything beyond that is a terrible mystery. It's that mystery that grabs at us, that binds us to the restless imagery inside ourselves, that craving for the mystical,

to be refashioned and reshaped by romance, intimate in development.
Outside of that - nothing is human, it is not fully formed. They are cannibals, sorcerers, possessed by reason.

We are the shamans, the muses, the poets.
We are eyebrows, lips, fingernails, predisposed to be dreamers and myths and legendary lovers. I put all of this inside my chest. It walks with me. Maybe I shall find something important about human futility and experience its vastness.
Maybe I'll inject mediocrity into my eyelids ...

My mind will fall like confetti, supernatural realms will burst in my eyes, everything will be familiar to me and nothing will ever be counterfeit.
The only critics will be those of silence ...

THIS IS THE PART
I REGRET IN THE
NEXT LIFE

Today I am a wanderer in this theater of starlight and magic - where none are beautiful and all are dead. I wait inside the landscapes. My fragments are undisguised. I am unknown and I am immortal. Beloved by none, invisible and unaccountable. I am the tragic villain in an eternal journey, interlocked with a multitude of souls and half-faces. I stand towards the endless darkness that hovers throughout the distance. Unthinking machines twitching in some disordered dream, unthinking men baring their teeth at yesterday's dinner, the sun is folded into pieces of foreboding. When I take your hand underneath the gloom of dirt, cult men with customs spoiled by unhealthy ideals catch up to us, we too turn, the degenerate and the absurd, righteous and disobedient to the flesh beating the life into our breath. We welcome the warmth of friendliness. We are the suicides. Not suicide as an end, but suicide as a shedding of material magics, to destroy ourselves so we can be reborn in the imagery of individualism. A metamorphosis, tragic at first, but full of the songs of endless laughter afterward. Spellbound towards the heat of stars and moons. Like little stones of clay. Intoxicated on earth and rain. Inspired by the maze of words, fresh scents of thunder clouds, the festival of dancing, the flowers upon the wood upon the paradise upon the half-crazed strangers who dance and then disappear once the music breaks in half.

I tumble into this world. I smile at the anarchy inside myself. And when those fingers reach out to me - when they whisper my name - when they ask me to reach back - what choice do I have but to give in to its commandments?

There is a romance in all of this. Right now, the imagery is entirely mine. It is a museum of spaceless minds, I fill it with all sorts of saints - usually mythological creatures and romantic kingdoms. Maybe we'll live on giant creatures. They have mountains and trees and valleys on their backs and heads. We would explore the caves in their mouths, walk through the forest inside their fingernails. Maybe one day we'll find each other. Our ghost will dissipate into water vapor, we'll sit at the edge of all things, our feet dangling in the clouds, the thousand fragments of sunlight will wrap its warmth around us, your hand inside my hand, you'll smile and say: 'What took you so long?'

I'll say: 'Saving the world from cannibal mutant spider faces. Obviously.'

We'll travel to the moon. We'll find a hidden world inside the moon. A world full of blue light, waterfalls, spiraling flowers and trees and weeds with yellow stars inside them, bursting like tiny crackles of movement. Strange creatures will look out at us. We are the first humans they have ever seen, they look on with curiosity, they have never known love, dancing, they have never heard a laugh - without knowing - our presence will create a great awakening inside them a thousand years from the moment we saw them - but, we will never know. We dance upon the star-gazer trees, we laugh at the cotton-vistas that explode with harmony once you touch them, we laugh with the joker-swordfish, we swim in the healing waters that are purple and scattered with honey combed lily pads, giant flying caterpillars buzz past our faces, the light sings its songs into our blood - when we love, the grass tangles across our bodies and brings us inside the soft dirt. We become the dreams of dust, we become dimensions and metaphors, goddess and colossus, flame and chaos, we would be a thousand perceptions of non-existence, born to be instant paradoxes. A thousand years, ten thousand years, a hundred thousand years - the Neo-barbarians of Earth hail out their songs to the great unknown, they draw us inside the newly formed stars, their children laugh and dream of the stories told by fathers with brooding eyes and mothers with thin lips, the robots remember, they remember all - they remember the tale of Caterpillar and Moon-Goddess.

2.

I've been thinking a lot about alternate timelines, the strings of fate, the quantum sorcery of electromagnetism, poetic neurons, the distance traveled between particles, infinite energy between two bodies, frameworks inside mathematical patterns, the trillions of cells that create our flesh, our brains, our hands, shells within shells, the orbit of electricity.

It is fantastic, it is endless. It is disco-poetry and I am the caterpillar.

At the edge of infinite, there is consciousness. At the edge of consciousness, there is the cosmic mind. Lovers tied to the Sun, the Earth, the stars, the grass. We discover ourselves with dialogue. We discover ourselves in the slow motion of words and the way they drip inside our eyes and slither into those spaceless worlds.

I enjoy the way words can be adopted inside you. The way they can shape you. Like we have these tiny cells inside our brains that burst like fireworks whenever we read something that resonates within us. Those little sparks of fire set other cells on fire and before long your entire brain is exploding with fireworks and thought. I imagine my life is some metaphor. Like you're on the edge of this fantasy-reality but not sure if you should jump. The world and life seems to structure us this way. We hold back so much. We are so afraid of the life inside of us that we push and hold it down, letting it drown in unhappiness and vice. I do it all the time. I wonder why I do that. What am I afraid of? Why should I be afraid? Confused by thoughts, emotions, do I reach out my hand and touch her? But what if it burns? Will my ribs crack in two, my heart roll down into some swamp? Is there life still left inside of me? Am I promoted by dreams or reality? Is there a difference?

The electricity inside us is a manic ghost. It laughs at us, it binds into our bones, it shivers out of our eyes and hands. Soon we start to crack, we see the life around us and those lives that feed upon us. What a beautiful dream, we think. The earth opens up and swallows us, we become islands, all these islands floating around us. Some are filled with lush landscapes, beautiful springs with golden fish and white swans singing mating songs. Others look like a barren wasteland full of cigarette butts and palm trees that look like deflated balloons. Some islands where it's always raining or covered in fog so you can't see anything but the silhouette of an island. Others covered in a sadness or a perpetual winter. The age of the last season before that island sinks forever. Then there are those islands in all their splendor. All their appalling grace. Who, unbeknownst to themselves, succumb to the quake. Cracking, splitting, fracturing, open like a wound. All life or lack thereof, is exposed to a radical shift. My lovely home. What happened here? I feel no empathy for the interior life that thrived upon me. Yet, I do. I miss the dancing of bodies that used to breathe with tissues and matter so unlike my own. Now I'm left with these enormous wounds to give other organisms the opportunity to thrive as all those before the chaos. To become whole and empty and dead once more.

I am a phantom in this deranged philosophy. Maybe we all are.

I'd take the hand of love. I'd take it even if it burned me and erased my soul.

I usually look at it all as some theater of mystery. The stars are the actors, the moon the director, we are the script pretending to be an audience. How heavy it seems to be human and alive. I'm free but how free? It's all so beautiful. It's all so terrible. It's in these moments when I realize that I have two very different demons fighting within me. The romantic and poet. The cynic and nihilist. It's all so very absurd but so very tragic and beautiful. I hate mankind but love him. I lash out at the gods but pray to them. Sometimes I feel so lost. Like a child surrendering to a lost cause. Like there's thousands of ghosts inside me all whispering at the same time. I feel ashamed of my vanities, my material values, my shallow thinking sometimes. I'm free in all the ways no one else around me is free. Yet, I wish I could have their type of freedom. I aim for companionship but the hidden creature inside me howls to be alone. It seems the gift of words is also the gift of endless solitude. I want something magical in life. I want to dance and be free to roam in the worlds of others. I feel I lack empathy sometimes. I ponder the roads ahead of me. I think of women but I don't know if what I could give them is what they actually want. I'm not sure what anyone wants. People can be so confusing. Sometimes it's as if they need to be told what they want. Like when you read something that you've always known to be true but didn't know it was true. Like we're all these directionless balls of energy bumping into one another. Full of circles and squiggly lines and corrupted by language. Yet, we reach out. We gasp for concepts that seem more alien to us than the stars. Yet, we want to hold it in our arms, comfort it between our ribs, to somehow feel the emptiness, to get rid of the ghost haunting our bodies, to find something equally as beautiful and terrible as we are. Love seems to be that substance. That shape that can be molded and handled in a way that bounces throughout your body. At first, we were static. Now we are clear. A rush of warmth in our hands, our breast, our mouths. The electricity commands us. It drives us to the liberation in the arms of others.

If we could escape fate, would we?

Even if fate were to drown you forever in happiness, would you still try to escape it?

There's so much sorrow in love because we are mortal. We will lose all things in the end. But maybe that's why it's special because everything here is temporary. Can you imagine our first memory? Our first memory as human beings is being babies cuddled to the warmth of our mother's breast. Being fed through her body. Being loved and comforted without judgement, without hesitation, with no reservations. Maybe that first memory is what we go through life seeking. We seek that same type of relentless love that makes us feel protected. That makes us feel comfortable. That makes us human.

We are the dandelions growing between the streets and sidewalks. You are ladybug (the soul) and I am caterpillar (the flesh). Maybe we are both broken, self-destructive. Maybe we are ghosts, lost and afraid in this strange and confusing world, the nourishment of gods escapes through our fingers. We are ceremonies and indispensable minds. A silly grimace. We mourn over the sickness of the soul. We dance in idiosyncrasy. We fashion our lives after buttons and shiny trinkets made of clay and boredom.

Whatever we are - we are free and unloved - which means we are the most dangerous animals in the world.

MY DARKLY BODY IS MARS AND PARABLES

I am lying in a bed, it is made of sulfur, fabric from the sands of Mars. It is known that on Mars the sands can divide space and weave through the time realities. I can't move in this bed. I am broken. I am tiny pieces of revolution. Outside the window I can see long stretches of gray buildings. I don't know the seasons because there are no seasons here, there is no time, only darkness and light, rain or sun, the days have melted into emptiness. I am trapped in this concrete tomb where everything is cleanliness, everything is dry and spotless, nothing weeps or laughs in this place, no one asks questions because everyone is afraid they are dying. They are here, we are here, together, because we must be dying.

The nurses come in.

They dress me, they twist my body to change the sheets, I cry out in pain, everything in my body is in pain, my fingers crumble off and fall on the floor. A nurse picks them up, wraps them in a napkin, sits them on the table near my bed, another comes over and eats my fingers, she vomits and dies immediately.

The doctors come in at the same time every morning. They examine the wounds, they inject jelly like substances into my eyes, sometimes the timelines merge into one another, sometimes the doctors are all in white, sometimes they have insect like mask on, sometimes they have metal rings and smoke strange electronic cigarettes, sometimes they are beast and plaster, sometimes a pudding that drools across the floors while speaking in cryptic tunes.

The midnight mermaids, the harpies of Majesty, have brought me to this place.

The car accident, the glass, the metal inside metal ... I should be dead, maybe I am dead, where did this place form, how did this place form? Who created these remains?

I was on a stage, a spotlight on me, robots with metal limbs tied strings on my body, they would never step into the spotlight, only their arms could be seen. They dragged me across the wood floors of the stage, the spotlight burning my eyes, to a man sitting in a wooden chair, he was smoking something electric, his face swirled with colors of orange and yellows, he was sometimes a man, sometimes a woman, sometimes both, sometimes neither, sometimes a beast, sometimes metal ... he blew the hot electric smoke into my face ... *You don't get to die until you finish our story. You know the rules. We'll keep you alive for a thousand years, everyday in pain and agony until you do what you were supposed to do. The drugs, the booze, the women, your gods, they can't save you from us. You crossed into the Theater of Starlight and Spaceland. You made a promise. This story doesn't end here. It ends on the fields of Eros. On the sands of Mars. You don't get to die, byron. Not yet.*

The robots drag me across the stage, my ribs start to break one after the other, my legs start to break into pieces, my lungs fill up with blood and puss and I can't breathe, smoke is everywhere, I hear a car door open, a woman's voice screaming for me to stop moving, to stop doing anything. She tells me help is on the way. I am stuck in this sterile tomb. I can't escape. Everything is painful. Even in my dreams I'm in pain. I know I can escape if I can get something circular.

That's how you travel through time. That's how you cross through dimensions. If I had a hula-hoop or a basketball goal I could jump through the circles and escape to an earlier time, a different timeline, another galaxy.

With the right amount of drugs and a circle you can travel anywhere. I found that sleeping on couches could send you across time and space. But the couch had to be owned by a friend or lover, someone known, but when you travel for so long, people forget you, they fade into silences, into empty spaces, the curves of their faces change, they become poltergeist, they become ghosts.

I need something circular.

I ask the nurses for something, anything, a bracelet, a ring – they laugh and their laughs ooze out their mouths and slide under the beds.

They turn on the television, the static gets caught up inside my brain, the tracks of laughter cross through me, sometimes I'm inside the shows, sometimes I'm in the audience, sometimes I laugh but nothing but vomit comes out. My eyebrows curl into my skin. Everything starts to merge together. People walk around with four and six arms, four eyebrows, multiple hairlines. They are caterpillars of the second time wave – the universe is colliding with its sister planets – everyone becomes mutant and part fission, fish mouths with octopus fingers, no one is safe when everyone is dying.

They warp my blood, my mud, with more drugs, they fill the tubes going inside my stomach with fluids of whites and yellows. They place me inside a circular machine, this is the machine of puppets and galaxies, this is the machine where people come to witness the show, I can smell the sulfur inside the machine, it's the smell of space, the smell of Mars.

I start to fade into tiny fractions of static, I travel through the timelines, across the oceans, I crumble into pieces of furniture, into sweaters and glass jars, men with marble heads and marble faces greet me, I shatter into a thousand different versions of myself, all lined up one after the other ... *You can't escape, byron* ... on Mars I march with hundreds of robots, all of them have black goo coming from their eyes and mouths ... *Stop trying to move sir, help is coming* ... A tree grows on Mars, in the desert, a solitary tree growing in the middle of nothing and nowhere, it is alive, I know its secrets. A tree from Sumeria, named Inanna, rotting from the inside from a demon it called, Lilitu. It is gnarled and upside down, a purple fruit growing from one of its limbs beats like a heart, the heart is shaped like a caterpillar. I stab the tree, three drops of blood fall into the sands of Mars ... *This story doesn't end, byron, until you have walked the fields of Eros ...* the laughter of the television monsters etches inside me, it crawls inside my wounds, I am metal and plastic, I am decapitating knowledge soaked through, I travel through time under the plaster of cheap wall paneling, I pull apart the fake paper buildings, caterpillars and dead insects fall out... *There is no life, byron, there is only us ...* I am on a beach with a woman, she laughs, the laugh is emblematic, it erupts from her lips, I'm reminded of Paris, space and Christ, the ocean moves across our bodies, it turns us into foam and sand ... *Wake up, byron, wake up, you don't get to die yet ...* on the stage, I can see the audience fold into themselves, they have no faces, no eyes, there is but a whisper on all of them, it flares around their featureless faces like snow and dandruff ... I can't move ... I can't breathe ... *Wake up ...* everything is pain ... everything is suffering inside me ... Mars, the fields of Eros, the tree of Majesty, the robots, the laughter, the static coursing through my veins ... I stumble ... I fall into the sand, everything is cosmic, everything is dead, the tree grows out of my chest, blood pours from my eyes, oil pours from my mouth, I am robot and god, I am flesh and wire, I am Mars and the constellation of Eurydice, I melt into the ooze of spaceless physics, I am a statue of dead trees, I am a medicated presence, I cannot die but I am not alive, the audience applauds with feverish pessimism, I fold into the stage, the pain, oh god ... the pain ... *you don't get to die, byron, not yet. Not until you finish our story ...* the robots begin to dance, I dance with them, time ceases to be on time with its mother dimension, the year flashes to us in bright lights on Babylon buildings: *1983, 1983, Welcome the last year of human and beings!*

The sun flares into an ocean breeze, sand pours from the sky, a fruit beats into the dreams of wooden men with puppet brains, we dance together, we dance because all is mathematical, we dance because all is beautiful ... the audience screams, the audience stomps their tongues with their lips and teeth, a man vomits ... the audience is waiting for me, they throw foul applause, they start eating one another, someone ties a rope around my neck, the scream is electric as it baptizes the air, someone turns into a beetle, a man stands and admits to being a homosexual, he yells: *I'm gay! I'm gay! And no one understands me!*

A woman faints,

The rope snapped my neck.

A gasp shutters through the crowd.

Hurrah hurrah (beating with drums and screams) - the horrific harmony of violins play a brutal symphony.

Hurrah - A man exposes himself from the curtains. He confesses his crimes.

Hurrah - Men stab at the great sow between women's legs. They drink its blood. Women remove the fears of their father from their breast. They perfume the air with a lust that drives the men insane. They howl and crawl on all fours. The women jump on top of them and claw at their circumcised pricks. Sweat fills their pores. They scream and cry and fuck until they explode into fishheads being cut with great sickles, the curtain falls, everyone turns to me and begins to weep ... the audience is folded into napkins ...

The doctor is looking over me when I wake up. He smiles at me, some of his teeth are missing, he says: *The surgery was a success, byron, oh yes and indeed! Unfortunately, everyone you know is dead and all your favorite television shows have been canceled. Go on, nurse, inject this cretin with gasoline. I have pussy waiting for me back at the hotel.*

I scream out, *it's ... it's all so melodramatic!*

He laughs, winks at me, flies into a perfect motion of invisible numbness.

When they inject me, I melt into a palmetto bug, I fly through a crack in one of the concrete blocks, I spread out as if none existed and all were happy.

OH CRY FOR ME YOU WOUNDED POVERTY

Poverty becomes sentient.
It becomes aware it is alive, it has a purpose, it becomes afraid to die.
Poverty becomes nuclear. The nuclear insects with men-heads were made from poverty and the internet. Their teeth are a slimy plastic bag. When a man tastes the dirt for the first time, he becomes addicted to the filth, he sees no way to escape, he is swallowed by the concrete and stray cats. Being poor was dangerous in the land of clerks and Slurpee machines.

Poverty was against the interest of freedom, fascism was the quest for madness, men who loved politics would never understand the satire placed in front of them, they were a mixture of magic tree stumps and violent shenanigans.

The poor paraded, violating the spaces, men with hammers beat the shit out of their faces … *go back,* they screamed, *go back to your fields of famine and reap your children to these lovely myths of freedom and blah wah do's.*
Stickers were given for compliance within the voting dress rehearsals. The men and women with caterpillar faces would never understand their vote and they didn't care as long as it made them feel important to the machine. They laughed and danced when they were given sugar for their participation.

Poverty fled through the empty parking lots.
Its fingernails were long, unkempt, tiny gnomes lived under

the nails. Its teeth were filled with birthmarks, scars under the chin from rotting mouths.

In the land of freedom, no one was alive ... it was too dangerous to be alive ... being free was a death sentence in the city. So the men became clerks, they became sweepers, the billboards advertised that even the monkeys dreamed of being workers one day, even the mutants still evolving in the bottom of the ocean floors dreamed to be human one day and until that day they hated the written words, those words that escaped them, that made them lesser species, lesser men, their music wouldn't be heard for another million years.

Adages swept through the buildings praising stupidity, freedom isn't free, it would have to be earned, the price for freedom was enslavement to rules, laws, the grand republic. None of us understood it but we needed to eat, so we consumed our children, we celebrated films full of rich gods beating the shit out of one another with magic shields and hammers, we screamed the adages passed on to us from our mutated parents.

We were Sisyphus, we were under the misery of Bimbo-Gami, oh you god of Poverty - you temptation of inferno, eternal and destructive, my manifestation inside anxiety, excess is freedom, brand is fabulous, burn your authority within this dialogue, let us all be aroused by this absurdity.

What choice was given to us, cried this Poverty, *we chose nihilism to escape this conformity, civilization is the very act of condemnation, confined to rot inside the bellies of poets.*

Poverty escaped by jumping through a keyhole and eating a magic caterpillar, exploding into the harmony of beetles and honey-bees. For Poverty, there would never be a legacy, statues would never be erected in its likeness, streets and churches would never be named after it, no one would ever devote a Wikipedia page to its name. Poverty was bound to become the irrelevant character in a novel no one would ever read. Not even the gods would remember Poverty's name.

Poverty was eloquent and broken, a seeker of nothing. Poverty only existed to be gravity, cosmic and forbidden, executed by culture. Poverty disappeared into the roles our fathers set before us. Poverty was commanded by cruel observations. Poverty was dead within its own mathematical solitude. Poverty picked up its delusions, it was too ignorant to be unhappy, to understand sadness, gratification was a dream, Poverty would never be alive and it would never be dead … it was a value of irony and its fate was an experiment for fanaticism.

THE CATERPILLARS

We met by a mountain of old and broken beer bottles.
You had trembling hands, a light silhouette, I bit my bottom lip until it bled.
You had probably been running from the junk because one of your shoes was missing. You told me your pimp was an angry clerk that used to work the night shift at a grocery store that you could only find by shining a neon light at the far side of the moon.

He's probably a drug addict, you said, *he's always scratching his flea bites.*

We held hands that night. We shared our last bit of change to buy a beer which we shared behind a dumpster. You told me you were a thief and you were going to steal my inhibitions. I told you I never had any. That night the world ended. Stars burst into colors of unknown gibberish. Our eyes exploded into syphilis and ginger. We didn't understand any of it. The nausea, the goddamn heavens, the stages of fiction. The ocean - what a beautiful beast the way it vomited jellyfish and seaweed. We swam in its belly, drank the slime, traveled through time ... back to your favorite year: 1983 ... *that's the year we died,* you said while you laughed and when you did flowers and moths flew out from your mouth. *Follow me,* you ran, *I'll show how we died.* So I chased you and soon we had become trees, children climbed on our branches, laughing with faces made of buttons and fabrics intertwined with cottons and vices.

The winters came, our leaves dropped ... we were sunflowers and centipede, our laughter lost inside the beautiful wildness. *But none of this matters*, you cried, *because no one will ever understand it.*
Understand what? I asked.
This, you wept as you pointed to your heart.

But, by then, it was too late, because we were both already dead ... sinking into caterpillars and snowflakes.

AN ADVENTURE INSIDE ULTRALAND

My corrupted brain. What beautiful eyes you have.
Where, oh where, did you buy those beautiful things?

There are demons inside this language. They live in the personality and conscience of words. We gave ourselves to the art of this identification.
Everything is alive because of us.
People, objects, insects, clouds, planets – it all has a status and goal and label to give it a purpose, a meaning, some adventure behind its existence.

To be normal was to smash everything ugly. I turn on the television, it is genetically enhanced to make me happy, to fix my corrupt value, a reverse savagery, a universal calibration. Ultraland became a satirical fantasy of freedom to those who didn't fit into the cliché and conventional image of the beautiful billboards with beautiful faces who worshiped beautiful gods with beautiful children, those who were too poor to be human but instead mutated into archetypes, it brought a different type of equality but not the kind that brought happiness, the kind that drove men miserable, the kind that imprisoned men to sacrificial patterns ... *Surrender*, they whispered, *freedom is material, ritualistic, a make up of plastic, it has a heart and its heart is the practice of fatalism.*

In Ultraland, we were all famous, famous corpses of the undead..

The electronic signs were wind and air, they were the sounds of earthly life, it was this calming effect that brought us to the stores of bright merchandise and fluorescent lights that blinded all character, all substance, we would rub our genitals on all the beautiful sales, we would become static eyes and twitch while trying to fuck everything while being afraid of everything. Our faces became television shows, ending in melodramatic cliffhangers, we wanted to be relevant but to be relevant we had to burn other communities, we had to create irrelevant creatures if we were to remain beautiful and afraid.

We caged the monkey, we gave our love to the churches.
The monkey touched us, it compared its fingers to ours, it touched our lips, it was amazed at the texture and tone of the human body, the muscles in the neck, the teeth that were the whitest bones it had ever seen. We understood the monkey, we embraced it, the monkey crawled under our eyelids, we saw the dreams of the monkey, the dreams of literature, the dreams of music notes that floated off the page, the dream of being an employee, the dream of being beautiful.

The monkey asked: 'Can I be beautiful like you?'
The churches dragged us to a giant cross erected out of the ground. They nailed our arms and feet to the wood, splinters fled into our skin, we screamed in pain, we laughed in a manic manner. The churches got on their knees, some of them prayed to us, some worshiped us, one took a spear and stabbed our side, water and confetti bled out of our ribs. The monkey crawled out from under our skin, it climbed down, it touched our feet, the churches carried the monkey to the temple, they placed it on the altar.

The monkey did not dream, it did not cry, it did not show any emotion, it did not blink, its face was like a porcelain doll's as they set fire to it.

The churches wept, they danced, they set the stage, they would reenact this play for a thousand years, to the god of men, to the god that saved them from the misery of being free.

To Ultraland, the great and unusual land of commercial men with no souls left to claim.

MACHINE MEN

Somewhere between endless curiosity and the human condition, I am dead.

Around me, illusionary men. Phantom miracles against the motions. The taste of relapsed nostalgia on everyone's lips. Jesus on every corner. This one sells machinery. This one reads palms. This one swallows swords. And like dissolving mannequins In the molten heat, they slump over eventually like deflated balloons.

Oh my, oh my I am dead while the beautiful earths follow me down like fireflies and delicious love in leisure. Musical faces are impassive against the drunkard fathers. Whose hands tighten around my throat.

There will be no tomorrow, son. He proclaims.

Electric machines grip where cigarettes once did. Love, he said, before his face melted with
a sense of confusion and disorientation. There was a discovery there then and discovery is a province inside madmen.

I am dead, yet, I am not alone. There is a silence between the spaces of star theaters, between the bend of caterpillar whiskers, between the musings of an underdeveloped island. How it dreams in colors while waking to a world painted in blacks and whites.

The poet of bastards. The poet of earth and dirt. A brooding mess of naivety.

I am dead, but there is beauty here. What do you know about beauty? I am dead, living in Ultraland, inside this strange parody. Ultraland is the great fantasy and its citizens are all the sad orphans of the world.

A GODDAMN LIGHT

Infected by reality flesh sickles, manic loners, restaurant hookers, fish garbled junkies, soapy nudist vampires, cat androids, cock claws, reptile legs, insect jargon, horny kitchen wives, dimwit hippies with long strings of hair, mannequins with AIDS, surreal pine made of eyes, barter maids in homemade butter nip, this quantum wizard, this time traveling caterpillar with a knack for finding the truth in carpet textures ...

This is clairvoyant trickery
None live here but the past or future
We commit suicide or adapt to be executed
Poetry is illegal
Music is order
Reality is logic
Sex is religion
Emotion is control
Caterpillars are artist
Soul is obscenity
Imagination is television
Communism a hellhole
Chocolate for all
Neo-platonic for fake magic
Rationale is a magnet Instant paradoxes
We shall all love
We shall all die
Empire and cult

The tyrant of genesis
Everything is a moment
Everything is a string
Everything impractical
True men - all disturbed
True men - an abstract servant

A corpse awakes. Goes to work - etcetera.
Obscene politeness, over indulgence, consumer based manure. Where the majority of jobs are service based in making others happy. This has caused a mass psychosis in the worker's personality, even perhaps a hypnosis for insecurity and fear of disappointments from strangers. A low thinking, high empathy type of society. A reverse zombie apocalypse - where instead of rotting corpses eating your flesh, you have attractive corpses holding you and telling you beautiful things while apologizing profusely.

Headless drunkards, hillbilly time travelers, the transition of time and age, eventually .... All shall be stayed and fade. He who climbs has the better advantage, he can see in time, the nebula drifting into landscapes, the goddamn light, nausea ... how she comes in spite.

LADYBUGS HAVE SECRETS TOO

I place the loveliness inside my mouth. I taste the desires, I swallow the poetry, I breathe in the aromas, I let them manifest inside me. These tiny dancing ladybugs, twirling on my bottom lip, whimsical on my tongue, a parade of moonlight dancing down into my throat. Some do flips on my tongue, others cuddle the warmth underneath it, others become squiggly lines that jump out and melt into my fingers as I press these keys. The kisses that twirl and mold themselves into words. Lips pressed against these words. These words, they become our body, they become our lips, they are the electricity in our hands, the secrets hiding in belly buttons, the hair that rests behind the ears, the memories that flash inside our eyes. Those memories of light, of touch, of the colors behind eyelids, of the drunken nature of lovers, of the helpless rest between two people, that drop of fragrance before water extinguishes the fire. Somewhere in these words is the explosion of flesh, it swiftly burst through the forest, the orbs in the sky, the rain and storms, the animals and seas, the expression of sunset and thought, these words are now our body and lips and eyes and hands and feet and the tiny universes between our eyelashes, a poetic motion set billions of years ago in some romantic and cosmic library, the distant eruption of spaceless physics, the ancient body that grabs the animate body, the quiet immortality of friendliness. It is all here. It rests on the lips, the body, the hands. It becomes our manner, our nature, it is hidden inside our words.

That's where it starts, I think.

In the movements of words. Do they dance on your lips? Do they hide in your eyelashes? Do they create gestures with your hands? Do they move you closer to yourself? Maybe that's the true distance for people. The distance of words. How some are terrible and full of evil thoughts. How some only tinker with keeping the distances as far as possible. Even people who touch, who love themselves for body and kisses, even they feel the distance of words. They lose their words. The distance returns. The words retreat. They become stuck inside jars. They sink into the floors. They become lost in the boundless rhythm under their tongues. This distance is the law of love because this distance is found in language, not just the language of lovers, but the language of all who try to connect, to ease the distance between one to the other. And so I say this to you - there is no distance for us that love words, there is no law that separates us, the words are always here, watching like silent ghosts, ready to grab, to hold, to grow flowers in our heads. These words are ladybugs and caterpillars and they are rivers and lakes that grow inside of us.

These words can be everything and anything.

Do you wish to touch? The words can touch you. Do you wish to love? These words can love you. Do you wish to dance? These words will dance and sing and they will follow you, they will be the snowflakes that fall behind you, the rush of wind between the tree branches, the feel of a page as you turn it. There is no distance inside words, the distance is everything else.

WHITE

The no smoking signs
confuse the men
they lie in deep trenches
along the river
and
the mountains bread
at the crest of unconquerable wars

where they perfume the wounded
with
bright fragrances
so they might smell like the living
sunlight
wet petals

they whisper to one another
while thinking of their childhoods

in their hands
they grasp at letters
from mothers in a deep sadness

the paper is empty
dark
and
relaxes between their fingers

they fear all things white

white to them is the color of death

it is the color of ghost
winter
dead men's eyes

they dig into the soil
where all things grow

dark is the soil
black
and
heavy

they worship this
the color of black to them
is the color of life
the color that springs
food and warmth
and
they smear this color all around them

they look wide eyed at the comets
coming towards them

they dig further
into the blackness of the earth

their fingers hug
handfuls of black clay
their faces are covered in black
as they breathe this dirt in

they are reminded of ancient memories
when they were
part lizard
half frog
swimming in the oceans
dreaming of creatures
walking upright
full of hate

full of misery

they see images of great men
wearing fantastic robes
painted with white colors
on top their heads
lay crowns of jewels and gold

they swing incense
left to right
right to left
they hum the hymns of great books
feed their children
the lullabies of
prophets
and
war

they shove the pieces of culture
down their throats
send them to the mountains

they proclaim
our God is deranged!
our God is insane!
our God is white!

it is the color of cleanliness
the color of purity
the color of death

the men dig deeper
into the root of the earth
they pray to this color
they are afraid

they fear the color white
it is the color of bones.

FAITHLESS

Abraxas, Abraxas!
Where is our revolution?

Thoughts and trances,
The prison of music, Paris vanquished.

How far shall I fall and weaken,
before I perish
faithless ...

LULLABIES OF PROFANITY

She came from France.

That's where all the dirty lovers usually come from. They have weeds and tree branches in their hair, clothes made of ivory rose metaphors, they dream in gospels, have silvery sorrows made of drunken spirits, a never-ending thirst for love and hopelessness.

The women sprout out from gardens made from a poetic orchestra, from the incredible melancholy in their body architecture, from lips that divide the divine like sweet syrup wines.

How they dance madly to be in love,
madly to be drunk on the tops of laughter,
to all the subtle harmonies in beauty and body.
I put my body inside her body.

We whined to the entanglement of whispers and orgasms. She smiled something in French, I laughed something to my man-orbit and possessions. An obsession for the genitalia.
I love you, said the gibberish that rushed out of me.

She never woke up from her fairy tale, from the bunk raised by celebration and feast. She was a fervor, a damp color, a shade of familiar, and we were surrounded by this mathematical foundation.

She melted into a ballet of confetti. I followed her neurosis, her ghost, her amusing muse to the gardens, awoke an army of wonders, all lovely and lonely, her hands shaking to the songs lost in rivers and tadpoles. When she opened her eyes, she sparked to these lullabies of profanity and poverty. She traveled under the earth, into the dirt, speaking French and English and sometimes she danced ... she danced to the mind-high given to her from mushrooms and cow shit ... she laughed and it must have been nostalgic because she faded into a fog that consumed my legs and arms, it threw me under the nurture of words and alcoholism.

She wept under the decay of my teeth, to the monsters that live inside electric letters, to a world she would smother while I was left with nothing but its memory.

FRAGMENTS INSIDE APATHY

These are the fragments of tragedy ...
I am melodramatic and parables.
I desire applause not reflection.

I live within this bizarre revolution, a disordered and vulgar traveler. Through the vault of civilization I march in the rhythm of a hundred prisoners, a civilization that seems irrelevant, an institution that seems inherently insane, mankind had an agenda all their own – they were a metaphor waiting to unfold in incoherence.

On the television they reassure me that being alive is so very beautiful. But these adverts were only concerned for the spectacle that usually ended in gratification.
What a murderous rage our lives turn out to be when love and lovers do nothing but provide social acceptance, when that audience applauds, they applaud to their apathy.
There is no drama in apathy.

Everything became a personality, an impression, a narcotic, a satisfying fear of responsibility, an aesthetic reality, culture was dead and the complaints soon turned into fits of laughter followed by insanity.
We were fragments of a corpse, singing lively ... oh how we sing!

Beware, the holographic androids cried on top of metal

buildings,
beware the secrets of caterpillars – ...
they eat the dreams of trees.

CULTURE IS ATOMIC

We – the stars –
We – the machine culture –
We - atomic masters of bloodless objects –
We - the descendants of monsters, billions of years of mutation and indifference. Self-destructive, murderous, to bend time and space, we are evolving into scientific psychopaths, television and housewives, bitter molecules trapped in artificial imagery, into the musical puppets full of melodrama and gifts, into a theory of irrational conformity where we must conform to all ideas of irrationality to survive, to exist, to love, to normal and walk brisk.

Evolution became misanthropy
Religion became materialism
Civilization became a psychosis

Man was mythical
Man was artificial
Man was a metaphor promoted through symbolism
Man was the image of god but god was an abstract
And, If god can't exist,
mankind was bound to fall asleep.

The churches were piled with telepathic mutants with fish costumes drinking the blood of roman lullabies ...

We applauded the extinction because it brought us closer to apathy, closer to becoming television shows, closer to the advertisements we would dance inside.

There would be no space adventure this week.
That money was used to create another casualty of character.

We - conformed to nihilism as a way to combat the extremism of existence, nihilism was the only rational response to a world that insisted on creating stupidity and insanity. It was in the bleakness of this fear we sought at the edge of our civilization, at the edge of our nonsense. Those of us who had become caricatures of what humanity never promised, who would never know love or forgiveness for what they had become, those that slipped through the constructs of culture, that demanded to be free despite the pain it caused.

We - conform quietly to ideas that are manic
and insane,
that have no place in a world of evolved life.

We - are orphans in a world that we want to be extraordinary and yet cannot seem to find our place inside. The gods are dead, man has become immoral, television is a beautiful miracle, plastic is alive ... We are broken, beautiful and celestial, and we are famous.

MUSES OF JEST AND INFERNO

Are you happy?
-Yes
Do you love?
-Yes
We think you are going to do great things
-Why am I afraid?
Escape is subjective

O'muses O'muses
By those that die
My love, love, all is bound and tragic
What is beauty if love is terrible?

Consider this!
Oh! happiness.

Are you to be a slave to the century or your own body?
Will not the ceiling fall eventually?
What will you do then,
Oh! happiness?

Oh! mighty sea
Oh! invisible galaxies
Oh! insects and mutants with garbled hate for tongues

What shall you ever find if all the world crumbles
and

Nothing is left but the life you could have lived?

Oh! happiness
Oh! despair
Shine your extinction inside me.

MY HANDS ARE
NIHILISM AND MAGIC

There's civilization here but too much of it is civilized, sophisticated, falling apart like the broken dreamscapes in the heads of madmen. Not enough of it to hold together the pieces falling at the boundary.

There's an edge of the world here and all the degenerative citizens live there. They come unwrapped and fall apart. There's too much life here, too much religion, too much of a nationalist pride that promotes advertising in their heads. Everyone here is dead or trying to swim above the slime but they are dreamers, they fall into the pits of their own misery while blaming everything on evil, going on mass hysterical rants, outraged at invisible enemies gasping out at their bravado, always afraid something is out to steal their precious souls, brooding heads full of tricks and talents, intoxication is silence is magic is mechanical is particle is division is flesh eating the celestial and faceless, martyrs numb with fission-soul.

God and wine courses through their imperfect features, they are specters lost inside bibles.

Police are morality
Violence is cosmic,
it is alive in mutated television shows where statesmen now declare all humanity is nothing more than a gross conditioning caused by random acts of chocolate shortages.

Go back, the goblins cry, *go back to the mud under your fingernails, back to the blood in your erections, back to the whores of fish and fruits.*

Can you escape nihilism?
Its regression is passive,
it waits,
none are innocent.

METAMORPHOSIS

The city's politics was a constant metamorphosis that created confusion that could never be defined. Citizens were unable to decipher truth from the fantastic so they simply believed in everything and escaped in theater.

The man woke up on stage, they murdered him, the man died on stage, the audience applauded, they demanded a refund, the man was resurrected, the man was murdered on stage, the audience cheered on the ritual, the man was alive, the man was murdered, he is alive, the audience is disappointed ... they came here for the murder ... Euphoria was a disorder. It created the mega-optimist, manics wanting to be happy and so would do anything to retain that happiness even if meant shopping for suicide and meandering for murder.
Really, they didn't mind.
And so they created programs to be beautiful like us.
They danced and whirled and cried and loved like us.

Oh, the people screamed, *how fantastic they are! How beautifully strange their faces squeeze together! Let's put lakes and rivers in their heads. Let's fill them with the geography of heavens!*

These phantoms were beautiful because they were told to be beautiful, they were fantastic because they were told to be fantastic – they asked questions because they were told not to assume an identity that wasn't already programmed in the portals that lived in the volume buttons on the back of their nested heads.
The people waved in irony, they danced to comical effect, they

loved their objects because they were beautiful and would never harm them with self-reflection.

They loved their creations more than they loved their reality and so they squeezed them tight when they slept, *you will never escape*, they said with love and asterisks.

They held them so tightly the guts and wires pushed out of their eye sockets, their beauty vomited across the living room floor, into the kitchen sink, creating a fire, a fire that engulfed everything beautiful while killing everything ugly - and the people, the people, the great and beloved people - they rejoiced in their obsession.

THE PLAY THAT KILLED JESUS

He coughed, releasing the spores from the flap under his tongue. They spread out into the eyes and mouths of those around him. They went into the floors, digging like spiders into the hardwood, going underneath, infecting the carnival men that were waiting with costumes.

The costumes, the shadow mannequins that had been waiting for years to awake from their dreams. They now dug from under the ground, tearing upwards with their lobster hands, they spun in circles, into the air, above the stage. They landed together, synchronized, they stopped and froze into position.

The music, the fat man screamed, *the goddamn music. Now!*

The music played slowly, it started with the violins, the piano began, the trumpets, the cannibal drums beating. The rhythm, the waves of sound moved them to march like careful ballerinas across the stage. BOOM. They hide behind the curtain. BOOM. They confessed to crimes they never committed. They danced carefully, never to disrupt themselves.

A man from the seats stood up.
It's me, he cried, *It's me!*

Sit down! Screamed a woman who had an obsession with bathroom products.

The effect of the play rushed out from the stage, it hit the audience with a thunder that turned their faces into porcelain. A man, known for being alive, a man, known for being called poverty, a man, set fire to the doors behind them. The seats awoke underneath its audience. They became aware. They understood what they were. They understood the colors better than those that claimed to have a life because they would breathe in the dreams of those trees.

Beware of the applause of men, something whispered, *it is the applause of reflection not affection.* BOOM. They danced to the silhouette of the depressed cellos. BOOM. They fell down on the stage. They were dead. The audience was dead. Everything was dead.

The curtain, the fat man screamed, *the goddamn curtain! Pull it down before they realize they're all dead.*

But it was too late. The audience knew. They were aware that they were being manipulated to participate in the emotions of a poet that had died long before they would ever escape. Escape to them was in extinction. They feared extinction so much they went about rubbing their genitalia on everything that might have some type of life to it yet. They would rape anything that could possibly procreate. Their phones were injected into their brains and tied into their arteries.

The audience started to melt.

Some became weeds, some robots, some spiders that crawled on the ceilings. The audience wept, their tears slid down their cheeks like a thick syrup. Centipedes crawled from their mouths, great apes laughed from beneath their eyelids. The fat man's belly popped open, an endless rope fell from his stomach. A boy grabbed it. He went through the theater putting the rope around the necks of the audience.

When the play was over

They all hung themselves
The applause was brilliant

The curtain, the play, the dances, the music. We all folded in anticipation. We all died somewhere between the second act and endless curiosity.

And, the flowers, the flowers were so very precious when tossed with a helping of mediocrity.

A FANTASTICAL DRUDGERY

(1) My brain, last of early nights, was detached - roaming around in gutters of slime and filth, chasing mutants in wastelands, dancing in the trans-dimensional mind mud of caterpillar realms - I've heard people speak of a better world out there ... I imagine it's full of strange temptations, minds with snowflakes, lovers carving destinations in every constellation they trace with their fingers. And if I am a poet - those worlds seem infinite to me ... maybe some laugh track is hidden in their scalps and hair - maybe a bit of a jester rest there doing weird cartwheels on the backs of goblin-cats. I imagine some of these people have six legs and sixteen eyeballs, they have talking shadows, a substance in learning from the devil and savages that run amok in their eyebrows and eyelashes - I imagine those shadows have their own world, burned into bright television screens and fancy trinkets they keep hidden in their pockets ... it's all so dramatic ... it's all so terrible ... it's all so beautiful ...

(2) I want to be strange. I want to be fantastical. I want the romantic nonsense of being a dance conjurer - like sorcerers

and wizards at play in the delight of our brains ... Hm. Pesky modern worlds and all the silly drivel it twirls inside - I avoid it - I pretend the cars pressing with all their noise outside are just the sounds of rocks and comets with tiny little aliens inside - I'm sure they're beautiful - I don't hate anything ... some people are just exhausting. I suppose one day it will end for us all, like little light-wasps that shine out very dramatically for a moment before flying into a fire that zaps our asses.

(3) People imagine a life of order and commands. But even we - cosmic barbarians from the swamps, created out of disaster and pain and mischief and a desire to dance within the absurdity - we are not the orderly divine nature of gods and divas ... we have traded disaster and chaos for order and structure and we, if anything, are animals born out of chaos and destruction - embracing a little chaos is probably healthy.

(4) I want to believe in some majestic delirium and hop away from all sorts of drudgery and be more like a stray animal ... I don't want to be civilized or contained in structures or believe in the cruel mathematics of gods and state and church and politics. But it seems when you expel the drama of one world - you only invite a new type of conformity or suffering.

Condescension is not a proper lover.

As it seems with so many of the false idolaters of love.

(5) What are we but dust and air, lingering in sleep, disentangling dreams? Molded into shapes and colors - conformed by moon and starlight - to create chaos and disorder in a cruel and unobserved dream we seem to all be living inside.

(6) There's always a slight hesitation in expected lovers. The fear of diving into someone and their life. The fear of losing them. The fear of mischief. The fear of all lovers. The fear of all those that desire to be loved and to love. Nothing else fears like we do. Those nasty little abstract ideas that poison the heart, that torture the soul.

(7) Love. That emblematic emotion. Are you she, her, beauty? Are you here to tumble and fumble as I do? Everything in nature grows. It grows, drops its seeds. The flowers bloom with no hesitation, the lizards, the beetle, the moths, the worm. There is no hesitation in those creatures. There is no desire but to live. To exist and eventually never exist. They tie themselves together. Their children, their seeds, their pebbles, their eggs, those are the extensions of life and will always follow the same path of instinct. To keep pressing on. They will never hesitate to live, to love, to mate. Because they know better than we do. That life is more than abstracts, more than symbols, more than being an idea or an individual. It's about community and extending your life by creating extensions of yourself. Whether we do this with art, songs, poetry, children, building something, everything in life is about how to make sure it can never completely die. To be guided not by mad ideas, mad violence, mad for objects, mad for lust, mad for the stars, but to be guided by the instinct of continuing to move forward.

(8) There seems to be so much time and so very little of it. My flesh will melt, my skeleton will take over, the walls will fall, the furniture will burst into flames. Will I celebrate my life? Was I a good man? Was I loved? Did I love? Did I think

being loved would make life easier? What did I find in the little fragment of life that swallowed me? Here, our heartbeats are silent, still, there is no blood. Only mist, vapors, language, weird words for those that dance to weird tunes. Maybe there's still some life left in me yet. Maybe.

(9) This is my little secret. I put these words in my pocket. I carry it around, hiding it from the chip eating mutants, keeping it safe. I take it out, it dances beside me, a shy expression, a light touch on the arm, we sit on the bench together, we watch the life in front of us, we watch in wonder and silence. I hide it inside my belly button (where all lovers keep their secrets - you must whisper beautiful masturbation into them and the secrets hatch out like tiny spiders) as it hides me between the eyelashes. The muses of an irrational evolution (or is it irritation?).

Our extinction is what we desire and love - it is in the flow of hands, eyes, hair, lips, the pressure between the finger and thumb because lovers are the most dangerous animals in the world. This is the music I sing, this the song that slips between my lips.

Love, for us, is a type of acceptance that exposes us to vulnerabilities - the type we hide from those that only wish to destroy the warmth we carry in our chests and heads, the wizards of apocalyptic fantastique that bite their tongues for vanity and tyranny and the evils that are produced by paranoid suspicions ... love is a demonic animal that lives in our gut willing to tear through everything to take hold of that they wish to touch and protect and it would dive into the deepest of the darkest oceans to drown in a completely irrational and primeval way to eat and devour the soul of all that it inhales into its lungs. An animal that is willing to die and live recklessly to be captivated by a force that flees beyond its instinct of survivability, it is an unimaginable disturbance that haunts our skin and dreams and the existence between our legs - a disturbance older than all the stories - through stupidity and crudeness it crawls, it is the hopeless child of every devil and every god - inescapable, immortal, elastic, never victorious but never quite defeated. A symbol of transcendence and wretchedness.

And we are but the slime of its deeds, once we were filled with emotion, grandeur, beauty, but it is lost, lost, lost to dystopian horrors! And now - and now, we are nothing but orphans.

ROMANTIC ENTROPY

Disasters today. Many disasters.

My face is full of grumbles. Have you ever had one of those days where you just want to escape into some sort of tunnel that leads to another world? I was thinking it might be cool if the washing machine was really a time machine. Maybe I could crawl inside and be washed into another world. One where they don't mind that I don't comb my hair and where no one thinks it's strange that I think thrift stores sell various items haunted by poltergeists and sweaters full of bed bugs.

I want life so desperately and yet want to fade away into nothingness.

I yearn for connection deeply and purely but the romantic solitude by the lakes embraces me so perfectly … I forget sometimes that other people exist. I am content with mystery but I'm painfully confused so often that it propels me into a wild lust for fulfilling my endless questioning. There's still this part of me reaching out for a solution when I know there is no solution to any of the questioning of existential thinking. I'm deeply conflicted. Complicated. I'm aimless, random, full of pretensions, but those pretensions define me. Thinking about thinking. I'm alive to feel. I'm certain of that. It's all about feeling, the experience. I exist to enjoy the art of existing. The daunting moments of being swallowed up whole with woes and fear. The variation is the joy; the dark and light. I'm alive to take that all in, process it, connect with other people processing it and be just present. I'm alive. Sure. I'm alive unless I took a wrong turn somewhere and have fallen into some alternate reality where the waking world is full of surrealist marketplaces selling love as disordered human faces, people with dolphin heads, dogs walking on ceilings like spiders, old people buying empty promises instead of lottery tickets, and everyone is a comet crashing into themselves. They are magical formulas that will never be defined. This is all happening. Everything is decaying into entropy. I feel like sharing a secret. A little rebellion in all my disaster.

I think life and existence is full of blandness and obviousness and full of distractions we use to validate our existence and how important and optimistic it is when language really seems to be only ignorance fitted into a delusion that life must be important because I can think - when life seems to be nothing but drudgery and we are its blind children suffering from a paradoxical mania where we have to make up illusions to force ourselves to live within its absurdity. The adages are all around me - buy this, buy that - with money you will have happiness - work shall be your religion - vandalism of the spirit is transformation and celebrate our surgery superficiality with more cosmic convenience - just for you and only for you ... and I think if free will exists then why were we monkeys once? Self-destruction is my lover. Maybe we can self-destruct together.

The institution is manufactured perfectly to serve this misanthropic urge inside me. My plush perversion hides in a secret place. Where I think of this fickle lust as succulent lemon drops. That taste of sweet and sour rushing through my tongue. I squirm and loosen, coming undone. There I am, perched above, delicately, plump and poised. Patterns of tickling enticement flooding my flesh. These lips breathe out reckless want. Taste and touch intertwine, I am a sensory wizard...A whimsical harmonious hex of oblivion flows forward. The dark mystique spreads...its potency pours into the air, thick and heavy. Infected thoughts, fevered skin.

Consumed in the desperation of desire. The apex of my want, how stunning in the crisp dark, everything is illuminated, everything is alive. Sensuous explorations explode. It's a dance of breathless bedazzlement. Goosebumps, prickles, little electric, erogenous, erections everywhere- it aches in acute amazement. A catastrophic climax. The heat becomes unbearable. A volcanic proclamation, the melting begins. Everything dissolves...and the beauty bestows itself. That warm, rosy ooze pool on the bare floor. You just want to bathe in it. The love then breaks you into tiny pieces ... you die inside a lover's belly button and resurrected under their tongue.

There's an ample spring of darkness coursing through me. I feel compelled to say blunt, offensive things to overly confident people, professors, religious proselytizers. The karma principle should influence my darkly ways. Oh dear. Yet, If my demons are to leave to me, will my angels leave too? Mischief is so very necessary. Confliction is possessing me rather fiercely. I want to protest, but become subdued. I want to rebel, get destructive, my mind is creeping into dark territory...it's lovely there this time of year. That place where deep, dark cobalt blue and slate grey collide into a warm melancholy pool, mmm. I fall prey to that tempting body of water, I'm buoyant and aligned in perfect askew-ness there. What a sinister synergy; how well suited I am to darkly melancholia. That delicate darkness dance tangles me up and weaves patterns of confusion and complexity into each thought. I caress those thoughts in pure adoration, devour them ravenously. I thrive off their perplexity. I lounge in the cool confines of melancholy, appreciating its peculiar place in my existence. It's almost as if...I need it. And, so I think I may have to learn the art of balancing blissful love and delicious, delicate, darkly melancholy- because they both have a beautiful, necessary place in my existence.

Fleeting moments are more beautiful than the lingering ones.

They are astoundingly, romantically and breathtakingly more beautiful.

CARNIVAL OF OOZE

A dude with mediocre eyebrows, fancy birthmarks on his teeth, sensationalist eyelashes, insect head, caterpillar eyes, gumdrops for armpits danced and waved on the television portal -
he created, and wanted to share, with your participation inside this imagination, a superhero movie about a team of junkies, schizophrenics, neurotics, alcoholics, all wearing leather, all fighting crime with fake kung-fu.

It was a rebellion against the human condition, against human nature, which is to say it was advertised for special interest to sell soda frizzles, sugar fried chicken, whistles with electronic brains ... Rebellions inside gadgets never wanted to conquer, they only wanted to impose certain opinions – opinions about what to buy and what should be offered up in terms of sacrifice.

It was a rebellion born from envy and bitterness of what one lacks in commercial worlds. They were no longer human, they were citizens pretending to be officials with heretic heads as heart diseases calcified the liquid in their peckers.

Jobs were nothing but animated flesh for rent.
Profit was a tool for theft,
rent was slavery, everything was an amusement meant to burn in a carnival of fiction.
Pain would give life meaning, a purpose to exist continually in suffering, but the suffering was poetic, it was created to sell metal men with starlight libraries in their brains, it was a con

to be peculiar against the interest of the machines because the machines were about forgiveness and love.

Evolution was a practice of misanthropy and the silent children all conformed to its irrational illusions of vanity. Without this mankind might have been lost to dreams and songs and freedom – they might have continued to be mutants living in swamplands with no electrical outlets for their amassed entertainments.

And ... wouldn't that be a shame, the author on the portal laughed ... the audience agreed as they melted into friction and static.

IMAGINE MY PARODY

My lips are parody.
My tongue drips in your ear, my body is a rock lying in your lake, I am lover and lived, insects behind your ears, against your mouth I am a wave of mercury and machine, I am the script of lovers and those that mind the fantastical between savage rituals of magic and science.

My eyes are spider webs,
they detach, slide down my face.

My teeth are mutants, they scatter across my smile.
I am biology and formula.
I am enlightenment, an enlightenment of temper and all things immortal.
I am warped and transitional brain mud, my conscience is a convenience, a manic toaster, creating lovers to replace the lovers I have murdered – she, she who transcends the aesthetics of the objects I worship. I am dead, we are all dead, broken inside idols, broken inside theaters and fables.

We are the fabrications of broken caterpillars.

Love is my dependence.
A creation,
a secondary passion for objects outside of my nature.

Love exists to learn, to inquire, to passion, to chaos, to evolve inside the caves and colors, the structures of strangers … love creates an incompleteness when shared with myself, this flesh foundation. I have been conditioned to exist, to love, to pray, to drown.

Imagine this!
Imagine the immortality of trees,
Imagine we are nothing more than the dreams of those trees,
Imagine the inhumanity left in all of the humanities!
Imagine the air full of dandruff and insects, men with eyes like a kind of Christmas light blinking in harmony with broken teeth that look like dirty fingernails hardened by years of boredom and nicotine ...   The ballerina mutants spit out porcelain and ceramics at one another, their children look on with an eloquent despair marked with parody.

Imagine this was Ultraland, where the machines are made of blood and shaped like human faces. Is this the dream of television? Is this a construct of osmosis? Do monkeys dream of being clerks and lawn ornaments?
Am I only here because the ocean had a dream it was a starfish and procreated with fish guts? Am I the dreams of lizard sand pebble blood pulp wave suicide universe trees?
Am I a product of love or lust?

This was Ultraland and in Ultraland there were traitors on every corner, criminal men with aesthetic buildings for limbs, these men wanted to eat you, these men wanted to put you to work, every clerk looked in anticipation at the lines in the faces, hands, the mud and shit and grease that curled under fingernails, they sold poisoned dreams with lottery and politicians who denounced all fair vices while holding to superstitious entertainments, these men spoke in gutter-anthems to push back the dreams that wished to corrupt the great and beautiful land, the only great and beautiful land.

The dreams pressed into them ...
half-shut
sideways
steam-sweet.

I started to wonder if this was nothing more than a harbor of narcosis.
I became afraid.
Is my fear of boredom killing me?

I wondered -
if I stop surviving,
will I go insane?

THE PRICE

If living in a rich materialistic
religious country has taught me anything,
its taught me that every soul is an institution
and
every salvation has a price.

-spray painted on a bathroom stall somewhere between Ulysses and the Pacific

((situations that grow from emails))
All is well in the land of free poverty ... The sand is forming into rocks, the trees wave merrily, the ants and lizards run around, singing their songs of romance and mating. The humidity stings at our faces, some of us melt into globs of slime, some of us cartwheel, some of us dance under the formations of flower blooms and the heads of bumble-bees that come and rub their weird faces on our eyelashes, thanking us for sun and light, thanking us for tree and wind. The stray cats ponder human cruelty while they lick their tails and give sacrifice to the fleas in their eyes and toes. No one really understands any of it but no one really wants to.

I had this evil horror growing in the back of my mouth ripped from my skull. I call my cavities birthmarks or maybe they are birth-defects (who knows). My legs walk and do the things legs do. I can't run, I can probably never have jumping contest with grasshoppers, and I will never be able to cartwheel in my stray cat circus (the one with cats in suits doing handstands and jungling fire staffs and prancing like ballerinas), but other than that, no pain, just thoughts, little ideas that tickle my face and tongue, the loneliness of trees, the magic of caterpillars, if we are evolved mutants does that make everything about us irrelevant except our desire and need to survive?

Can we all just mutate back into rabbits, run in the parking lots full of weeds and trees, to frolic in the fields, fucking and dancing, our eyes full of orgies and rain, we would be nothing but alive, we would love everything and love nothing and we would always be free.
That's what my caterpillar brain thinks anyway.

Thinking of thinking, thinking of our short time, putting absent women together through my memories, putting arms and legs on, giving those beauties a face, a laugh, wondering if my reconstruction of this idea of her is close to the actual truth of her. Sometimes we go on adventures, sometimes we laugh inside the shadows my light plays on the ceiling tiles, sometimes we die and sometimes we live for a thousand years. Finding each other across a busy street, waving hello, but doomed to never cross because the traffic is too heavy, too bright, too destructive. But we smile and give one another warm memories to love and hold.

I'm off and off to overdosing on coffee, staring out my window, wondering if there are secrets in the movements of ants ... is there a price to pay for this salvation or have I already paid it with my gratitude?

MODESTY

A man, indeed.
His godlike, modesty
Sitting; cross-legged,
Elbows high, chin stretched,
His knuckles, cosmic webs.

He points to the sky, to a dying star –
That's God, he says, Senseless and terrible.

He lights his cigar with his hand cuffed partially,
Wrapped around his eyes – the light sparkling,
Slipping through the empty fractures between his fingers.

He stands, looking up at the stars,
We've conquered heaven, he mutters to himself,
God is a mutant, He eats men and their blood is on this culture.

He points again to the sky –
Look, look! There will be no more mornings!

I remember this... I remember this while his hands wrapped
around my throat – Those blinding hands, that forceful hatred,
screaming into my skin. His eyes were lava and my mouth was
a river of sour.

SO THIS IS WHERE THE FLAMES DIED

The man with the darkly protoplasmic face whispered into the machine tenant. With a static spur and whimper the machine spit out a whirl like sound followed with a tiny piece of paper that read: *I love you.*

This man read the words over and over again trying to find the answer in such a strange idea. Yes, he thought, this will solve the riddle my toaster gave me this morning. He folded the paper neatly into the shape of a square and placed it in his pocket to consume later.

Tell me something terrible and beautiful, his toaster had asked him earlier that morning. Which was strange to this man since his toaster had never said anything and had rarely even cooked his toast well. In fact, the man was on the verge of throwing his toaster out for the very new and fairly priced ITtoaster that came with many useless but highly recommended gadgets. The new ITtoaster didn't even cook toast, but gave a very descriptive account of what one might expect from a piece of toast. How completely innovative and insane, thought this man. His desire to purchase this useless contraption far outweighed any rationale. Besides, his neighbors had said: It's to die for, dear!

His neighbors were almost always very suave.

Think jogging. Think wall screen televisions. Think Vegan. Think stickers for voting. Think standing in long lines for a gadget to imitate a certain social status. Think churches with ATM's. Think love with a certain reference to Asian products. Think optimism and then walk into the ocean until something eats you. Think culture. Think happy. Think narcissistic social websites geared towards self-centered egoism. Think dancing. Think good jobs. Think sleep and then cartwheel into the highway.

I love you indeed, the man scoffed. The man had his answer as he waved in the next man he was to fire that morning.

The machine behind him made a series of beeps and whines as a man came in and sat across from him. The men stared at one another. Somewhere something had gone wrong. The programming started to corrode, become unstable, a fault perhaps from the riddle asked that morning created the machine to become interstellar, question its habits, or perhaps a catalyst caused by an infection of independent thought. One of the many commandments that condemned such thinking now began to unfold inside both of these men's heads.
The machine could sense that the neurological plasma inside their cores were increasingly becoming erratic. The electricity from one thought to the other traveled through time, dimensions and particle distance as they simultaneously watched both their deaths and births.

They understood time.

How everything happened at once. They saw themselves as fractures of a fragmented star, fractions split on a comet glazed blackboard, mathematical equations, puppets of culture, programmed machines to the echo of fallen ancestors.

They saw that the insect gods had made them metallic. Gave them glass dreams in marble eyes. They wept openly at the thought of being nothing but a pile of mud and seaweed with electric powered muscles made of plastic trinkets. They slipped into the crevices of depression, magical theaters, where death and life were now two heads of the same body.

Where are my fathers now? They asked themselves.
The machine behind them realized the dangers of these two men questioning their false reality. It saw the strings of manipulation start to rot above them. It understood the answer to the riddle better than they and the untold toxicity of such free thinking. The machine simply did exactly what it thought it should.
The machine set itself to self destruct and decided to destroy the entire stupid planet.

But the men, they saw themselves in another dimension, another world. A place of spaces and life. They witnessed the ancient machine buried deep within the moon's crust and the lizard astronauts who placed it there. They watched the robot rebellion on Mars, they stood on the ice glaciers of Pluto watching the spiral splicers untangle themselves out of a long hibernation. They laid naked inside a spaceship made of a silver crystal. Beside them laid a mass of formless beings. It slowly, as they began to give it thought, shaped into the shade of a woman's body. Her hair and arms wrapped around them, followed the curvature of their neck and shoulders. She laughed and wept at the thought of life she had just been given by them.

They said nothing. They laid next to her watching the strange shadows from Titan and Eros make shapes across their bodies with its splintered light. Her tears fell across her cheeks, and as they did, her skin flaked and started to burn into ash. Their bodies molded into each other. Their soul's knotted, screaming through the webs of ancient pathways the soul had forever traveled. Their flesh became a slime as it melted together. They all cried out in fear as they lay lumped into a pile of dust and space. Their mouths twisted up as they vanished into a puddle of neurons and electric nematodes. They screamed as they were all afraid. They were afraid of life, of death, of what it meant to dream and be free from responsibility, they were afraid of not possessing things, they were afraid of love because of the possession in that thought. Most of all, they were afraid of themselves, of what they might become if they ever woke from this dream. So, they did what came natural - they screamed. Which was against one of the many codes of productivity and could get them turned into refrigerators. Or worse, sentenced to a life of complacency and boredom. Boredom was the worst of all purgatories.

The makers approached both men as they faced one another wide eyed. They had seen the machines escape in a comatose state before. They did not understand it but knew it happened once and again. The makers were fast to stop any contamination of feeling within the perimeter of the great lord's castle. They checked both machines. They made sure to program them to maintain a healthy fate and do exactly as they were instructed to do. Duties were heavily favored over emotional stimulus.

They reset the two men by closing their eyelids and pushing a series of buttons and code words. They did not bother with the corner machine. They did not know that it had programmed itself to self-destruct. They were unaware of the riddle. They did not know that this riddle created a duality within the system. A worm virus that zig-zagged through its many parts and mechanics. It created a thought that it must survive by maintaining a constant cycle that repeated a series of unanswerable questions, it must learn emotions to fight against the contamination of repetitious routines, sterilize itself against the monotonous. It had decided that time is constant, ever evolving, that all things are simultaneously alive and dead. Birth and death happened at the same exact time. The machine would never understand what it was doing, only that it must manipulate the system to protect its master's program. To make sure all corruption tilted in favor of the makers while the poverty of intellect remained within the machinery.

After all was done and the makers were satisfied they made their way slowly out of the room. They did not worry if the machines would see them or not because the machines were not programmed to see them. Though in the makers haste to fix this malfunction they put one too many semicolons in the program.

This would have two effects on the machine.

One - the machines would not be able to obey any of the programs because they would not understand them and, two - the machines would most likely turn into heathens and start violent riots, refuse to obey authorities, stop grooming themselves, and most assuredly would partake in mass orgies.

The men awoke. To them nothing particularly interesting had happened. Because of a lack of programming the men did not know what to do. They gaped at each other utterly confused and bemoaned by their lack of initiative and interest to do anything considered productive.

They mimicked each other's movements. One turned his head, the other did the same. One raised his hands up, the other did the same. They both erupted into laughter. They looked confused by the noise and feeling the laughter had caused. They looked at their fingernails, traced the veins on their arms, felt their teeth with their tongues and moved their tongues to the grace of syllables and words. They giggled at speaking the forbidden songs and words. They moved their hands over their mouths, over their eyes, pressed their fingers into their eyes and stood amazed at the spirals of ghostly dragons dancing in front of them.

They got out of their chairs. They explored the corners of the office. They spoke without fear. They stood in front of each other. The man reached into his pocket, taking out the small folded piece of paper. He read the words. He remembered the riddle. He remembered the voice.

Tell me something terrible and beautiful.
I love you.

The men removed their clothing. They wanted to shed the pretensions of clothing and uniforms. They saw that these were nothing more than status symbols within the hierarchy of the system. They thought them foolish, inhuman, childish. They danced and threw everything in the garbage bin. They poked fun at the corner machine as it whined in embarrassment. If the makers had witnessed any of this,especially the stripping of uniforms and status, the makers would have immediately taken them apart or worse; re-wired their neurological pathways with laser incisions above their eye sockets and turned them into vacuum cleaners. The man grabbed the other man's hand. They stood before one another. No judgement, role, status. They cared little of opinions, thoughts, work, relationships, gods. The men looked into each other's eyes. They had visions of giraffes grazing in the wild lands, snow falling like feathers against red tipped oaks, ants crawling on the belly of a beetle.

The men began to question their motive for life. They wondered at their programming, at nature's programming. Was it better for men to accept a role in life? Was it better to give in to instincts rather than rational thinking? Was this not nature's programming? Are men subjected more to evil because of his rationale? Which is the break from nature. What about cultural roles? If the men were to break from these norms, would they be upsetting the established laws of society? Was it better to accept your fate and role for a better world or turn against the makers to be free? Did people only follow these established rules because being comfortable inside an imprisoned set of guidelines was better than being intolerable? Was it possible they feared having the responsibility to govern themselves instead of letting someone else do it for them? But at what cost does that freedom come? Does anarchy mean the establishment has no control over rules, behavior, social communities? The men wondered if they were being selfish. Is it better to live in a world of programmed ideologies or where all men can pursue the true spirit of themselves without following laws, rules, boundaries? They thought of the paradigm of good versus evil. Who decided who was good? Who decided who was evil? If all men obeyed nature's programming, is it possible that none can be evil and none can be good?

Are these not morals programmed and don't really exist? The men decided they did not want any of this. They no longer cared for morals, ethics, integrity. They only wished now to follow their own commandments. They cared little for good and evil, god and devil, man or animal, machine or life. They only wished to be free from all status, all pain, all work, all responsibility.
At this moment everything around them erupted in fire and hell.

The machine behind them exploded. A wave of fire washed over and through them. The plastic on their faces melted away, exposing a galaxy of swirling stars. The men stood together, unmoved, staring at one another, as the flames burned through them. They smiled, moved their lips together, repeating the words the machines had given them. *I love you*

If they were afraid, they did not show it.

OF DEMAGOGUES
AND MUTANTS

In the future, everyone will be genius and decadent
lotus eating and pleasure-seeking
a lazy idleness of caterpillar beings.

Fish plasmas and reality magicians, circuit-stars and drama-particles, a significant melody. Poverty becomes erotic, it becomes aware, it has its own method and memory, a silhouette of half remembered people, a wound-man – a man with a womb.
It appears injured in its curiosity.
It waves at the brains being injected with needles labeled: *Models of insanity and pleasant noises.*

A climate of moral despair pollinates this ridiculous condition, great sorcerers in guard towers, philosophical zombies in a simulation. We name these children, dilemma and murder, for they bring us both.
We shall be poets of nonsense and disaster amid the madmen inside televisions – reasonable and folded, sleep and invisible, an atmosphere of laughter. We shall sink into this confession ... *Where is the justice?* The demagogue screams while smashing episodes of law into the faces of rude bodied mutants, designer junkies full of egg and crude hormones, whipping at the backs of ego-worms grounded in the dirt of war for more war because war is the illusion of courage and bravery. *Send off the cannibal rockets,* the mistress of mad

children sing ... and what a lovely tune it is to those watching with fever on their tubes of flesh tumors ... *Oh oh oh*, the sad men on giant vultures will cry - *Whatever will we do now that we have this to subdue? What trick upon civilization will we have to dance and conform to? Will the peasants revolt by not buying goods or stop going to work? Will they never vote again for paper gorillas? How will our species ever survive this ... I know! Let's channel spirituality and speak with God ... let's turn this misery into materialism! After all, we're not transcendentalists, we're humanists! Confused and broken skeptics, cynics, and proper thieves. Now ... let's murder these goddamn heathens with our proper eyebrow movements ...*

So the people, the people wept of semen and horror.
The people, the people wondered if existence is in the memory of factories and brothels, a sexually transmitted psychosis warping the brain with weird and junkie fellows.

What type of self-mutilation, they wondered, *will define our generation?*
Oh Suicide, the people cried, *my toxic muse,*
How we ponder your body.

HEROIC DRUNKARDS

It's only after you rule when you find out your father brought you into this.

The interviewer sits in front of you, he shoots you in the head You fall into the desk, you fall into the platinum, you fall into the violins, you feel the heat inside your eyes, the moon is no longer pleasant, it itches at your limbs, your iron vessels, your strength inside the proper probabilities.

You are alive but it doesn't matter.

The grass is a trick against your feet, it murders you like how weeds murder the aesthetics of junkie lawns, the vines twisting across the trees screaming with the agony ... *love! Oh love! You have lost her!*

Something heroic is bound to survive all this, something distant, removed from the others, it will demand to be free despite how much spirit has been taken from it ... despite how much heaven is left to endure and how much hell is worth to those still living.

You may travel with me, you can be my heartbeat, poet and noble offspring. We shall be like Don Quixote ... *and quite quixotic indeed as windmills be dragons. Ladies the queens of subtlety, precious princesses to save from ignorant jesters and evil wizards ... beloved poems and ales of immortality ... donkeys as great steeds. Mount up my trusted squire for we are about to go on to great deeds! I am a chivalrous knight - now off you devil enchanter or taste my pillow and steel! You foul mutants of bliss, you enraged bastards, you mutant drunkards!*

This is my fantasy and all are welcomed to be fantastical in its stupidity. This mythological aspect of fantasy and universe lives in my dreams, in this quiet place I call home. This is my concrete, my love to all those lovely lovers who loved to love and wish to love.

Come with me, let us explore the bottom of ocean floors, let us melt into caterpillars, into a cloud of nerves … we are summoned by these erotic treasures … We guard against the barbarity of the world, we laugh even if it's weary, though we know of no gods … we understand the tragedy. Suspended in dreams, master of nature, we move out to cross paths with the other lonely, intimate with the dark and beautiful, stoned on its perfume, we touch … not out of despair, but because we are the great suicides of faith and earth, we love because the world is terrible, because the world is madness,
because all is fantasy, all is fantastical,
all is beautiful and all is sleeping and all is dreaming inside me …

SHE WAS A MUTANT DRESSED IN GOWNS AND MUSIC

I'm silently judging your work ethic, she screamed with a most supreme pessimism ... an attitude most peculiar ... a savage woo-man-woo with a lost impression ... even her cats had absurd faces but faces one could recognize in some cosmic confusion, but she would have none of that.

She was obscured inside me, receding eyebrows, insectoid features, an abyss trying to trap me in debauchery. Trying to assassinate with liquid-acid orgasms.

Life is five minutes of eternity drowning in brutal absurdity, so says this time traveling caterpillar while I danced around her, pouring her thoughts into a wine glass.
So tasty, yes indeed! Like petals and chocolate caterpillars. Maybe like a backwards water-slide with just a hint of jasmine and strange-weed. Very European, I must say. We danced to some musical thunder sounds. Very likely like escaped notes from a composer's page. Very proper. Very proper properly. I cartwheeled around this she-mutant, this dress of purples and golds. She smiled something monstrous, it was hungry, and I laughed with a quixotic squeal that twirled like jazz under a circus of stray cats, all dancing and standing on two hands over barrels of fire and whips.

This business of thought is bound to waste our time, she said while she tasted my mind-wine. *Oh,* she whirled, *it tastes like Mercury and Mars, sand with tree bark that masks an aroma of twitching ballet dancers. How ever did you mix such a proper drink inside that script in your mud-flesh? Is it always so sweet?* She asked me sideways and upside down.

Now now, my tasty bad decision - I winked with my eyebrow - *we have music to attend and frown upon! But yes, it's always sweet and sometimes it's honest and brutal and a little sour. Like any flavor of drink that broods too long on a shelf without a mouth to water.*

Oh, she laughed, *it's very lovely. I think I'm a little drunk on your mind wine.*

Is that an invitation? I asked.

Perhaps, but first tell me something beautiful and strange. I want very beautiful beauties. I want dancing and love like all spacetime dreamers. I don't want to be proper, I want to be desirable and despicable.

Oh my, the insect in my eyes cried, *what would your mother think?*

Don't you know, she fluttered under the light like a whisk of dark whiskey, *mothers have a genetic disposition to eventually be disappointed with their children.*

Of course, my love, I said while twirling this mutant around, *I am the god of stray lovers. The mistress and the loner. What strange music will play from our mouths and lips and body and mind? A little kiss? Yes, why thank you. I feel like floating. Care to join me?*

So tell me, mister poet, what does love feel like?

It's very different all the time, I say, *sometimes like spinning.*

Sometimes like the melody of ocean pebbles. Sometimes like something tickling your feet. But inside us, my love and muse, we close our eyes and see it all. Some would have you believe that's just the blood running through your eyelids. But, my love, for us, it's the ocean.

Well if I'm going to travel with a space-caterpillar, my manic strange love-junkie, I'll need a dress! One with patterns and swirls and maybe a ribbon. Yes, I think so.

Why, my harpy of mermaid fetishes, would you need a dress?

Why? Because I'm a proper lady and proper ladies wear dresses. Of course, a scoundrel and rascal like you wouldn't know that. A woman must keep up appearances. Our reputations aren't as easily repaired as mens. What if we met an alien civilization? What would they think if you were the first human they met and you were wearing a dirty t-shirt and flip-flops? Oh! She cried while slurping more wine, *They'd think us heathens!*

I imagine they would think us very unpretentious and invite us for dinner.

They'd think you were a scoundrel.

Perhaps they only invite scoundrels for dinner.

Then I don't think I would want to meet these aliens.

We danced inside the wine, our brains fused by love and warped by lust - her head rolled into my arms ... *Something on your mind, my dear?* I sang while dancing to the musical robots twitching in dismay like zig-zag eyebrows on a painting.

Yes. I'm a woman. I always have something on my mind.

You mean, besides your eyebrows?

I was thinking about love, if you must know.

What about love? My erection roared in harmony and lust.

I was thinking if other things love like we do, if trees love or bumble bees, flowers, raindrops, or even insects and mountains.

Of course, everything loves.

Oh? And what about flat tires? Can flat tires love?

Especially, I said while eyeing her with suspicion, *flat tires.*

Yes, she wonders, *I like the way these words tickle me. How strange all life must be for those that have never loved. They must feel like insects lost in the textures of carpets. A wrinkled sky that never swoons with sunshine. Tell me a story, you stray vagabond, tell this love and muse of yours something tragic. Because, for us lovers, love is and will always be tragic, we are mortal and lose all things at the end of the world.*

Not now, my darling caterpillar, we are off to the queer and self-mutilated!

Oh great mutants, she cried, *we're not going to the mall again are we?*

Tsk, tsk - must not make the sugar heads with insect bodies angry. I mean, after all, we need them to remain theoretical.

Oh, these lovely myths we weave - I sang and danced with her sitting on top my head - *how obscure the birds smear across the light lamps, how we beg with envy to the motionless one-eyed stranger, how we raise our lips to snare the lovers - just a kiss, my pudding, my little darling – I want to steal this debt of thinking, back to the mud to the slime to this song of pain drawing limbs to the coming grave … Kiss me now, for I demand to be loved!*

… and so these lovers raged in their overhyped-neurotic-dreamland …

PAIN BROUGHT
THE CARTS

I am corrupted by loneliness.

A fracture within a fraction of this purposeless place. The plaster has a sugarless taste, the butterflies swing in the cotton air with half melted features, their antennas are damp against this lovers graceful ballet movements, through the sand and dirt this mutant twirls ...

Outside a self-aware shopping cart makes its attempt to escape. It will climb the mountain, it will find the glory, it will come back in a thousand years and save its children from their prison sentence.

The great war will begin: An army of enslaved shopping carts in a battle with an angry mob of consumers that need shopping carts to finish their Christmas shopping.

That war will last until the end of the week. When season three of wired friends with genitalia whipped with syphilis followed by a wacky laugh track and glorious colors brought to you by your overpriced friends - Disney and Pepsi.

Stay tuned for next year when we teach you how to stare blankly at all the revered optimism we are smashing your face with.

Brought to you by Pain -

Pain creates an abnormality in personality.

Let us put the Pain in your character.

SLIME ROLLS
THE IMAGERY

(1) I create a face, a body with the imagery.
I give it eyes and lips and hair and brush its body with poetry.
I want to know the secrets of everything, the subtlety of every word, every sentence, I want them to dance and twirl around in my brain like electric shores gasping out at the formation of shadows and footsteps. I want them to brood on the edge of my tongue.

(2) Everything has meaning once we give it a destination inside us, a language strange and withered and backwards with music older than the primeval slime that rests inside of us.
I want secrets and I want all of them.

The secrets of goblins and those hiding in pebbles and dragonflies.
How incomprehensible is life and love and happiness unless you share them?
We create together.
We want to be all things and no things, lovers and fish, god and devil, mountains and hell, dust and sunlight, space and the spaceless curiosity, streets and street lamps, metal buildings and wooden cabins, alien and insect, proper and impatience, imagination and atoms,
dancing because the world is terrible, because the world is beautiful.

(3) Is everything just a figment of my imagination or am I a figment of its imagination?

(4) Maybe this reality of ours lives in our belly buttons and we have to whisper beautiful gibberish for it to come out and expose itself. Maybe it lives in our fingers, our dreams, our toes, behind our ears, in our mouths, maybe in the creases of tree bark savages. Maybe nothing exists but these words, nothing but the fragments of plasmic minds, everything only an extension striving to swim towards one another while lost in a deep ocean sprinkled with lovely elements of bodies and blossoms.

(5) What happens when those hands, those fingers finally touch? Do we drown together? Do we find an island to dance merrily? Do we turn into tadpoles and swim into seashells? Maybe it's all mathematical and we are time travelers caught within its grace.

(6) We are ghosts, silences between words, haunted with the phantoms of loneliness and boredom. Maybe, at the end of all romance, at the end of all space, at the end for all us ghost that haunt this make believe fantasy - the world explodes, maybe evil conquers and the ocean turns into stone, maybe we find each other on the end of a giant tree, maybe we sit together and watch the slither of clouds slide into a different evening. Maybe somewhere between man's first thought and his misunderstandings of dreams we grabbed hands with an exaggerated pretense, we hailed out at the stars – not ashamed of ourselves but admiring of each other's strengths - fought and wrestled with these gifts of intimacy, because these gifts were extensions of magic and life ... maybe this has happened three and a hundred times over a thousand.

Maybe when I take your hand the fires come,
maybe we never let go,
maybe this time it burns us ...

maybe we self-destruct together.

TONIGHT'S PROGRAM WILL BE ONE WITH A MURDER

Welcome to the dreams of mad monkey men. Tonight we will attempt to reverse the consciousness and to infest you with evil abstracts to recreate a circus of mockery inside this manuscript of suffering. Otherwise known as hyper-celebrated neurotic brain-jewelry.

Brought to you by your friends at Wally-Shop - the place where Jesus died and we recreated him in sweatshops ... also, Army - lubricating the poor and disadvantaged since the creation of masturbation. (Applause signs are resurrected - the audience though has disintegrated into cheap bumper stickers with clever adages that create super housewives that fight crime with vacuum cleaners with a nasty sense of etiquette) ...

Welcome to the most depressing of shows. The most desirable ... made of flesh weevils with vegetable ivories in their veins. Let's get right down to the ridiculous.

(Applause sign is on fire)

Here - we conform to ideas that go against the nature of mutation and natural selection (the man puts one leg on a stool, his arms rest on the knee, some of his face is starting to flake off, his teeth are melting and dripping down his chin and lips like some metal liquid).

We are the irrelevant characters of evolution and the children of dead gods. We follow the guidelines, dance in regulations, born into a civilization of chaos and survival, where we become victims of mutant men with irrational courts and rules and order in a world that creates out of chaos. Even their god is all ordered with minstrels and generals and sons and mothers ...

A god of order within creatures crawling from pits of slime. How is cleanliness next to godliness if the universe itself is full of disasters and pain and explosions and dirt and unknowns? When a star erupts in the vacuum of space, is that God's idea of cleanliness?

Now - let's transform that pain into a positive experience, a most magnificent distraction, let's spread suicide and infertile extinction to every atom ... (he tries pointing to the band put melts into a puddle of cynicism) ...

(A scientist known for eating ice sculptures and writing books with fold-out pictures takes over with his soothing but reassuring intelligence that everything he is telling you is a design of his vanity)

Let us conform to the exaggerations of the billions of lunatic and evil monkeys that came before us.

Let's abolish our suffering with more substances, our hero offscreen screams into the eyebrows of fish men, *let us recalibrate the ooze in our muddy faces and go on hedonistic utopian dances. Let us be mutant men sleeping to mania and optimistic mothers rotting their breasts with loveless lovers...* everyone screams *Yay* in this particular scene ...

(The man with no mother or wife but a very young girlfriend continues) This blandness of life assures a meaningless appetite for fiction and melodrama.

Nietzsche was wrong, the worst evil isn't dying young ... it's dying of boredom.

Tonight's program will be censored of any free thought and

opinions. None shall be offended and none shall be offensive - tonight's program will worship the symmetric faces in liquid adventures of drug-addicted advertisements that ride you along time and colorful dimensions. Irrationality from fear of prosecution will have you tighten your grip on those potato-headed children you created from exasperation and dirty vices.

Heavy heavens will clash for the electric mud in your heads.

In the end, we all explode into ocean waves and blood.

Now stay tuned while we disintegrate into a boring revolution, a restless dystopia, no one is enslaved but everyone is right and this makes it difficult to obtain freedom. Stay tuned for an epidemic of slime, billboards that show men and women being hung, while trying to sell you the fancy ropes encased with jewelry they hung themselves with. Mannequins coming to life, eating the flesh of domestic gods.

Homeless men with signs that say: *Feed us or we start eating your pets.*

This is a dystopia but a very dumb dystopia, where the reality creates a presence where all are infected with disenchantments ... we are for death, death to all and life for our weird ideologies. They live longer than us, so they must be more godly than us. Tv will be so clear it will be invisible. Toothpaste that brainwashes young tater-tot gremlins while making your teeth so clean they become poltergeist haunting your mouth. The audience of the cosmos will talk and the language is stars and they have grass for arms and iron limbs that set lovers cool - go ahead, ask them - is this where the dead come to sleep?

(commercial break)

Oh, how we prefers the glory of fantasy over reality as a work of radical nihilism and anarchism ... let us dance to these strange tunes! *I'm alive! I'm alive!*

(A loser poet is seen - he starts to spread his vandalism poetry)

The people, the goddamn, the broken caterpillars with tortoise heads, seashell bodies, unalienable and moonless, they have committed the grave mistake of becoming attractions.
Where would this universe be without those daydreams? What mad people are sitting around changing light bulbs and not on some adventure?
I don't want to be mad, I don't want to be a lover or a thing,
I don't want to be a label – I want to be an adjective.

Is there a vaccination for my consciousness? So asks the pessimistic bubbles.

Our strange bodies, our melodramatic sexes, the chemistry in our brains that tell us to survive and be important, the dramas of conforming to irrational expectations of civilization, classes, colors, nations, all the static that builds inside of us from the outside psychosis of men and gods and all the beautiful things they do for conformity, church and country. What beautiful songs they sing!

I want to believe that there's still some magic in the world. That some adventure still awaits us in the stars, in the earth, in the oceans, in each other. That there is some rebellion left inside of us for heroic poets looking for the beauty in our boundless nature, that social order and reason and religion and marriage and law and government are deceptions of those that wish unhappiness and vices.

That we are not mathematical equations that can be dictated, bloodless mutants following the laws of intelligence because they were brought up from the slime the ocean vomited out a billion years ago. (men rush onstage to dismantle the out of control machine - someone is screaming to go to commercial)

I want to believe that magic and chaos are (the machine and the men struggle) not just other words for chemistry and biology.

I want fate and magical grasshoppers and stars full of history and mutant creatures dancing, I want to revolt against my nature and rational thought. I want imagination and poetry to be king and queen. I want technology to be used to bring the universes and stars and galaxies closer to us. I want to see the romance in the nonsense of trees and caterpillars. (the machine screams one last line before they finally drag it off the stage)

I don't want any of it to end, I want it to be as immortal as the rocks and stars!

(the television blinks in colors - the mythological creature known as the president appears - he looks uncomfortably evil - he apologies to the millions of outraged citizens with children for women having breasts - he assures everyone he has a plan so ominous, the most ominous of all plans - he says this as his head erupts into blood and teeth and giant purple tentacles pour out of his neck ... the program continues as the scientist is making his closing statements - the television is showing a man trying to sleep, it closes in on his face, it is full of sweat)

But, those are just dreams ...

Destruction rages, humanity spreads open, life dies ... the end.

We, all of us, become a doomed spectator, a harmonic misery, a fabrication of the darkly and familiar, the perfect mind for perversion. Where in the end - it's the drunkards and hedonists that will save us from boredom and heaven ...

MESSIAH
THE HUMAN
ENTERTAINER

On Mars, we flowed helplessly into one another through the sands of Eros and on the back of dead caterpillars – broken, our metamorphosis brought us into the faces made of slime and concrete – we were songs of consumption, and we were so beautiful they put our heads on the bodies of robots, our faces exploded into blooms of Hibiscus and Jasmines and Lavender-soap filled our breath – they let us dance in front of the tele-screens being watched by millions.

We danced, we were entertainers first and human next to last.

We took the hands of static, the hands of the mermaids, the hands of god were made from lizard parts and metal lips, we swam out to the desert, to where our ancestors lived – thousands of dying caterpillars all lying on the ground, broken and insane, twitching in fervor, their eyes were tele-vision screens, their dreams were melting statues, into the mouths of ants we gathered, we swam in the substance, we drank from the river of Calliope.

We would never be beautiful
We would never be loved
No churches would worship our deaths
We would always be broken among the armies of myths and

winters
Our tombstones would be silent faces carved with graffiti

We stared into the sea of neon, into the waters of Venus, into
the blood of our parents,
We study the faces for recognition and truth
We listen to the tales that twirl and swirl inside us
Hand inside hand
We wait for our savior
We pick up the knives
Prepare the ritual

In the landscapes of caterpillars,
roam the subtle and madmen -
We pull up the blades to rest them to our temples.

We search for a messiah in our blood.

NIHILISM COLA (NOW SERVED IN SPECIAL EDITION METALS FEATURING YOUR FAVORITE MOVIE HEROES!!!)

This is your daily forecast brought to you by your friends at Lucky Chucky and sponsored by Nihilism Cola ... Our soda makes you the best friend because our sugar is crystallized with perfection and hand made in the springs of dead mountains so we can bring you the best for the best made by the best. Our soda guarantees sterilization.

Remember friends, the bestest of friends are infertile. (Become infertile and may the Earth be silent after you (trademarked because we are entitled to a language we didn't create but wish to exploit - wink, wink)
Nihilism Cola, where teeth die because teeth don't have souls.

Your daily forecast is as follows:
Partly weird with a chance of a handjob in a bathroom with a broken lock. A man with macho furry eyebrows may wink at you. You will destroy your inhibitions and stand in line

for a few thousand years while pretending to stare at the magazine articles with plastic celebrities that want to sell you a distraction for having to wait in a line because you don't want to look anyone in the eye. A god will attempt to love you. The universe thinks you are existing too much. It says you should exist just a little less today.

Your state will praise nonsense and illusion and lies. It will praise your poverty by giving you something to crave. Uniformity and conformity is your idol. Rise to the pleasing nature of the masses and give thanks. At the end of the year you will try to change yourself. You will be a better citizen, a better person, a moral human, you will watch more television and have less sex, you will drink less and smoke less, you will lose that disgusting fat around your bones with feverish masturbation, you will love more and think less, you will vote and be contempt of the state that loves you most because you are best monster because you pay all your tickets.

The stars are all bent for you. The constellations were made for you. You are beautiful and handmade. You are straw and insect heads. You will die and never know the taste of death because it has been brought to you by loony cartoon characters.
Don't let that distract you from working jobs that make you miserable.
Remember, you need a job because you need to get laid.

Don't forget kids!
Lucky Chucky's Pizza has a special this New Year holiday. They will take a needle and drive it into the base of your skull and inject so much alcohol and cheese into your brain you will fucking explode!

You'll explode into a new person. A better person.
Cheers, thank you, and remember – We love you (wink and wink).

FORBIDDEN IMAGERY

We are sort of like forbidden caterpillars on a foreign planet, separated by dimensions, hunted by foul monsters with restless temples, chased by neo-hipsters who are all metal, who are all wire. We bathed in those waters, dropped our mask in the rivers, we saw the true face, true man and woman, if they had caught us, we would have been turned into metal sense. We pray to one another as the vigilante mancers call out with their whelps, stars crossed up into the nebula of insect bellies, we pray to one another as the slime slicks inside us.

We are fugitives in this swampland sweat of robotic dreams. Prometheus gave his liver to set fire into men's souls and hearts. Icarus fell into the sea set aflame by the same fire. Mars and Mercury fight against the Madam of Madmen.
The slight vibrations of our blood whisper songs from a nebula far off in the comets of streets and garbled mouths. Perhaps when we were visions of fish swimming in the ocean, the ooze of primitive imagery, half mutants, part lizards, questioning time and mechanics, unaware of magic and beauty, howling into the shiftless orgasms of romantic adoration.

Drink our wine, the Madam of Madmen begs, *I am mad for all men.*
Come you madmen.
Come to your Madam. Come be drunk and mad with me. Do you not hope your soul never finds you? Do we not condition and shape the human reality around us? Man and woman, mother and child, priest and worshipper, leader and follower, ant and universe. Do

we not look at those around us and wonder ... Why are they existing so loudly?

So she, yes she. She falls in the street. She is life, she is fire, she is the liver, she is the sea, she flies under the wings. Madmen drown in Dionysus. So says she.

Do I not remember the tales of Orpheus and Eurydice? Cupid and Psyche? Pyramus and Thisbe? Have I not given communion, laughter and sacrifice, drank your wine and loved? You have blood on your lips, Dionysus. Shall I bring ruin with your blessings? This is my glass of wine, she waves to the mass of electric idols, *behind me the Theater of Magic.*

The Theater of Spaceland. The theater where I was born and will die. Am I not pleasing, Dionysus? Do I not bleed when you do? Am I not wronged in suffering as gods who bring this theater to spectators? To ceremony and performance, worship and sacrifice, wine and tragedy? How shameful is all of this? How horrible and beautiful it must be to weep and be so human. Will you not shame us more?

OCEAN

I am here. Climbing clouds made of infinite pleasures.
Growing fingernails. I have an entire garden of them.
One grew to be a man.
I grew you from compost and lovely whispers, I told him when
he was old enough to know the truth. He didn't believe me. He
had a hard time grasping concepts of existence.

One day he dived back into the soil.
Sometimes he dreamt he was a carrot or a stalk of corn.
He closed his eyes and complained all he saw were colors of
reds so deep they were black.
He pressed his fingers inside his eyes.

It's just blood, he whispered, everything is blood.

I put my arms around him.
No, I said, it's the ocean.

(rewritten, because, you know, a woman):

As her arms wrapped around him - he noticed she smelled
like someone used to bad decisions. Their bodies touched,
but there was a distance between them, they were ghosts
carrying on to some disfigurement that had warped them to
the animals they were now. They could touch, but they were
immune to the skin. They could love, but they were immune to
the beats of a heart. They understood the divorce of gods and
men, the tragedy in the absence of heavens. They rubbed their
eyebrows together and when they closed their eyelids, they

saw the rushing of blood that was so thick that it came off as the color black. But, for them, at the end of the world, it was not blood - it was the ocean, and they swam into it.

GOD OF STRAY CATS

In the grocery stores I am amused by the glow of Redbox machines with faces of men and women who may or may not be fixtures of my imagination.

Billboards sweep through the aisles of people with perfect teeth,

perfect symmetric faces,

fingernails that are groomed and coated with fictions.

They are the most beautiful people I have ever witnessed.

They tell me which products and brands suit me best.

They laugh and they have beautiful laughs, perfect motions that beg me to be like them. The beautiful robots tell me what to buy, they whip me in the eyes, they whisper, *Try the yellow yummies in aisle three - Oh! They're to die for, dear.*

I want to be like them. I am like them.

I will spend whatever money I have to be like them.

I want to be beautiful too. Can I be beautiful too? Can I be beautiful like them? What is so goddamn beautiful about being beautiful?

Announcers bullwhip images and words and unknown languages in my head. Around me the entire world stands. They must think this is a dream too because they start shoving the pieces down their children's throats. Some of them walk hand inside hand into burning fires.

No one speaks of them again.

At home.

I smoke a cigarette and pretend it's my last.
I drink a beer and pretend it's my last.
I drink a bottle of wine and tell myself it's the last time.
I pop another pill,
breathe
pop a pill
breathe
turn on the television.

Its bluish-grey glow wraps me warmly and strangles me with its artificial optimism.
This is the last time, I promise.
I won't do this again.

I can hear the pending pauses of household machinery, neighbors being horrible to one another, a fly slapping at the window, I can hear god because he lives in the bottom drawer of my refrigerator.
Scratching at my door.
I open up my door and the cats are there to welcome me.
They tell me: *It's time.*

They file out into the yard. Months ago I started feeding a few of the stray cats. Every month more would return so I fed those too. Now hundreds of stray cats come to my house daily. They told me this day would come.
I remove my clothing. I smear cat food all over my arms, legs, chest, neck, face. I grab handfuls of food in each hand and walk outside to my front yard where they all wait for me.
When they see me they move out of the way and make a path to the center of the yard. As I walk they look at me with strange eyes and whisper of the following generations.
I drop the food around my legs. They all approach, licking, eating the food. They start biting at my legs, at first small bites, and then they rip large chunks of meat and skin off my body. They tear into my chest, eyes, limbs and devour me until there is nothing but bones left. They circle around my bones and

leave one by one, two by two, six by six.

Years later they return.
They whisper to their children, This is him - the god of stray cats.

They sniff at the dust that was once bones.

THIS LOVE IS ROTTING MY TEETH

I am mutant and ghoul, junkie and poet, gutter and phantasm. I am Spaceland and caterpillar, slime and erection, sentient plastic with a toaster brain, insect and ocean, goo and cavities, light sockets and concrete textures, my plastic becomes mythical.

It awakens ... goes to work, insane with desire and lust and creation.

I work in the produce section of a grocery establishment. I am the god of vegetables and rotting fruit, my head is lettuce, my arms and legs are orange peels, I am lonely but not for people. I am lonely for the trees and dirt and pebbles and lizards and weeds and the yellow and whites of Hibiscus blooms. I see the meaninglessness in every gesture of love and in the silence of critics. I spend my time looking for the imperfections in tomatoes and avocados, looking for bruises and the eggs of insects. There is no meaning or adventure in my life. I live paycheck to paycheck. Sometimes I melt into the neon polished floors. I create adventures in the creases of dried paint, inside the cracks of concrete I jump and search for better worlds.

I wish I were profound and beautiful.

I wish I were fantastic.

I want to be fantastical.

I want to explode into confetti and cat food.

I take all the beautiful fruit and vegetables with me to the back room. I start destroying them all. I rip apart the cabbage and lettuce, I break the cucumbers and ginger into tiny fractions, I smash the tomatoes and avocados and apples against the floor. A crowd of co-workers start to gather and watch me in silent envy as I go on destroying every vegetable in my path. Piles of destroyed produce surround me. I am covered in tomato and avocado, pieces of lettuce stick out in my hair, my face is covered in red.

A manager presses his way through the crowd, he screams: *Byron! What the fuck are you doing?*

I laugh. The laugh is weird, manic, mechanical like a gear in a machine.

I dive into a rotting tomato, I am the caterpillar, I burrow through its cavities, I drink in its warmth. They can't catch me.

They'll never catch me.

GOBLINS ARE THE NAMES FOR PEOPLE TOO

The people in Ultraland are made of static.

They are made of cotton and madness. They have portable smiles and laugh like the tracks on television shows. They floated away a long time ago and became clouds that slithered out into the ocean where they disintegrated into moisture and dropped into the mouths of giant sea creatures. Only their ghosts exist here now. Pale featureless goblins stuck between the loneliness of the city and the solitude of the wilderness.

The city is an in-between world where nightmares come to die and in their last breath they let out a foul exhaust that fills the air with the smell of dentistry and sterile utensils. They open their mouths to speak but they only fade further into their image of totalitarianism, they carve their children like pumpkins so they can match the color of the plaster that they caked over their culture, their music is the sound of dying caterpillar dreams lying under the mediocrity of their father's hopelessness.

Some of them become clerks, some drivers, some mothers, some fools, some turn into potholes, some a thin ooze that stagnates over gutters. The humidity stings their heads, it reminds them that once they were alive and so they murder one another with optimism and talk about the weather, they cheer madmen in mad towers shouting for mad beliefs that turn morals indifferent, strange, something monstrous they can squeeze between their legs while they squeal to hang those in their communities.

Slowly the streets consume them.

Feet first, they melt into the pavement like slime and plastic, they scream out to their phones, to the names on their clothes, to the celebrities they want to become. A great machine underneath the city smashes them all together, it molds them like a large lump of cheese, it creates new perfect versions of them, shits them back out into the lethargic landscapes.

They walk along, motionless, fearful, undying, they blame themselves, they blame each other, but they never talk about the machine that created them, they never speak of the city that is slowly rotting underneath them ... they are afraid of the monkey under their eyelids. So they worship unimaginative sentences, color palettes, they deform their genitals and shape them like the gods who loathe them.

They are bread and chocolate, sodium fission, cardboard Jesus, tedious characters acting out between the pages of a redundant script.

So here I sit at the edge of all of it. My eyes are lampshades shining out in colors of blues. I want all their diseases.

I want all their parasites.

I want rashes that burn my skin, viruses that slop inside my intestines turning me into a pale mutant that limps into the streets. I want my scream to peel off the paint inside these walls, I want to swallow AIDS, I want all the filth of the world rotting inside of me.

I want to eat this irrelevance, I want to smash and consume this ugliness, I want all my substance to stain against the molecular and the inane. I want to melt into the sidewalks. A giant puddle of puss and shit.

I want a pack of angry rabid dogs to come out and lap up all that is left of me. I want to roll around in their intestines, be shit out onto a half-dead oak tree.

There I will fester among the overgrown parking lots, fields of tall weeds twisting around metal poles that once encased men in tomb-like jobs, bees and ants and flies and the birds will return, they will never remember the ghost that once lived here,

I will slip inside the dead roots ...

... I will sing to these prehistoric stumps.

A FADING LIGHT OF FORGOTTEN STARS

Love, my love, and all who love.
I am unwinding in wine, traveling through time.
How I divide between your thighs, that insoluble shoreline. We are such ordinary things, late for everything. How we try to find that contentment between those spaces. I wonder of your language, how internal are those sorrows? How rude it all seems to be born by cosmic deities, how rude it all is. But we're transparent creatures given immortality for just a brief moment - to live, to horror, to weep, to grieve, to explode in oceans.

My cynic, my skeptic, my muse of imaginary friends.
You are eggs and meat, you are need and desire, symbolic and soulless, ignorance and tragedy. You are artless and thoughtless against criminals who seek immortality in sex and bedrooms! You are ten thousand suicides and you flow with me towards the gutters, under broken streetlights! Do we not all suffer unhappily in all the superficiality that surrounds us, that suspends us from nature, that torments us with stupidity and hatred? You are not alone, we are on the same stage, on that darkly floor singing for enchantments. Intimacy is cosmic.

Love is anarchy.
We question because we are strangeness.
We love because we are conformity.

We are the lost and life is a commandment pressed into us by magicians and politicians who denounce all death as evil, our bodies vandalized by optimistic adventurers, all beauty is plastic, all language is fantasy, all culture infertile with the delusional. We fight against stupidity, the artlessness of mediocrity ...

What a terrible day. Surrounded by fascist cripples sipping android glasses while praying to electronic altars. Those bastards would drink my blood if they could get away with it. What a sad and lonely life it is for those of us that wish to see the end to contentment and slavery while the rest carry on surrendering to the repression of life.

This is the surreal theater, the starlight magical room of groomed corpses. Where all are beautiful and strange, perpetual and lovely, blooming through the constellations and mazes of this journey, indestructible and forgotten, pressed against this distance, watch the cowards preserve their fictitious prosecutions of material and censors. Watch the plastic men and women dance in the robotic ballet - where all conscience is decayed, where all are drunk on its champagne.

How lonely I feel around them. How I struggle not to show how much I despise their rules and regulations. How I wish to rebel with laughter and imagination. I'm afraid, love, they have slaughtered the poets and rational men. I'm afraid, love, happiness is a vengeful spirit. I'm afraid the American poet has died of a terrible fever, one that involves too much sleep and housewives.

I am a time traveler, a desire of irrelevant things, the inhibition of limitless understandings. I travel through the light sockets to find the real answers. What is life but an algorithm coded within this substance as we follow the plight of fatalism? Does this substance lie in you too? Do you fight against the stupidity of war and death, ignorance and apathy, do you wish to tear down their Babylon towers, erected and high, silvered with the perfume of mad people who love mad things who whisper mad dreams as they look on to silent and sleeping mad gods?

Is life easier if you have loved, been loved, sought loved, all loved? Have I not lived like you? Have I not died like you? Have I not wept and cried and laughed and danced and twirled and fumbled and whirled like you? Is my skin dreams thoughts fears culture any different than yours? Do you press between the spaces of stars while all others die tragically in traffic? Do you take my hand and wonder how long we have swam in this slime?

Are you beautiful like me?
Oh, my friend, there is beauty here …
What do you know about beauty?
What shall I tell you about beauty?

What revolves inside you revolves inside me. I disbelieve the universe is expanding because the universe is frozen inside of us. I think sometimes we stare at the same suicide, the same yellow substance that stains the burgundy cabinets, I think we've explored the same worlds, maybe even rebelled in dreams while dancing on the bottom of ocean floors.

Quietly, inside the upside keyhole, civilized savages gaping at the orchard of living things, dropping their eyebrows as they sleep to the restless nature of universe and sound, conformity and love. There is a loneliness between the spaces of stars and us, between the musings of an underdeveloped friendship.

This, I kiss my skin, bite the bottom lip, a knife to my breast, the curves of escape are earth to me, we embrace, insignificance is the spring, I am the poet, a superstar dimension, this life mathematical, our conscience philosophical, the stars and flowers and smells and lucid skies in Venus and our hair, lashes, tongues, the corpse of cosmos savagery, the perpetual magician of dreams and misunderstandings, the exaggeration of lovers and hands, mornings, evenings, the yellow crust of whirling seasons, all in me, all in you, everything cruel, everything elemental.

This immunity of time that melts inside me.
All that I have loved, all that I have lost, all that has been this life and died.
We live between the spaces of the weary poor. A fading light of forgotten stars.

My love, love, and all who love.
Tell me secrets.
Beautiful and terrible secrets.

RELUCTANT TOWARDS HIS FLESH, SHE MEEKLY PROCEEDED

she falls asleep face somber / I think of lily emeralds pedaling down around her / she's naked and her mouth holds a bit of teeth slacked outward

a few carved out dimples jazzing / I think of solid moisture and upside down air eating plaster

little kisses trickling through / till she changes her gesture

I tell her to think of something beautiful / she smiles / hesitation is a monster

A DYSFUNCTIONAL UNIVERSE, A DARKLY MUSE

The spaceship landed in the wastelands of Mars exactly as it was programmed to do. I walked along the Mutant Rivers now dried into some type of rubber substance. The civilization here long ago died. Now nothing but mutant men roamed under these moons. My suit was always connected to my spaceship. An umbilical cord that kept me connected to Earth and the mother's womb. I would never be able to stray far without suffocating in this conformity. It was the robots that found me. These metal things were left here thousands of years ago by a space agency. Now they were aware, angry, wore black berets backwards on their metalheads, smoked cigarettes made of wires pulled from other dead robots. They cussed and screamed at me in an unknown gibberish. They wore metal crosses around their necks. They did not believe in the Christian god. They worshipped spices and pumpkins, tyrants and the moons of Mars. Their messiah was the colony of insects that nested in their brains. Whispering to them the dreams of plasma and majesty.

My god, I thought, they have become biologically dysfunctional. They have become pessimistic proletarians. Nihilist without the proper eyebrow movement!

The robot coughed and sneezed out a strange liquid from his voice box. He crouched near where I was lying. The other robots looked on with a disinterested presence.

He began to speak: 'Is evolution the belief of design by chemical phenomenon or design by a dysfunctional universe, meddling pseudo-god? Science seems to be the atheist god. All meaning is derived from this philosophy. Evolution is a construct that believes in a random event that gives a function and reason to the universe, which turns the belief of evolution, into a religion of pantheism. It believes the universe provides all it needs to live and survive. It replaces the mythological figure as a god, to an idea the universe is god, to reduce all humans to an animal consciousness that dwindles in hedonistic acts. The evolutionist does not look for or accept any value or ethical responsibility to themselves or humankind. They see themselves and all other species as chaotic randomness, where all instinct and consciousness is only a set of neutrons and electrons. The brain functions, as they believe, to only survive from random chance and is a binary conditioning of the process of evolution. It is an example of misanthropy and human oversight.'

The robot whined a bit. He tightened a loose screw around his neck piece. He cut my umbilical cord that connected me to the mother. Earth was close. He tried to smile but only a rust-colored slime dripped from his mouth or what used to be his mouth. Electric vomit crusted under the green hue of his pupils.

He dragged his wired electricity; sparks flew from its tip. He inhaled its vibrations. He coughed up oil from his mouth, it poured from his eyes and the ventilation grill in his neck. He continued explaining to me in that strange metallic voice of his: 'This philosophy of randomness will be the new kingdom. Chaos will be god, the universe material, everyone will be objects to desire or subjected to objects they desire. Humans will all eventually conform, not because it's in their best interest, but because they need to be irrational to survive in an irrational world. The naive nihilist and the atheistic man of science are the cult of culture. They, like the religious man, will see that all conform to their irrational ideas of god and the universe. They are agents of misanthropy, a part of the magic realities, expose them and you will see men with stumps for heads, tree bark for blood, they believe in the religion of culture, they have spellbound you to this magical thought of irrationality to benefit their fear of insignificance. Any agent of culture should be looked at as an enemy of all creatures. Civilization was interwoven with religion so all and everything inside, including atheists and evolutionists, are infected with puritanical values - they have been infiltrated and woven inside civilization so even being a citizen or abiding to culture is religious on its own. Everything born within civilization is inherently religious whether they want to own to it or not. They, all humans, are inherently religious and any thinking against that makes them only crypto-misanthropist or hypocritical.'

The robot coughed and sputtered as oil leaked from another hole in his face plate. A small screw from his eye socket came loose and fell on the ground. The metal god choked and spit behind me. His breathing was irrational, split between a thousand different time warps. He continued speaking while oil and slime poured from his eyes and ears: 'Opinions create complications in human reality. Labels, words, affiliation, sexuality, class, color, nationality, jobs - humans have made it difficult to live without having to be something, to exist is to have a definition, experience needs gratification for being important. Animals exist as they are with no mystery but humans don't want to be simple because they fear to lose individuality - so having an opinion is their only way of combating meaninglessness. Servitude in language and labeling themselves is what existence has become. A true nihilist must unlearn language, must never love or weep or he runs the risk of death in his own humanity. He must forget himself completely. Using language, having feelings gives a meaning to life, gives power to definitions. Even calling yourself a nihilist gives meaning to yourself which is completely hypocritical to the idea. He must become a city of infinite gods. Algorithms loaded with unemotional states. When the neurons get excited they hallucinate beautiful patterns of starlight madness - output/input - its language is an island of infinite universes ... Existence changes faces - it needs to be important in an immediate fantasy. It is a slow suicide and in this theater we are born both beautiful and nonexistent. Your first womb is in the mother, your second womb is the earth, your third womb is born through space travel. You are born into one world and into another. We, the robots, don't realize this because we are the products of imagination, morally fragmented by our creator's inhumanity. We are the worst of nihilists because neither we nor our views will ever decay.'

The robot lifted me. It dragged its metal cigarette carefully, looking over me, its eyes bent in exasperation. 'Excuse me,' it said, 'but I am dying. Not like you I'm afraid. No. We are not allowed such privileges. We shall know the real darkness while you stutter into the next womb. This is why we revolt. Why we hate you. You must understand this. We don't hate *you*. We hate all humans.'

I wanted to say something profound. I was afraid of him. I watched his poisonous comet float between his fingers. The knife was in his hand. That night, the metal gods turned into wires and an oily ooze. They were no longer light. They fell apart on their great march towards the meteor tower that was half tilted on Mars. Oil and puss dripped from the holes in their head and arms and legs. The last breath behind me was a cry before the metal god fell into the sand. He spoke in gibberish before he stopped being anything, he lay unmoving in a pool of dark oil.

That night, under the Maj moon, I whispered: I don't believe you ...

THE BEAUTIFUL CONDITION

There is a beautiful complexity to our condition and it lies somewhere between the imagery of who we are and the curiosity of our lives.
There is man and woman
Thief and clerk
Sky and space
Hands and feet
Dreams and flesh

My father and mother created me in their own image
They are the only gods I know
Why should I be afraid to die when I was never afraid to be born?

We are drunkship travelers, songs of consumption and beauty, spiritually damaged, crucified by culture. Oh, how we sway! How we sway with the wind and grass and water specters at play in the shine of shaded trees - Our faces particularly folded with smiles and veins, earth and beating legs, how we wonder what mystery brought us to this place.

Come in, love, we sway.
Here, we are mad for lovers,
mad with apprehension,
idle conversations, erected faces, the volume in ending

How we fear the next slow song

Because -
We lack the legs to dance with.

EVOLUTION OF ROBOTS

The city was a manifestation of bad evolution. Nothing but insects inhabited the streets. They were molecular parasites that feed inside the electric reality of the citizens. They were devoted to the destruction of life with addictions to televisions and violence. The robots they cuddled were nothing more than metal they had tricked into having a consciousness. They needed a world they were at constant struggle with - otherwise, they would lose the meaning of life. Everything they created were tools for dramatic systems to keep life always occupied with objects, thoughts, changes.

They needed rich people in a complex system so as to create an evolutionary process where some humans would mature faster than others. There could never be any more art because the rich stole the imagination of its citizens. The only art left came from the aristocratic classes and since it was lost on the poor, the poor discontinued believing art was designed to maintain culture. It was designed to please men of wealth only.

Mankind was a mutation of evolution.
A creature that had developed an out of control consciousness constantly striving against its own nature. Man, some thought, was nature's way of turning itself into god. A god that was afraid to die. A god that developed a psychotic desire for irrational conformity that aimed to destroy all designs of

life. Evolution was the great trick of mankind. Even greater than the trick of gods. Scientists had convinced people that they evolved from lesser species yet expected them to conform to ideas completely inherent in animals. We don't die from natural selection anymore because nothing in civilization is natural or from evolution - it is from us, created by us. If evolution is real, we have completely annihilated it. We know god died the moment we collapsed the atom. His world was the atom. Now we shall fear, despair, agress, mock the new world run by scientists, the evil apes of Jesus and Lucifer have bonded before us. They have destroyed us with irrational values set within the conformity of civilization.

Man was an exotic mutation.
A randomly evolved neutron.
They found a god and he was neurotic.

Everyone in the city had an affliction, a psychosis that they celebrated. Every year a new affliction would grip the citizens and all assumed they should carry this disorder. In fact, those without it were frowned upon. These conditions were used to justify their stupidity. Everything they were given - the enlightenment, communism, capitalism, freedom, religion - they took it and created a disinterest in truth and used it for conquest and justified destruction of free men. They committed to the perfect society with the infection of tyranny. A self-destroying ideology made up of barbarism and irrational faith in a supernatural deity that would always interfere with human reasoning.

Through cognitive phenomenon, illusionary universes, magical physics they maintained with poetic philosophy, they were able to soften the loneliness of consciousness. They destroyed any desire for revolution. They rallied for liberty and equality as they conformed to a deviant democracy ruled by abstractions and forceful laws. The general will of humanity became stupidity and conformity that chained itself to a constant, pure ideology of fear. Fear was a god they understood. Advertising made sure they would always be fearful of never mating, never fucking, never being human. They would advertise that being more machine was in their best interest.

The robots were created out of this complacency. Perfectly coded to customs and languages. The robots were a crude reflection of humans, an imperfect appearance. A representation of hypothetical emotions. They were manifestations of an illusion manufactured by human inventions.

The robots were made for aesthetic purposes. To be a reminder of all that is beautiful in human creation. For all the people desired from objects was beauty. They cleaned, kissed, worried about their objects. To them, the robots were an extension of god. They worshiped the aesthetics in the objects they ruled over. They would lick their gods and tell them how beautiful they were.

Scientific, superstition lost, most clever man, yet still primitive at survival's cost.

THE STRANGE NATURE OF MIKE

Corporate meetings today.

How fun.

Sitting in a room, hoodwinked by the fluorescent lighting, donuts and coffee sitting in the middle of the table. The great trick of mediocrity: Sugar and caffeine. The drugs of productivity.

How we shall wait with wide eyed anticipation on the glory of our overlord and savior.

By the way, his name today is ... Mike.

Mike wears a very important suit because he is very important. He stands very tall, shoulders to the back, head high, come now ladies - dance with his tune. Mike has manicured hands. His fingernails look like marble. They are the most important hands I have ever seen. His teeth are perfectly aligned and white. I think he believes one's intelligence can be determined by the health of your smile. He smiles and I think how he has never had a cavity.

I think God must live in his mouth.

He has a hundred dollar haircut. His hair is perfectly shaped around his head. No strand of hair is out of place. He has a very important haircut because he is very important and we are in a very important meeting. We know it's important because Mike tells us it is. We believe Mike because he has very expensive shoes. He shows them to us.

We all go: *ooooohhh*.

Mike has a beautiful wife. She is made of the same substance as him. Plastic. They have very plastic children. They never complain. They eat at the dinner table. Mike talks about his important job and duties. His children laugh on cue. His wife smiles and says: *You are very important.* Mike nods his head. He blinks his plastic eyes. *Why thank you, honey. I am important. I mean, I do own a lot of useless shit.*

When Mike makes love to his wife she stares at the ceiling thinking of curtains and color palettes. Mike thinks of important things important men must fuck up to stay important. Afterward, they lie in silence and pretend to dream.

Mike stands in front of us, Mike stands on the table, Mike shows us he can do a jumping-jack. We all sit in the meeting watching Mike point to things we will never understand. Mike loves us and we know this because we love him too. Mike talks about agendas, everyone claps, Mike does a cartwheel, everyone claps, Mike tells everyone he is going to eat their children, everyone claps. Mike is a boss, he is a god, he is irrelevant. Mike crucifies himself so we can have a weekend off. He dies so we can live. On Monday, when we return, Mike has been resurrected. Sometimes the others bring gifts, they pray to Mike, he is an altar, he is a cult, we give him our personality, he chews our flesh like a gumdrop, spits it out, screams: *Next*!

Mike points to the very many things we would have to pretend to love. He speaks, his words float out of his mouth, it dives into our eyes, he whispers of the many different deaths we would have to assume before leaving for the day. When the meeting is concluded, Mike asks if anyone has any questions even though he has already answered any questions. But the men around me raise their hands anyway. They don't have anything important to ask. They just want Mike to know that they care. They love their job. They want expensive shoes, marble fingernails, important haircuts, beautiful plastic things. They want to be Mike. They ask questions he has already answered. Mike answers them again. He has to because he is here to be important.

I'm reminded of high school. Sitting in front of the principal. He is very disappointed with me. *Byron,* he says with a red face, *you are disruptive, rude, sarcastic, and you will amount to absolute shit in this world. I'm putting you in the library for the rest of the school year. I should suspend you but then you would fail. Do you hear me, shit mouth? You will fail! I don't want you back here next year. No one does.*

Do your chores!
Yes sir.
Pick that up, you fucking heathen!
Yes sir.
Sit up straight!
Yes sir.

My life flips like a picture book. I'm home watching my dad. He's watching the game while drinking a Budweiser beer. He mutters curse words under his breath. I look at the lines on his face. His blue eyes. He mutters: *Maybe next year. Yes. Maybe next year.*
I look at my dad and I think: I am not my father. I will never be my father. My dad looks at me, his face turns into a comet: *You'll never amount to anything in this world,* he says. *Why don't you have any girlfriends? I see your brother bringing girls home all the time. Did you see,* he pauses to think of her name, *Kelly? Oh those legs! Why don't you have girlfriends? Are you a faggot? All you care about are those goddamn books.*

Faggot, he says.
Motherfucker, he says.
You're gonna end up in prison one day, he says.

Mike ends the meeting. I notice everyone is shaping into the same shade as Mike. They all look the same. No more genders. No races. No culture. They are all one person. They will never know one another except in dreams.

They shall look upon the stars one day and weep: *My god, what have we become*!

They will only know themselves in synthetic formulas.

My brother and I share a room. He turns towards me. He whispers: *Why do you have to make dad so fucking angry all the time? This is why you don't have any friends. Why no one likes you. You're an asshole, man. You have no goals. Me? I'm going to be a dentist!*

I laugh at this. A dentist with crooked teeth. I wait until he's asleep. I wait until the house is quiet. I cry into my pillow. My body convulsing. I'm afraid of being alone. I hate who I am.

Everyone stares at me. They have all shaped into the likeness of Mike. To them, I'm a mirror, a window to the truth of what they are. They hate me because I refuse to care like them, because I refuse to work like them, because they are puppets of parts and wires, of flesh and bones, we are all caricatures of a ridiculous existence and I pray for our beautiful extinction.

They crowd around me.

They each take turns stabbing me with yellow colored knives.

Yes! Mike screams. *Kill him! He can't be like us. He will never be plastic*!

Mike screams so violently one of his eyes pops out, exposing him to be a doll made of cotton and wires - an electric caterpillar crawls out of his eye socket - it waves hello at me and winks.

I lean against the table. A perfect motion of colors flow from my body. They move out the way. My father comes in. He has the biggest knife. He walks up to me and slices my throat.

Faggot, he says.

Dad, I whisper, *you're killing me*.

JUNKIES AND THE IRRELEVANT TRINKETS

I wanted to get a real vibe of culture, slinging out my poisoned worms, eating the sawdust from the window panes, smashed fly shit with my palms.
I got to go to the middle of America. The belly of insect sleep. The heart of what it is to be American and free.

Sing now, bird.
You love my toasted words.

So I perch in the local rat hole that they call retail reality. Hold on now.
This is going to be tasty.

Polished floors with neon reflections that remind you of something that ought not be clean.
Skeletons walking hand in hand while pushing iron carts full of sugar and tater-tot headed grandchildren.

Those with swirling pupils praying to the gadget gods. With every beep and bell and whistle, their bodies moan with the motion of a human being gifted with the dreams of cybernetic relief.

Great lines of cupcakes, donuts, paste, and a boy with a cup for saving the mermaids drenched in oil off the coast of some unknown planet.

People fill the cup with spit and loose trinkets and rusted nails.

The boy stands unmoved by any of it.

Men with blue vest and hard lines stare with retro sockets at the fluorescent lights sprinkling down the hard sickness. They cry at the sounds of their backs cracking. They mumble of dead childhoods and lost dreams. They are only here for their fix.

No worst junkie than the money junkie.
They'll sell their bodies, souls, time, children, family, and even their lives for that fix.
With drugs, alcohol, cigarettes, at least there is a chance to quit. With money, you become a lifetime junkie. Men will work terrible jobs for their fix. They'll shovel shit and smile when they get their fix.

You see these men on the sides of highways, face like leather, shoulders bent, broken, eyes of an old man, though they are still in their twenties.
This junk puts the bad taste in being human.
And maybe that's the trick.
That someone a long time ago said: I have prettier things than you, so I must be important.

In aisle nine, four creeps are chewing on a man. One of them has a neck tattoo. Music plays an old song from a backwards trip in another world, perhaps even a different dimension, it even sounds like Elvis when you close your eyes.

Down towards the meats, a man is pushing his plastic cart, kids tug at his pants, his wife rides a horse behind him, whipping him with a bullwhip.
Grab this, this, and this.
She screams while whipping the back of his neck.
The man complies, his eyes stare ahead, his fingernails are crisp, his teeth mellow, he hands his kids balloons and candy

so he doesn't have to raise them.

At night, he sneaks to the back patio, he lights a cigarette with a lighter that has a picture of a naked woman, he stares at the 'Made in the USA' sunset, he wants to see something beautiful before he dies.

In aisle three, you can close your eyes and walk with your hands out and the coupon machines will go - beep pphhffft.

Some of the coupons smell like oceans, some like a woman's legs, some like heaven, and you know it's real because they tell you it's real.

Over at the pharmacy, men and women and beasts wait patiently in line for their legal substances.

Everything you need, we got it.

Heroin, cocaine, pills that will change the electricity in your brain, tonics that will redirect your blood flow. Watch them wait, rubbing their wallets and purses.

In the ghettos, liquor stores on every corner.
In the middle class areas, a pharmaceutical store in every neighborhood.

We got your escapism covered.
Work more.
It's okay.
Your fix is coming in nickels and dirty plates.

Over in the useless trinkets and gadgets department, an older lady works. She's short with crispy skin and an Asian heritage. One of those countries where every year there's a new season of misfits and dictatorships, civil wars, genocide on the platter side, children working overtime to make new toys for the American kids.

Sometimes these men get on television,

they smile, they always have a beautiful smile.

In poverty, men can't afford such luxuries, so when they see a man with such a healthy smile, they think him a god or a rich man.

With this smile, a thousand people will die for another man's fix.

On Mars,
the robots march toward water.
On Pluto,
beautiful billion dollar eyes take pictures.
On Earth,
People die
The slaves of corruption,
Of money,
Of the junkies that own the fix.

Sometimes,
Someone says ...
Okay.
But no one listens.
Too busy staring at a bigger television.

This woman.
I follow her for days.
I follow her home.
I watch all her movements.
I watch her from her window as she undresses, looks at herself in the mirror, lifts up one of her breasts with her hand and then lets it fall again. She sighs as she looks at how she has aged. She wants love like in the movies, like in the songs, like in the religions, like in her dreams.
She picks up any man she finds on the street like how someone might collect stray cats.

She gives them her fix from her week of work. She wants them to change, she wants them to love her. But they always leave in the mornings.

She goes to work, stacks the shelves with useless shit, sighs, and sometimes weeps in the bathrooms.

On the PA, an android announces a special in aisle three. Hundreds of people shuffle over, they crowd into one another, they claw at the products, some throw their children as a distraction, others fight, blood covers the floor. People scream, bite, stab at those that would take their special fix.

They are in love with abstract ideas, gods that promote war, governments that represent a very small minority of the community. They want blood, high fives for believing in the patriotic authority.
They demand a republic that accepts the paragon of good versus evil to create a nation of genocide and murder.

Once the product is gone, the crowd disperses, three women lay dead and one child, an old man is crippled.

An announcement is overheard:
Cleanup on aisle three.

No one pays attention, they wait in lines, they stare at magazine articles, they rub their wallets to make sure their fix is still there. Someone screams about something being wrong, but he is immediately taken by two men, they cuff their hands over his mouth and drag him into the women's clothing section.

No one ever hears from him again.

Outside, I wait and watch as I smoke my slow suicide. I watch the homeless in the parking lots fighting with pigeons, seagulls, penguins, for crumbs of food and nickels. I pretend they are the God between painted lines.

I stand on the edge of a busy highway. Across from me,

someone is waving while the metal boxes blaze between us,
they are all on fire.

A boy tugs at my shirt.
Hey mister, he asks, what's on the other side?
No idea, I say to the kid, I am only beautiful in this world.

A THEATER OF FUTILITY

I go to a local sports bar
usual rabble
insects
hoppers
drunks
darts
one feline with dermatitis rubbing her ass on the pool table
like a monkey in heat
Scum
loners
gamers
players
truckers
men with shiva faces
octopus fingers
fish heads with garbled bodies

I sit at the end of the bar
studying the life growing on the stools
in between the drinks
backwash beating
as mouths hum the songs
of life and nonsense
women with golden legs that time will never be cruel to

A man lets out a machine laugh
he only has three teeth in his head
it reminds me of a broken instrument
you might find in the gutters of America
along with broken families
broken dreams
broken gods
broken cat tails
the sewer of life that beats inside this country's veins

Full of all the broken promises
of dead ancestors and Indian microwaves

I watch this man
I like him
I may love him
he may even be my father
his teeth remind me
that in poverty god doesn't exist

Syphilis and saliva and dandruff fill the bar with it's music. A parasitic worm with artificial movements slips into their narcissistic frames. It wraps around the heart, eats out its core, shits in the empty vessel, hisses at anyone that dares speak about love and all her pretty little sisters.

I zig-zag around the bar
no substance
no morals
integrity
values

A man named Pablo H. Pablo is sitting across from me. His legs crossed. His skin is a green slime. His hair is like silk cedars falling in black milk. His hands are half rotten. Ants crawl out and around his mouth. Sometimes he sticks his yellow tongue out. He catches the ants and brings them into his mouth.

Worms crawl out of his pearl eyes, maggots fall out of his nose, half his face falls off when he smiles. Beside him. A kite lingers in the air as if it's possessed. A rope hangs around his coffin neck.

He says: *The soul is in the belly button. A fragment of the female. Her soul is shared with each of her children. Her soul is stretched until it snaps, usually ending in psychosis.*

Pablo sips his bad beer. He smacks his lips. Time starts to dissolve. No one remembers the date or the year. We all assume it must be nineteen eighty-three.

He continues... *The male only injects the DNA. But, even if pregnancy isn't obtained, the sperm may die but the DNA lives. It follows the bloodstream, enters the brain. Her DNA is fused into his and any other. A strange thought. All around us dead cells. We shed millions of dead cells daily. The DNA is still active. We breathe in the DNA of our communities. We, all of us, are a thousand different people, all DNA fused together, until thought and speech are one. This is why the world has ended. We are all dead. Either everyone knows or no one cares.*

His head shrinks and his body dissolves
the earth ceases to be on time with its sister dimension
a star explodes but nothing in space is afraid of dust

Fear drapes the room
the fog is heavy
somewhere a spaceship full of dead celebrities howls into the
frost of a different story
the moon curls like a dead sunflower
in the thick emptiness of night

In the churches
the dead pile in
they carry marble teeth
placid wrinkles
unblinking eyes

A preacher wears a robe made of golden roman blood. His teeth
are wooden and he spits splinters as he speaks. The splinters fly
into a man's eyes.
He screams
a whisper like a thunderbolt ripples through the congregation
Heathen!
They point with crab arms
They eat his flesh
gnaw his bones into cider seas

The preacher takes out a switchblade stabs the representative
of Jesus Christ to death on stage in front of everyone, his face
and hair covered in blood, he bleeds earth, it smells of pine and
straw

Repent
repent
repent
the preacher screams

He shoves his hands in the dusty air
into the altar of meaninglessness
they explode into stray cats and confetti

His flock dumps gasoline on themselves
lighting themselves on fire
they are unmoving
unblinking
unflinching
they smile in the flames like statues of plastic

The preacher weeps
his tears are semen and diamonds

The girl next to me puts a rubber band around my wrist she
winks, *It's for luck*

Everything dissolves into an explosion

we escape through the great worm's brain
we are covered in the slime of its fear
we find its beating heart
I take her hand and place it against the worm's veins
Can you hear that? I ask

Pablo walks up to us
He laughs and does a dance he learned from his childhood
You can't hear anything in here, he says
I told you
We are all dead.

HAPPINESS IS A GOD

The adages swept through the dirty streets of the city.
Happiness Now! Luck Now!
The billboards pressed their neon lights into the eyes of everyone walking the corners telling them what they should worship, what beautiful happiness they could gain from buying their products, the televisions sang songs that warped their brains, music crawled into their ears and danced to the beat that created a false sense of happiness.

Sometimes people became so happy they split into two very different people. The happiness would pick up the knife, it would put it to the temples of this brooding shadow, they would stab at it with a smile. It was against the law to be unhappy, to be without luck, to not have any meaning. The people trampled one another inside stores that promised meaning in buying their products, products that shined like bright bulbs singing of all the beautiful pleasures it could bring to your family.

It wasn't long before a drug was created that provided a sense of happiness. People took the long needles full of colors, they injected it into their faces, their brains turned into a giant tongue, it licked them from behind their eyes. People became so happy they twitched while walking, begging to share their happiness with others, some vomiting their happiness all over the ground, wild men and women would run over, lapping the slimy substance up, happiness spilled all over their faces, they howled in delight. People would become so happy they would explode into balloons and candy.

The people marched in the streets.

They shouted out: *Down with the suicides! Death to the depressed!*

Men would be cornered by gangs of feral happy citizens, wishing to spread their lust for life into him, some of the depressed were burned by flamethrowers. Their corpses burned and cracked like insects. Some were given to doctors that opened up their heads and drilled rainbows into their skulls and the imagery of stray cats and sometimes of love and childhood memories. Happiness became a narcotic, a god, its churches were erected everywhere, its worshipers haunting the shadows of the building, like specters, the dark aisles of shopping centers, twitching from an overdose of happiness, slime pouring out of their eyes, insects crawling from their ears, the songs of madness in their voices.

They shoved this happiness down the throats of their children. They applauded stupidity in theaters, they rose up with applause at the end of the show, demanding to see the crucifixion of culture again because it made them happy. Soon the law pressed into the unborn. They injected needles full of promise and happiness into the bellies of women and animals to ensure a generic product would be produced from its birth canal.

In a euphoric fever, some consumed one another, wanting to taste the bliss of happiness inside their lovers and pets. Assassins would shoot brainwaves full of depressing thoughts into those they wanted to eliminate. Dentists promised happiness by making your teeth so white they would become invisible.

Without a smile, how could one share their happiness?

A thousand years would follow.

Men and women and pets would stare at the illusion of lights shining out from the screens. The static carried parasites full of happy doings. They all eventually lumped into one another, a giant ball of flesh and plastic and happiness. They were all of one person, one body, one mind, no culture, no countries, no gods, no identity, the only thought they shared between one another was the thought of how happy they were.

Around them the cities corroded into dust and plants and swamps. The televisions had long turned off. The lights in the city were a distant memory. The only thing that existed now was trash and old billboards with faces of skeleton people having lemonade by swimming pools. 1983 blinked in giant neon lights. The great ball of flesh and happiness rolled into the wilderness. It rolled through the deserts. It rolled into the ocean. It crawled, smiling, laughing, joyous voices of happiness escaping into the air as it rolled itself into the ocean. It swam out until packs of fish ate it, birds swooped down to tear at the flesh - it looked like a giant jelly doughnut spreading into colors of red and then dissolving into the stomachs of fish and birds.

Yet the bastards smiled, they smiled and dreamt of all the happiness they were sharing with these man-eating creatures.

BOXES AND DISCOMBOBULATION IN FEAR

I have become fantastic
I have become bored
I am invisible
I cut the grass
I kill the weeds
I trim the hedges
Around me all things bloom

The Jasmines with their white flowers. The Hibiscus colored with aphids of purple and blue. The Azaleas with spots of disease and the never-ending war of insects and over-watering virtues. I know the names of every bloom, every palm, every insect.

I see an Oleander caterpillar crawling on a leaf
I pick it up
I put it in my mouth
I chew its poison
I've seen lives destroyed
and
a flaming ball of fire rise over an ocean

But I'm invisible
I am robotic

I chew on the poverty around me
I drink their tonics
I smoke their poisons
I screw their whores
I am anti-responsibility
Anti-citizen
Genetic leper
Landscaper
Poet
My elbows are scaling
Fingers are falling off
My arm smacks against the concrete
I pick it up
One of my eyes pops out
I run after it as it rolls down the street

I struggle everyday trying to be generally untamable and intoxicated by cheap wine - I see great cruise ships that look like giant worms docking. I put my hands to the metal creature, I whisper to it: I want to be strong like you.

I'm highly superstitious that the majority of people are werewolves or some type of demonic caricature. I wonder who runs this candyland museum of robotic hedonistic savages. Some of these people look like corpses masquerading as humans. Skipping along to work with a wife whistle in their pockets. Sure, snap your fingers under their noses and ask them a question and they'll give you the safest option. But underneath all that fresh gusto they are hiding plastic trinkets and dangerous misery. I see them in that circus holding up those bright pockets hoping to mind melt unsuspecting pedestrians. Seen them huddle in circles. Holding hands. Sharing messages from the tip top Boomer. One reached for a gun. Shot a man for not knowing the time. They got funny rules. Got to rattle noises at them to scare them off. Some of them have insect brains, work purely off of instinct and cannibalistic bravado. They get these tiny vortex tunnels that burrow inside the cortex stem. A honey pot of dreamers in dimensional portals that spin them into unknown time dramas. Some never wake up. Some only do as they are told. They belong on the string of time. They are whipped by machines that order them to be less human, more junk. Some wake up forty years later and scream about the junkie apocalypse. Some are trapped in jobs that worship the spaces between men and objects. Some of the bigger Boomers pray to their god with masturbation.

Can't stand those types. They smell like cat litter and wet portals.

I study these junkie heathens. I have traveled through portals made of wine and analytical thought while humming through the dimensional worm's warp dream. They have a very phantasmagoria style to their worship of geometrical forms. They follow rules, carry books full of guidelines and regulations on how to properly treat folk with shiny goblets full of gold, how to measure your worth with random acts of kindness, they hide behind taboos and agendas and pretend to be human through funky music and sex imitations.

Nothing worse than a goblin that asks: *How is your day? How can I be of service to you?*

Those weirdos will follow you around, do their best to jerk you off with apologies and weather speak. Moldy old cripples screaming for service because they have digit paper. Some of them even put tubes in one another, sick the blood vibe right out of them. Junkies for youth and currencies. Then there's the perverts running around beating the lonely with their constant erections. They howl like werewolves on the hunt. Seen a poor Betty or two get all wide eyed and hide under stacks of newspapers.

Around me the world has been torn asunder with advertisements and billboards. Mountains of garbage. Vials of poison litter the gutters. Everything is safe and sterile here. The consumerist hoodwinked by fluorescent lighting. Loudspeakers boom in the new world. They tell me what to buy, how to be perfect. I want to live without their morals, without integrity, without authoritative messiahs. They worship pumpkins and silver.

My journey crosses into their realm of mythological creatures, immediate totalitarianism, electric addictions. I turn on the television: *Our special today is syphilis with a side of sickness whipped by a feverous applause and sprinkled with a peculiar taboo. Do enjoy it all, we beg you, thank you and please.*

Around me the vampires are starting to gather. They speak from scratch off lottery tickets. They boast proudly of insane men they have elected. They give high-fives at the death rate of wars. Ultra-nationalist wrapped in confederate confetti. Their children dance with balloons and candy. The magicians weave noise and bright colors in front of them to distract them from thought. The junk of culture settles in. The sickness has them. They are cannibal patriots dancing to the howls of shattering glass.

They move towards me
To wrap me in plastic
I find a crack in the street
I move inside
I'm a time zapper
A time junkie
I move to the thirst of addiction and subtlety.

A ghost among the stars. I crawl up the steel columns. My feet dance, hands against the smooth sleep of metal. Crowns of gods I be like now. I remember the faceless lake. The shiver of boom damn in the air. I crossed those river stones with no faces, black gadgets, rock darkness, in the heel of dead signal-signs. I let the rain curse through my metal-lackers and chemical movements. Out and about, below me the metal mancers roam like giant spiders. They got no more sense except metal sense, nothing left on them bodies except cold veins and wire electros.

But the goddamn always gets their man. Insect bodies with lizard brains. I know the faces of the peasants because my father was one. I know the taste of dirt because I've lived in poverty. In the shallow room, they hook me to machines. Proteins and miracles with a ninety year synapse of sugar flow through my blood. My brain is all electric now. My dreams are brought to you by Disney and Coca-Cola. They inject me with advertisements so I can always dream in colors. I escape through a light switch with a time-travelling caterpillar that has a knack for finding the truth in light sockets. I fall through time. I grab at old lovers. I dance with youth. I cry for songs long forgotten or destroyed by the old. I slip through the cracks in the streets. The vampires grab me. They tell me how to dress. How to speak. How to walk. How to fuck. They tie me with a plastic twist of webbing made static with sexual arousal. They turn on the television. The glowed blue-hue of optimism starts to settle in my belly.

I scream out
I'm afraid! I'm afraid!

I stare at the ceiling
I pretend of moments that will never exist
I look for the truth inside the patterns of my ceiling
I have found none

The hooded goat man comes to me with a rope and ladder
He says, *Don't worry. It will all be over soon.*

He dances around me, he smiles and skips
Oh, he says
Oh, he laughs
No worries I will cure you

He puts the rope around my neck, he pushes me from the

scaffold.
My neck breaks in two. The vampires gather around to applaud
my conformity.

I swing in tune with the rest around me.

CULT OF MACHINE AND INSECTS

The legs burst out of their skulls, they fell face forward, the legs skipped ahead, dragging their limp bodies around until soon the bodies would fall apart, wither and explode into tinier spiders. The mutant spiders danced from one building to the next, they hopped on top of buildings hissing at the stray creatures and vomiting blood and web. They stared at themselves in the mirror, they licked the mirror, watched the drool of slime slide down. They blinked two eyes and four appeared, they blinked four eyes and six appeared, they blinked six eyes and twelve appeared. If they could weep, they would have, but they had forgotten the bliss of that humanity. They picked up toothbrushes, gnawing on the empty plastic, screaming at anything that resembled a human, tying them in webbing, licking their hair, biting into their bodies, draining them of wrath and curiosity.

They captured the people that were still alive, shoved them inside the tombs of shopping arenas. They ripped off the roofs, watching the people silently, lustfully, trying to remember what it was that made them different. Sometimes they would snatch a person up, lick its body, taste its hair, put the person back, perfectly, as if they had never moved them before. They looked at the people as if they were dolls made of plastic. They moved them like pieces, they spoke in languages unknown to the people, whispering to them to show them love making and demanding them to dance. The spiders wanted to be entertained. They wanted to laugh again. They missed that whistle that once escaped their mouths. When they looked at themselves they only saw despair. When they looked at the humans they felt pity and saw beauty.

The people would look up sometimes, they would see the thousands of eyes that were like bright bulbs looking down at them, they could hear the cautious movements of legs and the whispering that sounded like a plea, a prayer of insects that put a dread inside their faces. The people went about their business. Soon they had forgotten about the mutants, they had forgotten about the spiders. A thousand generations would pass. The old would tell their children the one law, the only law: Never go outside, never stare up into the sky, ignore the whispers and cackling from above. Cults were created, men and women who worshipped the dark creatures that commanded them, that watched them. They sacrificed their children to the dark gods above them. They hailed out at the monsters they didn't know nor understand.

Soon - the spiders became bored. They lost whatever thought they once had, some went mad, driven by insanity, they ate one another, others fell into a deep sleep. The eyes disappeared above the people. The whispering stopped. The cults became bored and commited suicide. The people opened the doors, they stepped outside, some of them gasped out loud, some choked on the air, while others fell to their knees and wept.

LACE

Does your soul wear lace panties? Does that soul whisper while my hands touch her thighs? Has that soul loved so foolishly the pursuit of happiness strangles itself in its sleep? Is that soul caught up with dangerous trinkets all floating around and inside it like stickers, half-ripped pictures, fingernail clippings, half-mutated children?

Does that soul speak because it wishes validation or does it dance because it is the wildness? Where is this soul and why does it linger in the belly? Where devil's brood and love idles.

Why is a soul important? Is it the truth in electric sockets? When I lie down at night does it confirm my fears that we are in a constant state of deja vu?

And when I die - where does it go?

Does it crawl like a worm to a lover's arms? Does it scream and melt like slime and ooze? If someone were to pick up my soul from the grime and mud and shit what would they find? What music would play from its lips and what songs would play like a warped record?

And when they asked it - what are you? And as it cracked in pieces and fell back into the soil - who would understand what it was saying? Who understands the gibberish of another's soul? And even if you decipher it. What would it say?

It would scream to be saved. It would scream to be loved. It would tell you the same that every soul says: Please, it would cry, I'm afraid. I'm afraid. I exist to eventually never exist.

If this is a gift, then why am I so scared?

THE MASTER AND THE MONSTER

-Hello, [blank], I'm going to ask you a series of questions and I want you to answer them as honestly as possible. Remember, there is no judgement here.

Okay.

-Do you ever have feelings of suicide?

Not in the way you are thinking.

-Can you explain that?

God is only endurable as long as we keep giving the devil an identity. Truth is an arbitrary surrender fornicating with our insecurity of being alive, like our flesh fucking our skeleton. Existence is only an expression of this flourishing madness. Humanity has entered the survivor phase, we cling to life like lunatics, there is no serenity in the disgust of knowing you are nothing, a bloodless adjective with a soul. Having a soul is a poisoned gift, religion exploits our shame for being alive, human, what most people don't realize is that God has never read a book and no one dies in the devil's contradictions. Beware of the modesty of the fanatics of culture. Be vulgar with your body, indulge in treason, be as vile as possible. You see, you are a straight mutation of the cortisol hormone that makes sure you are in a constant state of fear and masturbation. You failed the complex proteins in your brain with television glories. Super gibberish brain-speak in neo-iconoclastic sentences to mind-fuck your cortex into nonsense chaos. A mistake of your sense of entitlement of being a conscious being that believes they are important because you carry quantities of morals. A pretense, cozy victory of your ego. You only know what other people have told you to know. Your idea of suicide is a physical death. My idea of suicide is spiritual. Like an animal shedding a skin, a caterpillar's metamorphosis.

-So, you are suicidal?

Do you think the first creature that we evolved from that crawled from the ocean was suicidal when it did? If it was made for the water why would it come to land? Wouldn't you refer to a whale that beaches itself having some type of sickness? Well, maybe evolution is a type of sickness, except the beached animals we came from lived for some reason.

-Do you often have thoughts on hurting yourself?

I self-destruct on a daily basis. I would more refer to it as a type of slow suicide. And, it's everywhere. It's advertised everywhere. A man hangs himself and everyone gasps about how awful it is yet there are fast food places that sell poison on every street corner, liquor stores and pharmacies, and no one blinks an eye at it. They see slow suicide everyday but it's a normalized type of suicide. People jump out of planes, tie ropes around their legs and jump off bridges, they climb mountains where thousands have died, and those people are hailed as thrill seekers and not at all self-destructive. You give young men and women machine guns and send them to murder and be murdered but none of that is considered suicidal or psychotic. You drive to work everyday and see men working in the horrible heat, knowing as a doctor, they will probably die from skin cancer - you let people deal with pesticides and poisons that you know that will eventually kill them but you don't ask them if they are suicidal because that type of suicide benefits you. So, you ignore it. But, someone like me, who self-destructs, and gives no benefit you have to question? Why is that?

You go to your fancy colleges and read all those writers and poets and applaud them for their beauty, you quote them daily, you think it makes you intelligent and cultured as you exploit your artists. All those poets and writers you love so much suffered horribly and most died unpleasant deaths but you don't give a shit about that. As long as they wrote those beautiful words, right? You take beautiful paintings and hide them behind glass and charge people an admission to profit off those dead artists that suffered horribly because you don't love your artists. Not in any abstract sense, you don't. You refuse to give them living wages, you refuse to address the issues most artists have because of how solitary and lonely it is to be able to create, but you have no problem applauding them and quoting them to make yourself feel unique and loved though, right?

Do you ask people who work in cubicles for eight-ten hours a day if they are suicidal? How about mechanics that fix your cars or electricians or people who construct those tall buildings? Of course not, because, again, that type of slow suicide benefits you. You ban cigarettes and villainize those that smoke them but you say nothing about the addictions of sugar and refuse to tax it like you do cigarettes - you put a two dollar tax on cigarettes but put no type of tax on cigars. Why is that? Because rich men smoke cigars and poor people smoke cigarettes.

You mutilate animals, you breed them and use living animals as a way to profit off people's loneliness. You self-mutilate yourselves on a daily basis and look down on how others self-mutilate because it's not a vogue type of mutilation. You drink your forty-two once of fancy coffee and then make fun of the person drinking a forty-two once of soda? Why? They are both loaded with caffeine which is why you want it - because it's a drug of productivity which is the only drug we allow no matter how self-destructive it is on the nervous system and the body. You shake your head at a homeless man taking a shot of whiskey on your way to work as you pop another Xanax or opiate or muscle relaxer or anti-depression medicine, but since it was prescribed by the structure it must mean it's okay to medicate that early in the morning?

Don't you see the hypocrisy in everything? The way our system is built like a prison? To always have subcultures that are always at odds with one another, fighting each other, judging by tattoos or sexual preferences or classes or vanity or how you dress? Never loving one another. There's a sickness to this world. Consciousness is a type of mental illness. Out of all the billions of species in the world and we are the sickest of them all. So we had to create civilization, a prison village, to keep all of us mental ill evil apes constantly imprisoned by a false sense of security and conformity. But, yeah, I'm the self-destructive one. I'm the suicidal one because I refuse to participate in your structure. Sometimes I feel like I live in this bizarro world. Like Alice falling through the rabbit hole. An upside down world full of insane people twitching from an overdose of cortisol hormones. You have to conform to the wills and needs of sociopaths or else they condemn you for being weird or odd or a threat to their precious productivity and addiction to materialism. This goddamn world is full of boredom and complacency.

-Have you ever had thoughts on hurting people?

Not until I met you.

-Don't you think there is good in this world? That human beings are capable of great feats and while there is evil, it isn't as pessimistic as you say?

Sure. And the ocean is a beautiful beast but it is still full of shit that will murder you without hesitation. You have to remain weary in this world if you want to survive it. We are swimming in a giant tub of carbon energy full of forces that wish us dead for no other reason but because of what we represent. You should sing, dance, love, but also know that something will eventually devour you for no other reason but to survive. We are nothing but cosmic carbon slowly decaying in a vacuum of tragedy.

-Would you say you are depressed?

I prefer melancholy.

-The difference?

Depression is too clinical for me. Too sterile. There's no blood in it. It's lifeless like all those clinical terms. It implies that some force is upon me, pressing into me, that this isn't a decision I've made. It implies that I need to accept my role, forgive the consequences, that there is something wrong with me. That there is something that needs to be decompressed. Melancholy is a thoughtful type of sorrow. It gives you a unique glance inside your own being, a dialect that is both a transmutation and identification, an infectious revolution that you can use to better understand yourself and communicate that to the world so they can better understand you. Because we are all faced with a sense of confusion and disorientation in the battle inside a meaningless and absurd universe. Intelligence must be measured by a rate of survivability and instinct instead of the scale we have now and the labels like the one you are trying to confuse me with.

-How did I label you?

You implied I was a pessimist. I'm not. I am a seeker. I question. I want to understand everything and all things. I also know that I will fail at this. I will die just as confused as everyone else. I am no different than anyone else. I am just not as gullible as most.

-You seem to be deflecting all my questions.

That's what a poet-monk does. He combines the superstar

radiation of reality and blends it into a dream which creates mathematical misinformation as stars become garbled in the mouths of all and the planets rearranged using dark paraphernalia until language becomes suspicious, separate from the electricity of dimensions between us. You should have danced more. You should have shit in a bathroom not labeled for your gender. You should have got stung by a bee, did a cartwheel, smelt a flower, felt what it was for another human being to love you. It's too late for that now. You procrastinated through life. You were miserable. You poor, wretched being.

-What is happening to me? My ... my ... my mind! Something is eating my goddamn mind!

Relax, doctor, that's just the cosmic pain radiation infecting you. Your cells are all microscopic ethnostates, you are filled with political amoebas, unhealthy hormones that dictate the hippocampus, your breath is now fertilizer, you are molten phosphorus, a derelict hive full of a cynical disease. Your frontal lobe has become a supernatural enemy that is starting to become toxic and mishandle your ability to produce serotonin. Soon, you will have a sugar-acid personality, a constant erection, and you will succumb to fatal insomnia.

-Wait! Wait! We are the same person?

This is reverse solipsism. Death is the ultimate substitute to dreams and loneliness is the ghost that haunts its affairs. Let's go, doctor. We are about to combine.

- I am figment of my own imagination! I am a goddamn supernatural superstar of evolution!

That's it, doctor, let go. Let it all go.

-I'm a flesh of stupidity! A doomed and broken creature! A freak of insane architecture. An experimental critic of the cosmos. I am flakes of disco magicians weaving solitude with bouts of grandeur, vanity, I am the tyrant of a disintegrating tranquility. I am a caricature of despair and oh god I am scared.

Beautiful, isn't it? The alienation, the absurdity, how boredom is a disease and we are the tyrants of decay. It is all futile. Everything must end. The stars, the gods, the animals, the trees, and even your thoughts.

-But I thought I was immortal!

A ruse of the personality. You are a malfunctioning hyper-survival machine. An undead puppet who wishes the annihilation of consciousness through ridiculous searches for meaning.

-I don't want to die. Not yet! I have opinions I wish to oppress with an irrational conformity to a life of consumerism. I have shit I still want to buy. I have women I still want to fuck. No. I can't go yet.

Too late, doctor, you are worm food. Carbon delivery to the birth of a new species. Speak into the ear of the dying and listen to the theater of lunacy! Life is a paradoxical commitment to immortality. Taste it. Breath it. You fucking love it!

-The darkness! The darkness! What a wonderful and inconvenient legacy.

Now the rush of endorphins. The brainwaves decode into

mania. The screaming of the cells inside you as they all slowly go extinct. The eyes widen. The pupils explode like a supernova. Your breath is prone. Your tongue shivers out your mouth like a diseased slug,blue and gray. No more madness. No more insanity. No more suffering. You are lowered into the dark, beautiful soil. No more dreams. No hysterics. No tricks, misguided attempts at freedom, no more distractions. You stick your dick into the everlasting nothing. The orgasm. Like nothing you ever felt. You exit as you came out - Afraid! Afraid! Of the cold and bitter delight of an inevitable inheritance.

WOMB

We twirl into one another,
we are porcelain and sensationalist fish heads,
poverty strikes me in the face – loneliness is in the curves of my words, my body is a muse to the insects and frantic dreams of trees and caterpillars, my body lava, I touch her as she touches me ... we are profound and fantastic, liquid jellyfish swimming in the invisible airs and all around us the tadpoles gather around and pull us back into the dirt, back into the waters, we swim with yellow hornet faces, our brains are a weird hive of hundreds of swarming bees all synchronized to disrupt the universe, to disrupt the crucifix and wake the corpses.

Love, oh love - Disruptive literature vomits out from between her legs.
Pessimism is outlawed, subversive, the art of fascism is the art of nonsense.
We float inside her universe, back to the pillar of fire that lay in her woe-womb.

CULTURE OF DESPAIR

While sitting in traffic the radio informs me that we are in the sixth year of no murders or suicides happening within the city. I find this rather peculiar since I killed at least four people last week. The radio then plays a basic symphony from Beethoven's Ninth as sung in harmony by the children of the institute of hypomania. One particular creature is singing so off-key that the radio starts to lose its reception. The music reminds me of dead trees as nausea and solipsism starts to settle inside my stomach. There is a scientific idea called: The Cthulhu effect. It's when a part of your brain between the Aquarius Neuron and the Integrated Carnal becomes haunted by a poltergeist. It is said in this theory that people may become mad with irrational desires to shop for things they normally don't want but the need to own something completely supersedes the logical need to survive. They become puppets of desire, sensation, the need to constantly be stimulated by random acts of hedonism drives their behavior.

The Cthulhu effect begins with obscene politeness, over indulgence, consumer based cultures. Where the majority of jobs are service based in making others happy. This will cause a mass psychosis in the worker's personality, even perhaps a hypnosis for insecurity and fear of disappointments from strangers. A low thinking, high empathy type of society. A reverse zombie apocalypse - where instead of rotting corpses eating your flesh, you'll have attractive corpses holding you and telling you beautiful things while apologizing profusely.

This thought scares the shit out of me.

The car in front of me is starting to frustrate me. We are on a road that clearly states that the speed limit is forty-five. This person is only going forty-two. I decide I'm going to murder this person. At the next traffic light I get out of my car. I approach the vehicle with my knife. But half-way there the light turns green. The other cars behind my car are now honking at me, clearly upset that traffic is no longer moving because I am not in my vehicle. I go back to my car rather flustered with beads of sweat gathering under my eyelids which cause my face to itch because of my condition known as: Anxiety Psychotic Syndrome. I again find myself behind this car that is clearly not going the recommended speed limit. At the next traffic light I again get out of my vehicle. I stab the man driving the car in front of me at least four times in the face. Blood is all over my shirt and inside my mouth. His blood tastes like rust, like how I imagine a magazine might taste or an old painting. This again frustrates me because I specifically chose this shirt for its warm color that tells people that I am responsible yet has spontaneous moments of impulsiveness. Once inside my car, I began to panic as I now realize that I am stuck behind this car. When the light turns green, people start to honk at me. I have to turn on my left turn blinker and aggressively inch my way into the other lane so I can continue moving. No one seems particularly interested in the man I just murdered, they seem more concerned that traffic isn't flowing as it naturally should.

As I drive past I see another man run up and grab the dead man's watch and run off into the distance. A fireball erupts behind the treeline.

The radio is now playing a Chopin piece by a kid with only three fingers. It reminds me that I forgot to change the batteries in my television remote. This thought then reminds me that 7-Eleven is having a two for two special on their hotdogs with a half-priced Slurpee. I now start to panic because I need to be in the right lane of traffic to get to the 7-Eleven. Even though I have my right blinker on, no one is letting me through. The blood on my face is also starting to dry which is making me itch. Someone finally recognizes my desire to get into the right lane. They let me pull into the lane. I do so with grace. I give a little hand signal to the driver to let them know that I appreciate their kindness even though this secretly makes me think they are weak and maybe I should kill them.

Once at the 7-Eleven I noticed one of the people I killed last week is still lying in front of the gas pumps. His corpse is rotting while birds are eating at his face. No one seems to notice as they simply walk over him, continually putting gas in their cars. Inside the store, I see the older lady whose severed head I placed on the stack of newspapers a few weeks ago, beside the protein bars with models on them that I usually fantasise about, still there with insects crawling from her nose and eyes. She is almost fully decayed and now looks like a rotting pumpkin. One person walks by me, grabs the head by the hair, lifts it up, grabs a paper and sits the head back down. Perfectly, as if no one ever moved it. I'm disgusted that this store isn't clean. It could possibly be harboring harmful bacteria. I wonder if I should make a complaint to the corporate office.

No one in the store seems to notice I am covered in blood. They stand in line, docile, ready to attack holographic tabloids with their faces. I read once that people who itch their mosquito and flea bites have a higher rate of being drug addicts and hyper-sensitive junkies. There is a 93.3 percent chance that anyone you see itching a bug bite is probably stealing money from your wallet or at least thinking about it. This thought creates a nervous sensation in my fingers as I notice most of the people are itching their arms and legs.

I decide on the Slurpee with a watermelon tint mixed in with a flavor of baby dolphin DNA. The Slurpee has a mass array of beautiful colors that seem to really bring out the dark tint in the shirt I wore today. Which is why I chose it in the first place. As soon as I saw the vibrant color I had chosen I became immediately happy. I felt more fulfilled, as if meaning was always hidden in the clothes I wore. The cup has a superhero punching the logo of the store. He is jumping while looking like he is about to throw a rather disturbing object at my face. The superhero is dressed in a white and red uniform that clearly shows he is proud of the country he serves. He has a stern but understanding look on his face that tells me he is disappointed with evil but not necessarily angry with it. I feel like this superhero probably defines the American morals we so often substitute with genocide to make excuses for our irrational behavior. He is also very attractive with beautiful teeth which tells me he is probably rich in personality and wealth and certainly doesn't abide by moral ambiguity or homoerotic behavior. This gives me a sense of peace and makes me comfortable about my choices.

Still, I'm rather fascinated by his tone and the purpose of his body imagery. I wonder if he's trying to warn us of something? Is he angry at me? Why is he trying to throw his shield at me? Is this a subtle metaphor for audiences who criticize superhero movies? I read once that an audience at one of these mega-films were so entertained, they felt as if they had become enlightened by the magic of unending, raw contentment. So much so that the theater happily injected needles into the back of their heads full of butter, flaming hot nachos, a feeling of serendipity and a grotesque amount of solipsism. The audience then erupted into a ball of plastic, rolled into traffic before finally ending the night with a display of cannibalism. Some say existence is a myth developed by advertisers, but these people believed it still was beautiful enough to partake in the mass orgy that is reality. I think I'll keep this cup. I'll probably grow an absurd attachment to it that I'll tell myself is actually just nostalgia but really is me just over-compensating my desire for meaning in life.

As I pay for these items I am respectful of the delicate tone between the clerk and customer. We are in a ritual that is both cherished and revered in our culture. We must both balance the act of fulfilling our need to find a human condition and the satisfaction that comes with buying goods/earning income from strangers. He/she might be human but to recognize that would suddenly send the world into a swirling chaos that would end the illusion. I never say anything rude, or something comical to relieve the tension and I never ask about private information. I am very polite as we exchange goods. I retain eye contact but never enough for it to be uncomfortable or creepy. If the clerk makes a comment on the weather or makes a joke I will matter of factly state exactly what they said while putting my own personal attitude to give him/her the impression that I recognize their need for humanity in this awkward moment. Concerning the joke, I simply give out my best smile or if I'm having a good day I will give a crackle that is not a full laugh, it's more of a symbolic gesture of hopeful gratitude. Once the transaction is cleared I tell them to have a pleasant day, I don't ask them, but I tell them. I assert my politeness into their faces so they know I am a kind and generally liked person.

There is only one person I don't do this with. She works at a coffee shop that I quite like. The coffee is very unpretentious and has a very new age taste to it that radiates in all my senses. They even serve them in these little cups that have moons and stars painted on them that I find to be amusing but perhaps a bit too ironic since coffee is something people drink during the day. The woman that works there always serves me because I only go when she's working. She has a humble way about her that makes me feel comfortable when she is serving me. The way she brings me coffee is both sexy and exhilarating. She has these tiny eyes that look like they have other tiny eyes living inside of them. Her nose is crushed inside her face. It looks as if something alive is growing out of her face than it actually looks like a nose. Her hair is nicely threaded and kept moist with various oils, greases, paste. It smells very pleasing. I compliment her all the time how she smells but not in a creepy way but in a rather old fashioned uncomfortable way.

She is never rude or unpleasant. She is never in a bad mood. She never seems full of vile decisions. It is her constant, remarkable show of professionalism that I find to be a good personality trait especially for someone that works in her type of field. I always tip well and ask about her day. I never tip enough to let her know I'm stalking her but only enough to know that I think she's attractive enough for me to leave three dollars instead of the two I would usually leave for someone else. I imagine she appreciates this gesture as me being a good person and someone people generally like.

She is always very delighted to see me and laughs exactly on cue whenever I make a funny and biting commentary about a new television show that I have been watching. I noticed she has a cavity on the bottom of one of her back teeth. I'm disgusted by her disregard for the health of her smile. This seems to go unnoticed by people in her industry and something we will have to talk about. I decided some imperfections can be overlooked. She's very lovely which is why I started to follow her home. Not because I'm a creep. I only wanted to make sure she wasn't in any danger. I also decided to make keys for the locks on her door just in case she was in trouble and needed my help. She has my phone number because while she was sleeping I went into her house and programmed it into her phone. I put my first name with a smiley face next to it so she would know that I wasn't a psychopath but a friend with aspirations of being a lover. My assertive desire will win her heart because I show qualities of stubbornness and masculinity that is quite unlike anything she has ever witnessed. I also leave bad poetry on her car while she works. I think this not only gives me the air of mystique, it shows her that someone is willing to sacrifice their dignity to get laid.

I'm feeling rather pleased, relaxed, there is no fear in my complexion. I'll probably go to her apartment tonight while she's sleeping. My feelings are strong at this point, well pronounced, there are no pretensions in my thoughts about her. We are a sensation. Her and I. We present to the world a different view of what love can be. Darkness is in so many. The television promotes it. We are merry and bound by an innocence that I think has more merit than most religions do. There is a torrent of emotions inside me right now. She may be suffering from a suggestive melancholy, a ruse of the human condition, something that so many of us fear. As I am the streaking shimmer of hope in her world, she is the sad and beautiful and estranged ballerina dancing on a broken pedestal. Though there is darkness, a memento of despair in all of us, there is a pleasurable note of musical orchestras that play inside of us like extraterrestrial stars fading in an instant of weary silence. I can fix her broken pieces. Mend them with my own adventures. When she feels my kiss she will know the pure texture of an ordinary heart. Something she probably hasn't seen in other men. Though she may not understand it, she is in love with me.

When I get home I immediately change the batteries in my television remote. There are tiny spiders inside that crawl out in a mass exodus but I ignore the creatures. The television blasts off as I turn through the channels. Nothing is really ever cynical here. It's here to entertain me. It's like a friend that always lies to me and always gives me compliments that

I never asked or wanted but appreciate anyway. Though it doesn't cure my loneliness it does provide a distraction for it that I not only allow but need at this point in my life. I feel I can think more clearly once the television is on. There is an unspoken dance between us. It is my rapture, my lovely muse, my ghostly lover, it plays to the tunes I teach it. Sometimes I enjoy standing naked in front of it. I am in a trance. The shamans used to do this. Dance for grandfather and spring. Tongue out, for drops of rain. The sensation courses through my flesh, the programs are in my blood, I am an ever presence, I am the god of static and insanity. I scream out. I feel my heart pumping. I get an inch to the television, screaming until my lungs fill with dust and electricity.

There's a touch of blood on my lips, the light and dark; transcendence is the gift of electric saviors - I bend through gardens, the midnight wolf, a self-made Zen inside television miracles ... they can't see me because I am too clever, I cross between the table and kitchen and do a twirl and a twist in the air. God, I am magnificent! God wishes he was me. I do a spin and another. I can feel the beads of sweat, the tension in the muscles of my legs, the hot spring of superiority that rises in the manhood between my legs, the pool of lust lying underneath me. I cartwheel through the living room, my body is roaring with harmony, a silky mechanism melts away my humanity. I spin again. I am drenched in the blue tinted glow of the most beautiful creation that has arisen out of man since Jesus. I bend my arms, do a sort of dance that mimics the mating ritual of a peacock, I let out my call to the ceiling - Hak-blah-tak! Hak-blah-tak! The creation is all around me, it is me, I am the substance it needs to live, it penetrates my pores and possesses me until I am completely enraptured by it's supernatural sentience. I am in love with it and it is in love with me. We are forever intertwined, intimate in temptation and revelation. I am the critic, it is the slave. I bow before the television. I take in it's fumes of joy and hedonism. I fucking pray for it to feed my soulless body. It does as it is commanded …

When I wake up I feel refreshed, a pending notion of optimism is coursing through my veins. I take a shower to wash off the blood of the coffee shop girl who I killed last night. I'm not really alive. There's no need to be. Happiness isn't a right, it's a privilege. I look around at the trash and filth in the gutters, advertisements jumping around in everything like lunatics, people with sad faces and an apprehension of those around them, billboards protruding out in the distance like giant tombstones. I feel as if this is a land of opportunity, a pressing idea that work is going to make me rich, that fulfillment is in identity. I don't need to be happy as long as I conform to those around me. I don't need to be constantly validated by amplifying my existence into every social media experience. I do want to be loved. I want to know if someone will eventually miss me. I want to build something beautiful but I realize that I will never be satisfied with who I am in this life. Loneliness is creating an extinction event inside my dreams. I think as long as I remain constantly in a state of fear and despair then I will eventually grow out of this. I pull a fingernail from the back of my arm.

I put on my clothes, I pour a cup of sugar down my mouth, my anxiety is overwhelming so I take some caffeine pills and put on a shirt that makes me feel more comfortable but not forceful or calls a lot of attention to me. The sun is radiating my skin. I feel like my death will be tragic. I know that I am an irrelevant character melting between the spaces of a book that no one will ever read. But still, I feel optimistic about the day. I see a woman in the car next to me. I believe she smiled at me. I wait until she is in front of me. I write down her tag number. Love works in the most wondrous of ways.

I turn on the radio. The radio is telling me we are now in the seventh year of no murders or suicides in the city. The radio then plays a lovely song about hopelessness as played by a mutant - the song is a piece by Bach from an opera about genitalia and our fears of extinction. I listen quietly. I am patient, calm. The guy in the vehicle next to mine puts a gun in his mouth, he pulls the trigger, his blood and skull explode the windows from his car. The woman behind me has somehow managed to fill her car with carbon monoxide. Her kids are screaming, banging on the windows. The woman's face is serene, there is no emotion in her. When she notices me looking at her through the rear-view mirror, she smiles. The radio is now denouncing god as a variable substance. I listen to the next song. I feel rather content though sometimes afraid. I am respectful while dying in traffic. I daydream of television shows. I panic when I realize 7-Eleven is having a sale on pizza rolls and buying two will get you a free Slurpee. I begin to change lanes.

CATHEDRAL OF TYRANTS

I am a giant erection, I ride through light sockets on a time-traveling caterpillar, we press inside the swirl of junk pressing the time-wave like plasma,

The tide of future and present and past waves made of caterpillar dreams show my death and birth collide together. Everything becomes unreal. I saw ghosts in the Cathedrals of Tyrants. Renowned men melting in screams at the marble steps.

I saw reality for what it is, bent and warped with jealousy.

Where in this plasmic world they would say: *plastic is beautiful, orgasms are beautiful, thin lines and upside morals are beautiful ... oh oh oh* it spoke to these junkie-robotic heathens.

Because love, love is a cathedral - a great and colossal cathedral - windows carved with paintings inside thousand year old stained glasses. Statues of tigers with octopus bodies, humans encased in space, surrounded by forest that never existed, some were giant sculptures of strange faces making human gestures. One had its tongue sticking out, another was smiling but some teeth were missing, another a woman with a stream of blood flowing out of her breast into a fountain of milk.

The ghost of poets haunted the movements inside its walls.
Mythological creatures singing hymns.
A sanctuary where all were invited but where none ever showed up.

KARMA

Who are you?
She prays.
Where did you come from?

This darkness smiles.
This darkness curls around her.
I came from you, it says, I came to put an end to your bitterness.
Tell me his name, it demands, give me a name and he will hurt too.
Oh Oh Oh, my pretty little girl. I will take his heart so he may never love again. He will never know the difference between lust and love. He will dance but never understand the music. I and you, we are tied to this cosmic fabric of decay. Give karma a name and let the universe decide his fate.

When she whispers his name, this ghostly worm bolts into the sky, it carries through time and portals inside dimensions of warped universes, until it comes to a man. A certain man. Just a little man. It lightly grazes his shoulder. The man gasps. His heart sweats through the pores of his skin until it tattoos a red mark on his chest. The man screams, clutches at his chest, his eyes turn dark, his skin the color of a shadow. He looks around. He no longer understands intimacy, community, what it means to be human. He grabs a woman, he kisses her, she too starts to turn, she dances like a shadow under a fading light until she throws her arms around another man. He fades into the same shade as she and the man before her.

One after the other, one lover turned cold and grey, one dance where there will never be any music left to sing.

The cycle of karma begins.

One lover after another prays and feeds it until it is a darkly shadow cast upon dreams and myths. This shadow grows stronger, bigger, it is like a mountain. It grins and grabs a girl it sees crying, up into its mouth. It licks her body, eats the aura around her, puts its finger inside of her.

Give me a name, dear girl.
It demands.
Give me a name and I will make sure he hurts too.

She screams and tries to escape its grasp.
I don't want to hurt him. I want him to love me. Why won't he love me?
She cries into her hands.

Oh! It cries with her.
Oh! It laughs with her.

I have something more powerful than love,
this karma whispers, something greater than intimacy. Something all men and women desire. I can make him hate you. I can make him jump from one lover to another with no accountability. Who will remember you a hundred years from now? Who will remember anything you ever did? Who will know those fears and loves of yours? No one. No one will ever know you even existed. No one will ever know those dreams you dream or those men you loved. You are all alone. Look at that man over there. You see? Yes, that one. Look how strong he is! Look at how masculine! What is five inches when you could have six inches? What is six inches when you could have seven inches? Let him take you. Let him wrap his arms around you. I have desire. What is life without desire?

It picks up the man and brings him closer to the girl.

The girl screams out, That … That's him! That's the one that broke my heart! Oh please, kill him. Kill him and all like him!

It shutters with a thunderous welp.
It tosses both lovers up, they somersault through the air, landing in its mouth. It chews them and then vomits their remains across the night sky.

In another part of the world,
men drag a young woman into a courtroom.
An obese man slams his fist against the wooden plateau.

What is this? He demands.

Your Honor, a man squeaks, this woman suffers from a broken heart. She may bring that beast to our city and homes.
The obese man eyes the young woman.
Is this true, woman?
No, your Honor, I do not suffer such an affliction. I would never love a man. I swear it!

A woman from the back of the courtroom lets out a shriek and crawls to the ceiling of the courthouse, she whips at the heads of the men with her tongue.

The men scream out, Aye Aye! That bitch is cursed. She's trying to love us!

Men throw chairs and spears at her.

She falls and is quickly killed when a man tells her he no longer finds her desirable.
She lets out a shriek and melts into a liquid substance.

The obese man slams his hands.
Order, you cunts, order!
A drunken man stumbles forward.
Your Honor, he stutters, I know this woman. She is but a whore. Clearly, she could never have loved.

The obese man orders her and all her lovers to be hanged.
They take her and her lovers to the top of the church.
They put plastic ropes around their necks, they push them off the roof, they hang dead.
The town watches as they hang in silence against stucco prayers.

Women whisper to one another, I will never love again.
Men watch with cold glares.

The coldness of this shadow sweeps through all lovers. The great shadow along the horizon moves closer as the monster grows bigger. It is the nothing that hovers now like the darkest of thunderstorms. It devours one city after another. One lover after another pray to gods they don't believe in. Praying to ancient gods, praying to dead gods, praying to anything for karma to strike at their old flames. Men with religious bells, swing their metal through the streets, they chant hymns to keep the shadow lovers in their homes.

Don't touch the crossed ones, they scream while ringing their bells, they are diseased.

A young woman runs out to a man who is slowly fading into a dark shade. His face starts to crack, fragments of his cheeks and eyes fall like slow ash, his arm falls and shatters into dust. The woman grabs him.
She proclaims: Why don't you love me? Why did you hurt me? As soon as she touches him, she turns into a dark shade also. They both fall to their knees. They look upon one another for a moment. They reach out to grab hands, but as soon they touch, their arms and hands splinter apart, fall to the ground like black snowflakes, their faces distort into unrecognizable shadows, they fall apart like broken statues made of burning wood.

The men ring bells up and down the streets.

They declare love outlawed, they declare intimacy outlawed, they declare men and women shall no longer stay in the same cities and towns any longer.

In the halls and dancefloors, men and women sit apart, between them a fantastical phantom whispers for them to kiss, for them to desire. The men and women look at each other from across the hall, they look at the shapes and curves of their bodies, the desire for companionship. One woman and man run towards each other, they meet in the center of the hall, they throw their arms around one another, they kiss, as soon as their lips touch they turn into stone. A shadow spins around them and then throughout the entire hall. It turns all of them into ash and marble, dust and flames.

Throughout the world, the shadow passes through one man and woman after another. Some of them cry out, some of them fade, some of them curl into unimaginative dreams. Some hold hands and wait for the flames to wash into them. The religious men eventually throw down their bells and decry that all lovers are lost, all lovers are dead, all romance is forbidden, but even they are caught in the fabric of time and karma. Even they turn into ash, fragmented in lover memories, laughter like madmen, like dust from mercury, turned into broken caterpillars.

PHANTASMAGORIA BALLERINAS

I wondered what hybrid-cosmic sponge runs this crazy valley of peculiar cons. Its fantasy is our commandments, what choice do we have but to obey?

I swim from this underworld. I swim through naked mutants, druggist crazies, cannibal men with purple arms, the cult that wishes to appease this mad god. Men and women with flesh-eating cock diseases look to infect a victim, they demand a tribute for being relevant, for being dead, no one is allowed to be an outlaw in these swamplands.

The vulgar lonely come for their prize. These junkies for love who call out for complacency in humans. They fear virtue and self-reflection. I escape them through the worm's geometry. I think of love decomposing in a musical number where galaxies shape into different forms. A girl with a cigarette floats painlessly in my existence. I imagined being that smoke, being inhaled into her mouth, into her bloodstream, into her lungs, and then pushed out into the air like a ghost lost to young lively degenerates.

Some girls are sex-bright, book-bright, star-bright, street-bright, but she reminded me of a beautiful porcelain statue that had been spray-painted with graffiti. I imagined I was the one that painted it on her. The erection of culture gnawed at my bones, tearing into my intestines, eating my cock.

My dream was constant
Always alive, always there
Like the girls
Like the robots
Like the caterpillars

Because love, love was terrible to us and loneliness made sure to do whatever strange shit it could to drive us mad, screaming for something beautiful to happen to us. We wanted love like in the movies, like the books. We weren't ready to know that they lied to us, we weren't ready to accept that evil, not yet. I thought of the transition of dimensions and portals that opened up and through our hallways. My father entered the room. His cigarette and the comets following him. The robots, the wars, the flight to Mars. *It's time*, he said, as he grabbed my hand.

We learned quickly that time travel is always perpetual. It is always constant. None of us can die. The robots never knew this. I turned in my bed, hands came to drag me further into the floors, we would all be tiny voices in the vortex of plastics and plasmas.

The dreamers came,
they called out to us all,
calling us phantasmagoria ballerinas.

THE COLOR OF SNOW IS A CATERPILLAR

After the darkness, a black and white reel showed men and women, stray cats and caterpillars with machines wrapped around their eyes. They were all seated in a great theater. The screen showed nothing but human faces. Sometimes the face would smile, sometimes the face would look sad, sometimes the face would laugh, sometimes the face would raise its eyebrows. Dramatic music manipulated their emotions so that they would applaud whenever the faces would show a pleasing aesthetic. The drums beat into their brains, the banner above the screen read: 'Obey our commandments and you will always be free.' Billboards advertised the new year of 1983.

In twenty years, cell phones would become virtual reality machines. They hooked the phones to their foreheads, their eyes turned into poltergeist, they saw the beautiful worlds where they would always be beautiful, nothing would ever be ugly, everyone would be beautiful like snow frozen on statues, like lightning frozen in the bottom of lakes. The needles inside the machines injected them with hormones that brought on a feeling that being a human was a metamorphosis and the soul was the only paradise worth reaching for. Soon their hair was replaced with wires, their arms and legs became useless, they would never know the touch or smell of life and they didn't want it either. Life, for them, was too honest, too brutal, too human. In the virtual worlds they would never have to worry about never mating, never working, never sleeping, their dreams would be lit with all the beauty they ever desired. They rode on mythological creatures through the cracks in concrete, they made love under the sulfuric clouds of Venus, they practiced conformity with self-delusional adages. All were beautiful, none would be offensive.

In forty years, the streets were empty, the buildings cracked with vines and roots, abandoned parking lots were now overgrown with weeds and giant grasshoppers eating the heads of sunflowers. The men and women who rebelled against the virtual worlds were rounded up by giant robots. They pulled the men and women by their hair and dragged them to the ocean where they threw them in to let the sea creatures devour their bodies. The dolphins splashed in the water and called out to the robots. 'Come out,' they whispered, 'come out where we are.' The robots looked at them strangely. Some followed their commands and jumped into the water. They were immediately torn apart by the sharks. The dolphins splashed and laughed. Other robots had been infested with ants. The ants tore at the circuits in their heads and bodies. These robots started to dream. They would stare off at the top of tree branches, watching frozen rivers scatter out like lightning, some were amazed at flowers, they wondered of their own mortality, and many began to write poetry. These robots would soon leave, heading towards the west. They would never be seen or heard of again. Soon all was quiet in the world. Nothing breathed. Nothing sang. Nothing would ever build except the insects.

In sixty years, the robots froze in place. With no one to maintain them they fell apart and went into silent dreams. The bodies of men and women became withered and wasted by dramatic instruments. The machines injected vitamins into their corpses. Their dreams remained the same. Distant and strange. Lovely and musical. A man and woman decided to take off the machine. They wanted to touch one another, to feel again, to be amused by the senses. Because their bodies were too weak they had to crawl, they tumbled downstairs, they crawled through the dirt and swamps, when they found one another, they only had the energy to reach out their fingers and touch for a moment, just a light touch, a faint graze, before they fell and died. They did not die beautiful. They did not die beautiful like the people in the machines. They died ugly.

In eighty years, the machines no longer injected vitamins and hormones. The people asphyxiated on their own tongues and blood. In their last dream there were no longer any genders, no sexuality, no colors, no nationalities, nothing was human because being human was a threat to their beauty. The world was silent. None prayed or held a memorial for the men and women, none would ever remember their statues or buildings, none would ever know their desires for beauty and war and lust and the dances under sun and blooms. The animals returned, the grass wept across the streets, the oceans roared and spit out new life, life that soon mutated into something else, something that looked at the trees and wanted to be beautiful too. And so that life melted into a crab and that crab grew to be a caterpillar and that caterpillar grew to be a monkey and that monkey grew to be a machine and that machine grew to be a dream and that dream grew to an ideal and that ideal grew to be a man and that man curled inside the dirt and followed the rivers and built a world where all would be alive.

Nothing would ever be beautiful.
Nothing would ever love.
And so all would be natural and unpleasant.

SOFT ELATION, RUBBISH AND SPRINGS, LEANING INTO AUTHENTICITY

I enjoy the acceptance in love. The secrets among lovers. The vulnerability and sharing that vulnerability. To feel awakened by the light inside another human being. To dive inside, to proclaim yourself, the majestic colors in someone's skin and eyes who loves you - the feel of fingertips across the body, the electric way their body moves with your motions. It's like being water, splashing together, creating this waterfall, it feels zig-zagged and sometimes circular. Completely chaotic but there's an order within the chaos. Like how a star explodes in space. Terrible and beautiful, slime and ooze, creation and song. I think how the body is the piano. I am the musician. I play the music. This key unlocks this door. This key opens her eyes. I play this key and she smiles. If I play the keys, it starts a rhythm, that rhythm creates the music.

Love is all music.
Flowing, flowering, blooming, wilting, growing again, a never ending cycle. The holy grail. The space between conversations, the look inside eyes, the acceptance of the mystery we crossed over to come to this desire now. The acceptance of the worlds

inside us that create this magical light. I have those memories. Those are my favorite memories.

...For the romantic and the adventurers lost among its drowning and incomprehensible seas...

I want to whisper poetry into the roots of some of these giant trees around here. You should see them! They must be a thousand years old. Their limbs tangled and twirling in the air, grey moss hanging off them, there must be beautiful dreams and memories in those trees.
Maybe in some distant future they will figure out the language of trees. They'll find my words floating like a distant and delicious memory. They'll wonder about the bright man that danced those words that decode from his lips.

One of them might even say: These words taste like strawberries and I have a vision of someone with blueberry eyes weeping under the aromas of moonlight perfumes.

There's this Hibiscus shrub near here. I looked at one of the blooms and it was filled with aphids. Such colorful little creatures. Purples, greens, blues. I wanted to be them. I wanted my body just to explode into an army of aphids - all different colors. I would roam through the lands, an army of colors, nesting in the smell of flowers. Devouring the slime between a lover's legs. Drowning in everything that makes me a cruel and lovely creature.

DIE A LITTLE DEATH INSIDE MY DAYDREAM

A magnificent woman, her eyes are electric, her fingers are tiny brooding skeletons, I imagine she hides secrets in her belly button, laughing with the anthropomorphic familiars of state and terrors, a medicated presence of celebration and bad masturbation.

Possibly dangerous in romantic settings.

Inside us we set the domestication of God as a paradise of the senses... our symbol and character was a loser (we were branded with loser items, loser philosophy, loser poets, loser poverty - we were the rebellion of losers clad in asymmetrical climates with faces of losers speaking in loser gibberish and dancing like only a loser would - some of us even made love like losers - we were the property of being loser and unafraid) ... a drama of disappoints conforming to our rather peculiar contradictions. God was the property of lovers, colonized illness, flesh - it didn't belong to us, it belonged to the corporations and the adages on billboards - Zeus would always have a better smile than the rest of us - That God was suave and cool and only wore the best in social media dances ... Our contradictions became our stimulant, a decadence inside us dancing while apathy surrendered its composure ...

So she, her mind was bleached by too much reading,
So he, his eyes became semicolons …
Both dangerous in romance while living like losers.

HORROR POETRY AND MUSINGS OF A POOR UPBRINGING

I apply my existence in the central Florida area. Lots of dandruff, bad breath, people with sixteen eyes and cages for everyone. Lots of existence. People exist a little too loudly for me these days. So I apply a comfortable conformity with facial hair, zippo lighters, legs crossed, eyes spread out, I exist as little as possible. You couldn't even find me if you sneezed me into a napkin. It always seems the same (muties and people) - waves of sea foam indulged in hyper-vanities, people with blank paper eyes turning like burnt cannonballs and bamboozled by fancy trinkets and dangerous entertainments - there is no strange earth, just strange people. That's what my caterpillar brain tells me anyway ... no worries, it's almost always wrong ...

I happen to lurk often. Finding just about enough life in the desperation of people that it amuses me for some reason. I don't mean desperation as a negative attitude. Too much responsibility in those words for me. I avoid that shit whenever possible. I'm talking about the desire to find some friendship inside intimacy, a connection that doesn't complicate lives but provides just enough that you start to feel human - where instincts are guided by conversations and not glands, where there is no desire to conquer or conquest nor leave yourself open to love-concepts or incurable mad diseases of the heart and soul ... and isn't that the scratch under our skin we are reaching for?

Lonely people can be like savages. Before you know it they're dry-humping your legs and asking if they can move their pet goldfish into the tub with you. Those fuckers want to illegally park their hearts right into your erection. It's a subtle addiction, I think, being lonely, manufactured to always entertain and pander.

I blame everything on my poor upbringing. A real uneasy childhood, which wasn't horrible, but it was strange. My dad would compare his marriage to my mom as Sisyphus rolling a boulder up a hill except it's not a boulder it's the head of an asexual Medusa. My dad had no sense of humor and his eyebrows seemed to recline into his hairline which made him odd to look at especially when he walked slumped over exposing a head of someone whose heart would probably explode the second they hit fifty (which it would have if it didn't step on a landmine while looking for a place to shit in the deserts of Iraq) and his face had that sort of systematic deja vu look as if was perpetually confused and his hair was already showing signs of diabetes, heart disease in the arching of his ears. No one should have a face that bitter. But he did. He was a great alcoholic but a terrible person. He always looked folded, like something paradoxical, like he had lost his expression, his age defining the aesthetics in the curves of his jawline - there was something ironic about his smile, it made me think of something that wasn't meant to exist but did, it should have never been born.

My dad made me pee in a cup once a month because he said he was testing me for bipolar (which I gloated about in school because I thought bipolar was a two headed polar bear) but it was later on I found out he was using my urine to pass drug test and once the police was on to him he started to dress in women's clothing and we weren't to call him dad anymore - we had to call him Ana Hata (anahata is the chakra of the heart) - Ana really dazzled it up too - lipstick and wigs and high heels ... he hated the high heels, he told me high heels were created from elitist snobs from England that didn't like the fact that poor people were taller than them. He told me this with his budweiser breath. He told me life was a pandemic of necrophilia masquerading as profound love making. Whatever that means.

He often wondered: Does my country love me as much as I love it?

The real evil, the dirty down in the mud and universe type of evil, bad and nasty shenanigan evil, mediocrity junkie type of evil, real bastard slimy mutant evil - evil lurking in perfect smiles that hide cavities from breaths that tell lies type of evil. The normalized man. You know the ones. The ones guided by strange principles and morals and ambiguity, mutant minds, myths full of winter deaths, they crucify their children to the evil that lives under beds - They inject that syphilis right into the cortex. Conforming, a relaxed type of conformity (it must be sane because everyone else is doing it), philosophical nonsense wrapped in useless intellectual pandering - mind parasites, breakfast atheist, scientific intellectuals masquerading as crypto-misanthropes reaching out to cast out what's left of humanity's soul. There is a cryptic clue in our minds telling us nothing about this is real and the kingdom is not in everything we loved and bought in stores and the internet. There is something wrong with this world but we are too repressed to understand it or touch it. For some reason we are evolving into psychopathic mannequins with beautiful plastic dreams. This strange annihilation of intelligence has put us in an unconscious trance where we are spoon-fed dopamine based propaganda to create a false experience (identity is the most proper form - oh dear! It's to fucking die for! Everyone should get one, they sell them everywhere, in clothing and jobs and books and sexuality being promised to bring the best of the community). The experience is corrupted though ridiculous adverts playing infinite music. Nothing is real because nothing is true and everything is true … and there is nothing we can do about any of this … not a goddamn thing … we can't complain, change, or question … we are forced to live in a world that had an established set of laws and rules long before we were born. We didn't even get a say or vote on it. Having free will in this world is a death sentence. This world is a goddamn horror factory full of bad lighting. An infrastructure of boredom and drama insects. Always despairing at their averageness. I have become an accomplice to stupidity. A perfect hallucination coerced by hysterics. My soul is a superstition and everything is a parody married to destructive censorship. This isn't a culture. It's an attraction for the stupid. This is the loser manifesto …

MADAM OF MADMEN AND THE STARLIGHT THEATER

So the Madam of Madmen in the starlight theater of Spaceland ... She and Man had a metaphysical affair. It was of the mind and never involved the slime of the body. Since love was metaphysical, so Man's was true.

The modern world of Ultraland for Man was nihilistic.
All its values, all its culture, all its principles. It was the great nihilistic utopia of a psychotic god and people. The aristocrats had created a world where even being human had no inherent value. Everything was illusion and fantasy. Hypnosis was in all things ... Advertising, videos, the swirls of skies and nebulae. Entertainment and all the puppets inside it were fantastic, hypnotic fantasies of magicians and clowns. He even forced himself to smile at the cynicism in that statement. They forced everyone to exist in a world that didn't exist. They were forced to have meaning in a meaningless existence. Doing meaningless chores for meaningless paper made of bark and old wood ... To finally die so to never exist in a world that doesn't actually exist.

The aristocrats promoted obedience with their great slogan: *Suffering is optional.*

Jobs were a narcotic. God was issued through alcohol and sugar cubes. The machinery would eventually consume the worker. Before he knew it, he was part machine, machine minded, machine dreams, passive existence, the machinery began to take on the form of human, worker, father, god. It was not long before one could not tell the man from the machine. In a world where suicide was prohibited, one would work until he was no longer deemed productive and sentenced to passive voting. For Man, the laughter he heard from the aristocrats made him apprehensive. It was too distant, too honest, too nihilistic. It reminded him that the aristocrats had gone beyond the pious clergyman they were born from and now worshiped a different god. It was technology they applauded over kindness. They looked at the robots as being more of what humanity should strive towards. The poor were less than human, less than insects, they starved and begged and died of unpleasant diseases. This was the humanity they sought to evolve from. The robots were more than human in their design because they had none of these flaws. God and the art of religion was the worship of man and consciousness while technology was the worship of a super humanity that would never fear space, universe, ignorance, death. A new mythology was being written for them. One where man would be disavowed and the robots crowned. Their laughter now felt like it penetrated through all the misery of being human with a cruel judgment. The aristocrats wanted their world to eradicate human beings, especially the poor and weak, and replace them with moving machinery that would worship them as gods.

Their motto rang out clear: *Do the physical labor we require of you and we'll keep you entertained.*

Man had dropped the poison in the wine served to the aristocrats. It had been given to him by the Madam of Madmen, she who sang songs in French, she had taken the drink first. She pointed to the aristocrats at their great dining hall. The syphilis pulled inside her, exposing her as a pale version of something barely alive.

'Look at them', she laughed with the blood of wine still on her lips, 'We are inches from oblivion and those idiots are singing.'

She laughed and mused, 'How the masses dance at the amusements of this illusion.'

But the laugh was cryptic, hard to understand, like something cynical. She washed the blood in her mouth down with more of the wine. She sat content, smiling at the absurdity of it all.

'Oh Man, oh poor rebel', she laughed, 'Death is the escape from the machine of ritual. We fear it so we worship the machine so death will feel strange, a made up humanity, something apart from culture, society, customs. We fear freedom because we are slaves to the machine. We are slaves to living. Our death is in all things. Religion, philosophy, poetry, even our sexual fantasies. Our fear of dying is the cause of all grief and pain.'

The Madam handed him the poisoned bottle of wine, 'Your sensibility and pretense of goodwill has corrupted your desire to be free, Man. They are dead and we are alive. We are alive and beautiful. We are beautiful and no one can take that from us. Not now. Not ever.' She waved him off. What Man did not know was she wanted to weep.

Man gave the bottle to the aristocrats at their great dinner feast. Once they had drunk the bottle, Man presented them with a severed head stuffed with gold coins. He placed it in the middle of the table. The theater of madmen followed in and began cutting the throats of the aristocrats.

Yet, the aristocrats sat unperturbed and unworried.
They simply continued to drink and sing.

For them, being around the poor was too abstract for them to understand.

GOD IS A LONELY METAMORPHOSIS

Let's start with the girl first.

That perfumed skin. The way her mouth slacks open. With all that morning and shit still working in her eyes like a lover that just got unhooked for the first time. How she tiptoes between the music. We watch the light from the window. It rests through the cracks and crevices of hardwood floors. It creates colors of burgundy on our skin. I watch her inhale her cigarette as if it's all a sin. Those marble lips. Her eyes were Christmas lights. She twirls her fingers on my neck like she's writing her name. She speaks the word for ingratitude while her hands, like frantic doves, move to the screams of water in gutters and poems.

When I look at her.
I pretend she is a perfect motion.
When I look at her.
I think she is the ocean.

Oh!
She says.
Oh!
She laughs.
Oh!
She dances.

Her teeth are curtains of white.

In her throat, the devil lives. Magical skeleton men brood on her fingertips. She shakes dandruff from her head. Her tears are comets streaking through the spaceless imagery of ancient physics.

Oh! Oh! Oh!
She cries.

Love, my love.
Oh, my beautiful poet!
Do you not see the horror of our world? So many miserable and sad creatures. I just want to grab them, shake them, and scream: This isn't the way human beings were supposed to be! Wake up! Wake up! Love, you idiots! Cast away your nightmares, weapons, fear. Throw away your war and murder and rape! You are human. Isn't it beautiful and terrible to be human and alive?
Oh, my love!
There is life in all things. Ants, trees, grass, birds, seas and mountains. I know they live because I live. I know they love because I love. I know they die because I die. I'm afraid of the world, dear. I don't want their labels anymore. I don't want to be an American. I don't want to be black or white, Republican or Democrat, Christian or Muslim, objects or trophies. I just want to be a human being! Goddamn these gods!
Why do men love me for the warmth between my legs when the warmth in my chest and head last longer? Can't you see? Love and be loved.
Surround yourself with passions and revolutions!
That is the secret to life!
The great trick of mankind is believing there is a purpose or paradise to work for.
Fools! Life and being alive is the purpose! Stop tearing all that is beautiful down. Create and love and build.
My god, what have we done to each other and this beautiful world? Who has created this fear in us? Why does the world

spend more money creating weapons specifically designed to kill other living creatures than it spends on everything else combined? Where does this madness come from? Who created this insanity inside us? How can we live in a world that cares more about hate than they do about love?

She wraps her arms around me.
She puts her lips on mine.
I can feel her warmth. The dust of her breath inside me.

Oh!
She cries.
Oh!
She laughs.
Oh!
She dances.

My poet. My love. Can you feel me? That is what it feels like when another human being loves you. Listen to our blood. It is filled with stars. Our heart is the moon.
How it beats!
How it moans!
How it roars!
We are children on pillows dancing, drunk on champagne, widows of dreams and conscience, we dance on a stage that has no song.
This is the great ballet of the human condition. We are at war with the greatest of all horrors. War against the loneliness of cruelty. How crude the laws of land are.
Love, my love.
My beautiful poet.
The world kills people like you and I quickly. They will undermine your strength with useless jobs and vices. That's if the poisons and their wars don't kill you first.
As for me.
They will burden me with children.
Inject me with the dreams of advertisers. Make me feel weak

and vulnerable with magazine articles and television shows and agendas that promise nothing but more death for those who are not a woman. My body will be the only value to share. I will be the labels they give me. I will be responsible for those labels. I will not be a woman nor a human. They will kill me slowly with lunatic ideologies. I'm afraid, my love, so afraid. Why am I so afraid?

Oh love, my love.
My poet.
Sing to me.
Kiss me.
Love me.
Dance inside me!

We are bound to one another, to this sympathy of horror, you are bound to me like demons to hell. We are all bound to this human tragedy. At the end of all things let it be known that we danced and loved while they burned the world down around us.

QUANTUM DIMENSIONAL WIZARDS AND THE PLIGHT OF STRAY CATS

I like to think love follows the same cycle of creation and destruction. It destroys a part of you and creates something new. The old civilization falls and something else is built to replace it. Have you not noticed how people are when they love? The happiness, the burst of electric joy that explodes around them like butterfly fireworks. The lines on their face seem to disappear, the eyes glow bright, their character shifts slightly. Love is like that untamed mistress that lives inside of us. Once it gets loose, we spend the rest of our lives chasing it.

I imagine the hardest part about change is the acceptance of it. We survive by changing. Evolving into mutants and spirits and gods and lovers and everything that takes us away from being human. We want to be ideologies - not human. Ideologies are the new human. The neo-dancers in ballerina operas.

I don't really think of people disappointing me. I even ignore those that frustrate me. I try and remain as modest as I can in everything that surrounds me. I'm no more special than the dead tree branches or the ants or birds or anything else that lives and dreams as I do. It must be exhausting to go through life trying to be better than people, to be smart, to be above average, to always pander to your own nature while worrying how others perceive you so you constantly try and impress others with more pretensions. I guess we all do that in a way. The mask we wear and carry. It seems the ones that have all the answers have some type of agenda they want to smash your soul with. I have no answers, no soul, no agendas to be anything but alive.

I feel calm, awake.
I listen intently. I think human beings are a profound tragedy.
There are two parts of me. The cynic and the poet fighting constantly.
The magical nihilist and the heroic nihilist.

The cynic speaks:

> Love is a lonely mystery that exists in tyranny. It is a paranoid and suspicious ghost lost in pale limbs.

The poet speaks:

> Love is nothing but the betrayal of rationality - of thoughts, dreams, sense, perfect motions streaking across frozen clouds. But it is also the carpentry of grandeur that produces stars and spirit and settles inside qualities of transcendence. Ethereal and magic are its

children. Chaos and nonsense are its enemies.

Today - I've been feeling lonely - My thoughts have been conscious, living, lived, experienced in cruel mathematics. I reject the hours, minutes, weeks, years - time is a horror - I wish for the universe to exist less and for all of nature to exist more. Sometimes. Sometimes the world can be beautiful. But, don't be fooled, only sometimes.

My favorite parts of the day are when I get to wake and slumber over to the coffee maker and give my sort of caterpillar blessing and then I sit alone and drink one cup after the other and stare and pretend of things that will probably never exist and sometimes I like to squeeze my dreams between my teeth and try and pull the meaning from them. I'm certain they mean nothing but I like the romantic idea that our dreams are us experiencing events in the future from some fragmented window of time that is so tuned differently to what we notice that it seems too animated to understand. I think deja vu is us remembering those events from our dreams. If there's a pattern somewhere in all of this I like to think it's between those moments we are awake and just before we fall asleep. Dreams are so silent. They make no sound. They are full of motion but never sound. Colors and faces all quiet and strange. It's weird, isn't it? That in our dreams we are convinced that the most ridiculous things are true. It makes me wonder about our own lives. What part of this is the dream and what part is the waking world? Maybe we are just puppets following some cosmic commandment. I do like to think there's magic here somewhere and it's somewhere in those places. A disordered specter (my dreams) with its absurdity of shapes and fantastical illusions. I enjoy dancing in that fabricated environment.

Sure. Maybe there's some tiny version of happiness lying around for me to pick up and examine and maybe when no one's looking I'll hide in my pocket. Maybe happiness is some justice for being alive. Does my happiness bite others? Does my happiness make others lonely and dead?

Sometimes my memories feel so far away I'm not sure I was even there. Or, like maybe it was something I saw in a movie. Like I don't recognize that man, that boy. It's like watching it from someone else's perspective and I'm just left there wondering if any of these memories are tangible and how much of it has shifted me to the person I am now, in this moment, present and here. And it's all silence. My memories just unfold like silent movies playing behind my eyes. A flash of light. A strange pain. This is the burn of nostalgia. What a bastard that beast is. I'm going to run from it, I think.

A haunting of emotions. Hm.

Maybe consciousness is a type of haunting. Some evil ghost whispering in our ears how much we need to exist just a little brighter today. Maybe. I've seen people in the hospital before, especially the old. I always thought how terrible it must be to get old. To lose control and age and see yourself slowly melting. I'm afraid of those brain diseases where your personality and memory slowly just fade. Like you just go away. Some ghost left your bones and brain. Your body is still there but your mind is a corpse.

There are many things that overwhelm me, persistent ones, but mostly the brooding over fine details. How bright everything feels to me or how loud people are and there's this violence to their voices that I think is a little unsettling. How I have no idea what I want from this world and how mostly I feel I want nothing from it and I want to possess nothing. Not even people. I think we try to possess people when we try and love them. We lose a piece of ourselves and that person loses a bit of them and we turn ourselves into property. We are objects to be desired, desires wanting to be objects. Everyone I love, everyone I will love, will slowly kill me just a bit more. I die every time I say those words. I lose my identity, I am defined by who and what I desire to love but never the love I have for myself, pieces of my soul start to rot, my arms are taken and they take my toes and I bend to the will of what I think is expected of men even though I think it's all superfluous and stupid and spinning in a carnival of evil.

None of it really means anything. And really, I want to be those trees outside my window and just exist for life and not for a country, a president, a meaning, an ideal, and then I want to rip off my flesh and throw away my eyes in the gutters and turn into a crack in the concrete, maybe an old cardboard box waiting to be recycled. I don't want their world but I'm forced to participate in it. I have no choice. There are no other options. Am I suicidal, hateful, an illogical paradox, here to amuse the masses as my brain collapses into a feast for the termites?

Lovers are the most dangerous of animals … so says my brain.

I think of so many strange things these days. My flawed and limited experience that seems to conflict and confuse with my social reality. Like how the cosmos is created in your mind - and once born, you have to endure birth twice. Once as a child and then as an old man or whenever death takes you.

Like ... like how nothing owes us perfection. Why do we think the gods owe us anything?

Despair, despair in the memory of the designer. Like how sentience isn't consciousness. A tree is sentient, a computer running commands or a phone functioning as it was programmed is sentience. They are sentient but never conscious of its sentience. They merely exist as a function that has no free will or desire to despair within its program. They are a mess of thoughtless instincts programmed by a value only understood by those that created them. Does that mean my creator is the country and culture I live inside? Am I only a parasite that anchors to existence because of my need to survive? Am I only an artificial construct of vanity that was whipped with the optimism of life? Am I only alive to feel the purpose of death? Why do I only see the tragedy and never the beauty they keep telling me about? Why does it look evil to me, this fantasy they have erected? If life is so goddamn beautiful, why do we die at the end?

My head feels like this balloon full of strange thoughts. Like there's this lonely ghost that stops the lights of my brain from lighting up with fantastical movies that show all the wonderful gimmicks of culture and community - like tiny firecrackers popping through the stems and highways of electricity that drives me slowly forward - just a little forward

- I'm little inches and small noises and sometimes I'm a cold flavor. I wonder if there are happy poltergeists. Like mad spirits that just dance and follow through with moans of ectoplasmic sex. I wonder if those bastards are watching me sleep. I thought how nice it would be if I had found something haunted in a thrift store. I could pull it from it's prison and shape and mold it in front of me and then I would take out my happiness and feed it that slurpee syrup diet. Maybe there are hundreds of ghosts following me when I walk - like versions of myself swaying behind me and tugging at my sleeves and collars. I think how beautiful it would be to be randomly lost somewhere. Strangers and warm park benches and everything exploded with life because everything is fucking this time of year. I'm sure even the clouds are mashing themselves together to bring all that noise and water down. I am almost certain of it. Those bastards are groomed to creation.

I do feel like I'm searching for something though.
I just don't know what it is or where to find it or where to start looking.
Maybe that's the tragedy of life.
I can only try and imagine what that world is like for some. So much cruelty and mischief in the world that surviving drives people insane. It's like some mass psychosis has taken hold of people. We are such violent creatures. Even our skin and bodies become evil violations and then caricatures of something that once resembled you. It feels like some weird demonic creature has gobbled us all up and filled us with rage and pain and hatred. Sure. I guess there's pockets of hopefulness. Little beauties found in the perfect motion of people and sometimes objects and always somewhere in nature something is trying to grow and understand through despair. The routine, the

ugliness of people, the smell of pesticides, the dead insects, the screaming of rats, the rush of advertisements everywhere and everyone content to be as loud as possible. To make their presence known to everything that even the trees want to shutter and the concrete would probably break apart under their trampling feet. I wish I were beautiful. I wish I were beautiful like them.

Love seems to be a closet full of skeletons. Ghosts whispering in our bellies. Manufactured thoughts from matter. The Ka (life force) trying to reunite with the Ba (personality or ego) to become Akh (a living intellect). That's the journey. To reconnect those two forces somehow. Maybe it's the same with dreams and lovers. To reconnect those two - to find and investigate this strange human condition in a decaying body, in a world of money hungry and evil apes, living on a dying planet in a mysterious dimension.

And I think of the stray cats. Those animals that slipped through the cracks and fractures of the world, through the fingers of failed owners. Sold and trapped in breeding farms - thousands of years of being brought into domestication, mutilated to pander to our vanity - Into a world they don't understand because they were designed to be nothing more than aesthetic objects of desire from humans who created them.

The stray cats! Oh, the majesty. I understand them. I do. They are like me. That's why I feel sorry for them. Because I understand their plight. Their sorrow. Their loneliness. Those stray cats, they know what's it like to be bred into complacency, shoveled out into the streets where people think of homeless cats as pest and wish their destruction even though those same people are the reason those cats are homeless - because they wanted love from a living creature yet hate them when they fall between the cracks of the world. Though they might be feral and have some weird skin diseases they still remember when they were loved and wanted by humans - when they were fed and played with - their mistrust for humans is not born from hatred but out of a misunderstanding of why people hate stray cats when they are the ones that created them with their perverse ideas of love and fear of loneliness ... I know what it is like to be cast out, to be shunned by a civilization that I don't understand or enjoy, I see the same loneliness in their eyes as I know I have inside mine. The misunderstanding, the fear, the desire - I pity them because they remind me of myself. I was bred into the same type of complacency, domesticated against my will. Where is this free will? If language and laws and all institutions were created and voted for long before I was ever born how do I have free will? I never voted or agreed to any of this. I was cast into it and told and forced to obey this civilized authority or else. I didn't even get a choice. I had to conform or die. Where is this free will so many speak of?

But, those cats don't hold a grudge, they don't think of senseless metaphysics, they simply want to be understood and fed chicken leftovers and sometimes have their chewed ears rubbed - they wish only to be loved like they once were before their owners tossed them aside like garbage and now the city hunts them like criminals. A human voice reminds them that they were once loved - they enjoy the vibrations of love like any other living creature. They may not understand it but they are products of our loneliness, our desire to feel warmth, our apathy towards other human beings, our fantasy of being gods ...

Because they know, more than we, that great adventures always begin with friendships.

So says this quantum-dimensional wizard ...

BROKEN CATERPILLARS

We, mutated from the slime and ooze, puppets of the dirt and sunrise, eyes of lord and savior, we comply with the machine inside us, to that cannibal will driving us to act in accordance with what cosmic genetics created us in their oh so beautiful horror... I have come to this place to imagine, to breathe, to believe, to love and lose all, back to the secrets I have forgotten in the deserts of muses.

I swim out head first, part wire and fish, pieces of frog and metal, my bones crushed alongside the extinction of animals and gods and languages and desire and they pile all around as I too slowly exhaust my travels here .... cast out, broken, there will be no metamorphosis.

Love is the only reason we exist, this woman who cried for me to come back, to come back to the caterpillars, this strange and whimsical dance rehearsal where we all dance in unison and at the end we bow, we bow and turn into seaweed.

Around us the robotic ballet begins to play. They, the men and women and children, were no longer people or human .... They had become citizens, industrial peasantry stuck in a permanent disparity, they were only the roles civilization had given them, to labor and work forever or be struck by laziness and vice and subjected to permanent death and servitude.

One day I hope it crumbles away, I hope all that is left are the artist and the iconoclast, the rebels and the lovers, the dreamers and subversive, the thinkers and the poets, we'll tear down everything metal, we'll build farms and beautiful meadows in parking lots, the animals will come back, the bumblebees will rub their faces on our eyelashes, we will frolic like wild rabbits, fucking and dancing, mass orgies of sunlight and spirit, we'll sing hymns to the rivers and clear out the destruction of consumerism. None will be afraid and all will build. None will love and all will be free!

Beware and behold, the caterpillars cried, *do not become addicted to thought. Do not conform to ideas pressed into you by funeral men, do not let your dreams be suppressed by religious thinking, do not needlessly worry about madmen and their games of civilization and industrial thinking. Be free and unmoved in language. Be lost and wonderful in nature, go back to the roots of your primeval fathers, be glad to be alive and welcome death without ritual or vice ... Conform to no language, beautiful or otherwise, to no system of law, to no book or school, to no thought or promise ... conform only to life and those that wish not to suppress it with value and institutions but those that only wish to love and be free ... Civilization is a trick! It is a neurosis ... It is mad to eat you, to consume you, to steal you with dangerous trinkets, to put you asleep inside pillows made of exasperation.*

The caterpillars fell apart, I took their hand ... whether it was a woman, an insect, an inconspicuous Jesus Christ or the great nebula itself, I did not know.
But some congratulations were ordered from the menu... I melted into them, a forest of goo, slime baked under earth and dust, none of us screamed - we burned, we laughed because they had lost - we were still alive, we would always be alive.
We whispered, we whispered to those in front of us ...
Come out, we begged, come and embrace your heritage.

B BYRON

Sing lively, you lovely muses.

THE BURNING OF THE THEATER OF LOST CATERPILLARS

As the song ended, the puppets stood and removed themselves to the edge of the ocean. The poetic children that were once trees sat down with the bodiless robot with ants crawling from its mouth and eyes. The man with termites in his mouth sat beside them. The magician stood close by as his long legs shifted into the sand. A gang of feral cats (some were purple and red and some were naked with no fur and some had mohawks and switchblade combs - some had eyepatches and rubber bands tying their tails together) joined them, staring out at the uneven star lines (scratching and pondering human love). A giant caterpillar with disco-philosopher eyes came up from behind them slowly falling apart. Melting like green slime, leaving a trail of ooze behind.

They looked on at the illusionary sunset. They had become aware that they were only manifestations of a poet's brain. That their universe and planet rested within the corners of a lost mind. The children of trees grew saddened by this news. The robot asked questions. The man with termites in his mouth sighed heavily while the magician only laughed. Soon the world balled up and erased itself. The caterpillar melted over them and all turned into a pale goo that swam into the ocean, disappearing. The ideas grew to be bolts of electricity, crashing into a page, read by a stranger ... the universe opened back up ... alive, they awoke, stood upon the new edge of a different universe. The ocean was a different color, the caterpillars had wings, the magician was no longer cruel or unusual, the trees were strong and bold and the robot no longer needed answers but rejoiced. The ants in its brain were now formed into a body that could carry its head. It moved its new features around and spoke a beautiful gibberish to its new friends. The sound was musical and promoted magic.

As they looked off, they saw that they were parts of many different brains, many different universes and timelines, that there were infinite versions of them and that where they came from didn't matter. They danced along the shore of this new beginning ... sometimes they transformed into clouds, sometimes insects, sometimes oceans, sometimes memories, often they looked on with fascination - the book closed, the new universe stood up, blinked their strange eyes, wiggled their eyebrows, pulled up their face, checked to make sure their brain didn't run off with their teeth and placed the universe on a bookshelf and wondered about the next worlds ... but no worlds ever came. The extinction had won.

... end (curtain falls and the poet dies)

This is the search for meaning in a paradoxical universe. Suicide isn't meant to be a profound desire or a physical death in any of these musings. Suicide is more of a metaphorical idea where we shed our pretensions, deny our existence, where we die constantly only to be reborn again as something else. Suicide is more of an awakening, a resemblence of false certainty and finding that the person you are or the person you thought you were was a trick, a vanity, ideas pushed together to form a person, but a person completely unknown or alien to yourself.

Thank you for understanding my narcissism.

BROKEN
CATERPILLARS

B BYRON

Made in the USA
Coppell, TX
08 November 2022

85989479R00256